LAFORGUE, PHILOSOPHY, AND IDEAS OF OTHERNESS

LEGENDA

LEGENDA is the Modern Humanities Research Association's book imprint for new research in the Humanities. Founded in 1995 by Malcolm Bowie and others within the University of Oxford, Legenda has always been a collaborative publishing enterprise, directly governed by scholars. The Modern Humanities Research Association (MHRA) joined this collaboration in 1998, became half-owner in 2004, in partnership with Maney Publishing and then Routledge, and has since 2016 been sole owner. Titles range from medieval texts to contemporary cinema and form a widely comparative view of the modern humanities, including works on Arabic, Catalan, English, French, German, Greek, Italian, Portuguese, Russian, Spanish, and Yiddish literature. Editorial boards and committees of more than 60 leading academic specialists work in collaboration with bodies such as the Society for French Studies, the British Comparative Literature Association and the Association of Hispanists of Great Britain & Ireland.

The MHRA encourages and promotes advanced study and research in the field of the modern humanities, especially modern European languages and literature, including English, and also cinema. It aims to break down the barriers between scholars working in different disciplines and to maintain the unity of humanistic scholarship. The Association fulfils this purpose through the publication of journals, bibliographies, monographs, critical editions, and the MHRA Style Guide, and by making grants in support of research. Membership is open to all who work in the Humanities, whether independent or in a University post, and the participation of younger colleagues entering the field is especially welcomed.

ALSO PUBLISHED BY THE ASSOCIATION

Critical Texts
Tudor and Stuart Translations • New Translations • European Translations
MHRA Library of Medieval Welsh Literature

MHRA Bibliographies
Publications of the Modern Humanities Research Association

The Annual Bibliography of English Language & Literature
Austrian Studies
Modern Language Review
Portuguese Studies
The Slavonic and East European Review
Working Papers in the Humanities
The Yearbook of English Studies

www.mhra.org.uk
www.legendabooks.com

RESEARCH MONOGRAPHS IN FRENCH STUDIES

The *Research Monographs in French Studies* (RMFS) form a separate series within the Legenda programme and are published in association with the Society for French Studies. Individual members of the Society are entitled to purchase all RMFS titles at a discount.

The series seeks to publish the best new work in all areas of the literature, thought, theory, culture, film and language of the French-speaking world. RMFS accepts both shorter and longer studies. Around half of the titles in the series aim at a length of 50,000–60,000 words, in the interests of achieving a strongly focused argument. The other half are more sustained monographs, at 70,000 to 85,000 words. As innovation is a priority of the series, volumes should predominantly consist of new material, although, subject to appropriate modification, previously published research may form up to one third of the whole. Proposals may include critical editions as well as critical studies. They should be sent with one or two sample chapters for consideration to Professor Diana Knight, Department of French and Francophone Studies, University of Nottingham, University Park, Nottingham NG7 2RD.

Editorial Committee
Diana Knight, University of Nottingham (General Editor)
Robert Blackwood (University of Liverpool)
Jane Gilbert, University College London
Shirley Jordan, Newcastle University
Neil Kenny, All Souls College, Oxford
Max Silverman, University of Leeds

Advisory Committee
Wendy Ayres-Bennett, Murray Edwards College, Cambridge
Celia Britton, University College London
Ann Jefferson, New College, Oxford
Sarah Kay, New York University
Michael Moriarty, University of Cambridge
Keith Reader, University of Glasgow

PUBLISHED IN THIS SERIES

20. *Selfless Cinema? Ethics and French Documentary* by Sarah Cooper
21. *Poisoned Words: Slander and Satire in Early Modern France* by Emily Butterworth
22. *France/China: Intercultural Imaginings* by Alex Hughes
23. *Biography in Early Modern France 1540–1630* by Katherine MacDonald
24. *Balzac and the Model of Painting* by Diana Knight
25. *Exotic Subversions in Nineteenth-Century French Literature* by Jennifer Yee
26. *The Syllables of Time: Proust and the History of Reading* by Teresa Whitington
27. *Personal Effects: Reading the 'Journal' of Marie Bashkirtseff* by Sonia Wilson
28. *The Choreography of Modernism in France* by Julie Townsend
29. *Voices and Veils* by Anna Kemp
30. *Syntactic Borrowing in Contemporary French*, by Mairi McLaughlin
31. *Dreams of Lovers and Lies of Poets: Poetry, Knowledge, and Desire in the 'Roman de la Rose'* by Sylvia Huot
32. *Maryse Condé and the Space of Literature* by Eva Sansavior
33. *The Livres-Souvenirs of Colette: Genre and the Telling of Time* by Anne Freadman
34. *Furetière's* Roman bourgeois *and the Problem of Exchange* by Craig Moyes
35. *The Subversive Poetics of Alfred Jarry*, by Marieke Dubbelboer
36. *Echo's Voice: The Theatres of Sarraute, Duras, Cixous and Renaude*, by Mary Noonan
37. *Stendhal's Less-Loved Heroines: Fiction, Freedom, and the Female*, by Maria C. Scott
38. *Marie NDiaye: Inhospitable Fictions*, by Shirley Jordan
39. *Dada as Text, Thought and Theory*, by Stephen Forcer
40. *Variation and Change in French Morphosyntax*, by Anna Tristram
41. *Postcolonial Criticism and Representations of African Dictatorship*, by Cécile Bishop
42. *Regarding Manneken Pis: Culture, Celebration and Conflict in Brussels*, by Catherine Emerson
43. *The French Art Novel 1900-1930*, by Katherine Shingler
44. *Accent, Rhythm and Meaning in French Verse*, by Roger Pensom
45. *Baudelaire and Photography: Finding the Painter of Modern Life*, by Timothy Raser
46. *Broken Glass, Broken World: Glass in French Culture in the Aftermath of 1870*, by Hannah Scott
47. *Southern Regional French*, by Damien Mooney
48. *Pascal Quignard: Towards the Vanishing Point*, by Léa Vuong
49. *France, Algeria and the Moving Image*, by Maria Flood
50. *Genet's Genres of Politics*, by Mairéad Hanrahan
51. *Jean-François Vilar: Theatres Of Crime*, by Margaret Atack
52. *Balzac's Love Letters: Correspondence and the Literary Imagination*, by Ewa Szypula
53. *Saints and Monsters in Medieval French and Occitan Literature*, by Huw Grange
54. *Laforgue, Philosophy, and Ideas of Otherness*, by Sam Bootle
55. *Theorizing Medieval Race: Saracen Representations in Old French Literature*, by Victoria Turner

www.rmfs.mhra.org.uk

Laforgue, Philosophy, and Ideas of Otherness

Sam Bootle

LEGENDA

Research Monographs in French Studies 54
Modern Humanities Research Association
2018

Published by Legenda
an imprint of the Modern Humanities Research Association
Salisbury House, Station Road, Cambridge CB1 2LA

ISBN 978-1-78188-647-2 (HB)
ISBN 978-1-78188-648-9 (PB)

First published 2018

All rights reserved. No part of this publication may be reproduced or disseminated or transmitted in any form or by any means, electronic, mechanical, photocopying, recording or otherwise, or stored in any retrieval system, or otherwise used in any manner whatsoever without written permission of the copyright owner, except in accordance with the provisions of the Copyright, Designs and Patents Act 1988, or under the terms of a licence permitting restricted copying issued in the UK by the Copyright Licensing Agency Ltd, Saffron House, 6–10 Kirby Street, London EC1N 8TS, England, or in the USA by the Copyright Clearance Center, 222 Rosewood Drive, Danvers MA 01923. Application for the written permission of the copyright owner to reproduce any part of this publication must be made by email to legenda@mhra.org.uk.

Disclaimer: Statements of fact and opinion contained in this book are those of the author and not of the editors or the Modern Humanities Research Association. The publisher makes no representation, express or implied, in respect of the accuracy of the material in this book and cannot accept any legal responsibility or liability for any errors or omissions that may be made.

Trademark notice: Product or corporate names may be trademarks or registered trademarks, and are used only for identification and explanation without intent to infringe.

© Modern Humanities Research Association 2018

Copy-Editor: Priscilla Sheringham

CONTENTS

	Acknowledgements	ix
	Introduction	1
1	The Reception of German Philosophy in Nineteenth-Century France	21
2	Otherness and The Suffering Body	50
3	Germany and the Forest as Other	75
4	The Eastern Other (1): Multiplicity	97
5	The Eastern Other (2): Nothingness	124
	Conclusion	147
	Bibliography	156
	Index	165

For Mum and Dad

ACKNOWLEDGEMENTS

The doctoral research on which this book is based was funded by an AHRC Doctoral Award. During my doctorate and beyond, Damian Catani was a constant source of advice, support and encouragement, for which I will always be grateful. I would also like to thank Susan Harrow for her support over the past few years. Dave Evans deserves huge thanks for spurring me on at many crucial points during the project, as well as providing generous and insightful comments on the first draft; Zoë Roth, too, offered helpful feedback on early material. The Camargo Foundation hosted me at an important stage of the writing process. I am grateful to Laurence Taylor for his help with the cover design, and to Graham Nelson for his patient advice in the final stages of the project. Finally, I would like to thank Mum, Dad, Tom, Rae, Emily and Margs for their love, support and patience.

Parts of Chapter 5 appeared in a different form in my article 'Laforgue et le bouddhisme dilettante', *Revue d'histoire littéraire de la France*, 117.2 (2017), 273–82, and I thank the editors of *RHLF* for their feedback on that article.

s.b., Durham, May 2018

INTRODUCTION

On 21 July 1879, Jules Laforgue — then eighteen years old — wrote to the administrator of the *Bibliothèque nationale* in Paris to request a library card. In his letter, he states that he has been frequenting the library's publicly accessible annexe in the rue Colbert 'avec assiduité' for the past two years, but has found it wanting 'quant aux ouvrages des philosophes, des poètes et des auteurs dramatiques contemporains'.[1] With a certain humility, he explains that he holds no position that might justify his request, although he does not mention that this was because he had recently failed his *baccalauréat* for the third and final time, his crippling shyness having scuppered his chances in the oral exam. Instead, he wants to use the library to read and study in order to become a writer: 'Mon seul but est de devenir littérateur' (*OC*, I, 684). Although formal and ostensibly banal, this letter offers an important insight into the symbiotic relationship between Laforgue's literary ambitions and his voracious appetite for reading. Indeed, his mature work presents a veritable *bricolage* of terms drawn from the various works he pored over in 'la salle Colbert' from 1877–79 and subsequently, having been granted the library card, in the *Bibliothèque nationale* itself. Within this array of lexical curios — picked, magpie-like, from medical, Classical, technical, ecclesiastical, and other vocabularies — there are some that have a privileged status in his aesthetics. Chief among these treasures are the terms taken from his reading of the German philosophers Arthur Schopenhauer and Eduard von Hartmann.

The central importance of philosophy to Laforgue's writing is, indeed, evident from his letter, which places the works of 'philosophes' at the head of his *desiderata*. It is also clear from the earnest pessimism of his first, unpublished collection *Le Sanglot de la Terre* (written in 1879–82). But the special significance of philosophical terms in his later poetry and prose is not easy to discern, at least at first glance. This is because of the irony that imbues his mature work, from *Les Complaintes* (mostly written in 1883–84, but not published until 1885) to *Moralités légendaires* (1886) and *Derniers vers* (the title posthumously given to the free-verse poems he wrote in 1886), an irony that makes his references to philosophical concepts ('Inconscient', 'Absolu', 'Volonté' and so on) appear as unserious as his use of other jargons.[2] Indeed, there *is* a ludic aspect to his use of philosophical language: Laforgue himself states that he '[va] [s]'arlequinant des défroques | Des plus grands penseurs de chaque époque' ('Esthétique (*Je fais la cour à ma Destinée*)', *OC*, II, 168). Hartmannian garb is particularly prominent in this philosophical harlequinade, as J. A. Hiddleston has shown; ideas and images taken from Hartmann's work are 'transformed and given a new tonality, losing their philosophical or didactic solemnity and taking on that peculiarly strident and playful quality which characterizes Laforgue's irony'.[3] This playfulness might even be seen as parodic in nature.

In particular, the *Moralités légendaires* — where 'Laforgue's reworking of philosophy is most fully manifest'[4] — have been read as parodies of the use of philosophical lexis, the philosophizing of various characters (Hamlet, Salomé, the dragon of 'Persée et Andromède', Lohengrin, Pan) being characterized by an absurdly overblown or convoluted rhetoric.[5] For example, Salomé's *vocéro* — which replaces the erotic dance of the hypotext — is delivered in 'a ludicrous prose replete with puns, alliteration, verbal play, periphrasis, and an abstract philosophical vocabulary', and for Michèle Hannoosh this wordplay undermines the hymn's proselytisation of Hartmannian thought.[6] But parody does not necessarily imply ridicule; it 'can be critically constructive as well as destructive'.[7] The fact that Laforgue's references to philosophy are ostensibly jocular does not thus imply a lack of genuine engagement with philosophical ideas.[8]

It is in his private notes that we find the clearest evidence to show that he engaged with German philosophy sincerely, profoundly and persistently. In fact, these notes — collated in the third and final volume of his *Œuvres complètes*, published in 2000 — demonstrate that his reception of Schopenhauer and Hartmann was essential to the development of his aesthetics. Gustave Kahn, one of the poet's closest friends, emphasizes this point at the beginning of a pen-portrait of Laforgue in his 1902 work *Symbolistes et décadents*:

> La littérature, il la concevait non pas comme une chose par elle-même existante,
> mais comme un reflet, une traduction d'une philosophie.[9]

Kahn also indicates that for Laforgue, philosophy was a matter of both literary importance and deeply personal significance: 'il existait dans sa nature d'âme, un art, un besoin de saisir la philosophie comme une chose vitale'.[10] Although the story that Laforgue always carried a copy of Hartmann's Die Philosophie des Unbewussten (*The Philosophy of the Unconscious*) in his pocket[11] is almost certainly apocryphal (the two volumes of this work ran to more than six hundred pages each), there is no doubt that Hartmann's ideas were especially important to him. He even referred to the principle of the Unconscious as 'ma religion' (*OC*, III, 1149). His attitude towards the philosophy of Schopenhauer was more ambiguous, his notes showing that initial enthusiasm gave way to disillusionment; in his literary works, however, some of Schopenhauer's ideas continue to play an important role alongside those of Hartmann.[12] Indeed, the dominant themes of Laforgue's *œuvre* can be traced back to his reading of the two philosophers: pessimism in general and the sufferings of the body in particular; a nihilistic, atheistic view of the universe; the pervasive, almost inescapable presence of sexuality, accompanied by profound scepticism about romantic relationships. But despite the foundational importance of Schopenhauerian and Hartmannian ideas to his work, and despite his description of the philosophy of the Unconscious as his religion, Laforgue is far from being an unthinking devotee.[13] Indeed, he is always in dialogue with Schopenhauer and Hartmann, revealing himself to be a subtle and, at times, critical philosophical interlocutor: he redisposes not only philosophical language but also philosophical ideas, moulding them to form his own idiosyncratic credo — albeit one that is never solidified as a manifesto, instead remaining elusive and shifting.

Laforgue's transfiguration of philosophical concepts and language is part of the broader question of what is at stake in the crossing of disciplinary borders, in the passage from philosophy to poetry. But another sort of crossing is also crucial to his reception of philosophy: that from one national culture (Germany) to another (France). This book explores how the 'othering' of Germany and German philosophy — the perception of it as in some sense fundamentally opposed or alien to the French way of thinking — informs Laforgue's reception of Schopenhauer and Hartmann, and how ideas of otherness are in turn woven into his aesthetic principles. The importance of Schopenhauer and Hartmann's philosophy to Laforgue has long been recognized, as has his free-thinking approach to it. But the ways in which this approach is imbricated with the broader intellectual and cultural context have been largely neglected. Laforgue's thinking is not merely shaped by this context, but actively intervenes in it. In and through his engagement with philosophy, he deploys a range of strategies to challenge the demonization of other cultures: he celebrates otherness as a source of inspiration, reappropriating metaphors of 'othering'; conversely, he demonstrates that otherness might be contingent and thus fundamentally illusory, given the immanent presence of an underlying unity; he locates otherness within the self in the form of the unconscious. Moreover, his uses of philosophy are closely connected to a critique of his own culture. His work thus thinks through not only notions of cultural otherness, but also ideas of how society might be otherwise.

Le pessimisme d'outre-Rhin: the Philosophy of Schopenhauer and Hartmann[14]

In Laforgue's playful and parodic version of 'Salomé', the narrator describes the phantasmagorical cabaret provided for the amusement of the guests at the feast for the 'Tétrarque': it includes a 'jeune fille-serpent', 'une procession de costumes sacramentellement inédits, symbolisant chacun un désir humain', and 'des intermèdes d'horizontaux cyclones de fleurs électrisées', as well as clowns, some of them 'des clowns musiciens', others performing a kind of absurdist philosophical theatre:

> Et trois autres clowns jouèrent l'Idée, la Volonté, l'Inconscient. L'Idée bavardait sur tout, la Volonté donnait de la tête contre les décors, et l'Inconscient faisait de grands gestes mystérieux comme un qui en sait au fond plus long qu'il n'en peut dire encore. (OC, II, 441)

These three concepts — Idea, Will, and the Unconscious — are crucial to understanding Schopenhauer and Hartmann's philosophy. They are also, therefore, vital to Laforgue's literary project; but despite their fundamental importance for Laforgue, his published work only rarely makes reference to these philosophical terms directly (instead generally preferring euphemisms such as 'l'Un-Tout' or 'l'Absolu'). Their embodiment as clowns is, in a sense, a metonym for the parodic treatment of philosophy in Laforgue's work, a treatment that belies the underpinning role that philosophy plays for his thinking. For Ellen Sakari, the three clowns represent Hegel ('l'Idée'), Schopenhauer ('la Volonté'), and Hartmann ('l'Inconscient'); for François Ruchon and Pierre-Olivier Walzer, they represent the three principles of Hartmann's philosophy.[15] Both interpretations are valid. Hartmann's philosophy of the Unconscious is in fact an attempt to fuse the Hegelian concept of Idea and the Schopenhauerian concept of Will within his own concept of the Unconscious. This section explains Hartmann and Schopenhauer's systems and how they are related to one another, as well as sketching out, in a preliminary fashion, some of Laforgue's critical responses to his philosophical reading.

Both Schopenhauer and Hartmann base their philosophical systems on Kant's distinction between appearance (phenomena) and things in themselves (noumena). Kant argues that our knowledge of the world is limited to its phenomenal aspect, which we experience through the senses, and that the noumenal realm — the world as it is in itself — is fundamentally unknowable. But both Schopenhauer and Hartmann set out to discover the nature of this realm, the underlying principle governing our world. For Schopenhauer, this principle is Will: this is the driving force of the universe, 'the force that shoots and vegetates in the plant, indeed the force by which the crystal is formed, the force that turns the magnet to the North Pole' and so on;[16] in human existence, Will is manifested as 'will to life (*Wille zum Leben*), a kind of blind striving, [...] which is directed towards the preservation of life, and towards engendering life anew'.[17] Will, then, is 'the innermost essence, the kernel, of every particular thing and also of the whole' (*WWR*, I, 110). But this is not simply a variant of pantheism: Will is a *blind* force, governing the workings of living organisms and inanimate matter without any guiding purpose or rationality. The world cannot be divine, argues Schopenhauer, since its existence is meaningless. He asserts that 'there is no co-ordinated purpose to nature',[18] or, indeed, to history, which is merely an endlessly repeated cycle. Progress is thus chimerical. In this, he deliberately and belligerently opposes the Hegelian philosophy of history: as Andrew Bowie points out, 'Schopenhauer's main animus is directed against any attempt, like that of Hegel, to suggest that history can be understood teleologically, as the locus of the realization of reason.'[19]

In this sense, Hartmann's philosophy of the Unconscious constitutes an audacious philosophical enterprise: his explicitly stated aim is to reconcile Schopenhauer's Will with Hegel's concept of Idea, the very concept that entails a rationalist teleology. For Hartmann, Will and Idea are merely two aspects of the same force, the Unconscious. In this respect, he asserts that his most important philosophical predecessor is Schelling, whose *Philosophie der Mythologie* (*Philosophy of Mythology*) proves the inseparability of Will and Idea: without Will, Idea can only explain the logical essence of things, but not their existence, which is fundamentally irrational; without Idea, Will has no object, and is merely an empty striving for existence. However, Hartmann criticizes Schelling for failing to insist on the unconsciousness of the noumenon, which he deems essential in order to avoid lapsing into theism:[20] like Schopenhauer, Hartmann is atheist. Hartmann also argues that Schelling's principle is purely abstract, and requires experimental verification; this is the basis of his aim 'to restore again the proportion between the speculative and empirical aspects of philosophy'.[21] He thus deems it crucial to place his philosophy on scientific foundations, as the sub-title of *The Philosophy of the Unconscious* indicates: '*speculative results according to the inductive method of physical science*'.[22] Sebastian Gardner indicates the idiosyncrasy of this approach:

> In terms of his methodology, then, Hartmann is a naturalist, and his further peculiarity lies in his supposition that reflection on the results of the natural sciences is sufficient to warrant conclusions about the ultimate nature of reality which are thoroughly *anti*-materialist.[23]

The first part of *The Philosophy of the Unconscious* uses this natural-scientific methodology to posit a teleological metaphysics of nature, attempting to attribute purposiveness to all natural phenomena. Hartmann draws extensively on biological research into animal instinct and reflex actions in both flora and fauna, and he thereby argues for the existence of an unconscious will in every living organism (a kind of vitalism[24]). Indeed, even conscious actions require a process of which we are unconscious. This idea of unconscious will is comparable to Schopenhauer's notion of will to life, but it is crucial to note that for Hartmann, this will always has a definite aim, or idea; Will and Idea are both facets of the ultimate metaphysical principle, the Unconscious. Hartmann sees the operation of the Unconscious in every sphere of human existence: ethics, aesthetics, language, history and so on.

Laforgue's faith in Hartmann's philosophy is clear from the first 'complainte' proper, 'Complainte propitiatoire à l'Inconscient', which transfigures the Lord's Prayer as an appeal to the Unconscious. The poem's subversion of Christian doctrine also points to Laforgue's acceptance of the atheism propounded by both Schopenhauer and Hartmann, an atheism that is perhaps expressed most explicitly in his 1882 essay on Paul Bourget: here, he relates his belief that the garden of Creation has been 'débarrassé soudain de son Jardinier impénétrable' (OC, III, 127). However, Laforgue by no means endorses every aspect of Schopenhauer and Hartmann's philosophical systems. In fact, he expresses profound scepticism about the nihilistic eschatology that the two philosophers share; that is, both envisage the ultimate annihilation of human life or (in Hartmann's case) of the universe itself. For Schopenhauer, this annihilation is the logical end-point of his ethical doctrine of chastity (to which we shall turn shortly). It occupies only a minor role in Schopenhauer's magnum opus *Die Welt als Wille und Vorstellung* (*The World as Will and Representation*), but gained (perhaps undue) prominence in late nineteenth-century France through a seminal 1870 interview he conducted with the journalist Paul Challemel-Lacour, in which Schopenhauer discussed how sexual abstinence would lead to the extinction of the human race. In Hartmann's philosophical system, on the other hand, eschatology plays a crucial role, rather than merely constituting a by-product of ethics. For him, 'the existence of the world is a *mistake*'[25] and the purpose of the world is thus to return to the state of nothingness that pertained before Will and Idea were joined to form the Unconscious; this is to be achieved 'through the development of a collective human consciousness which, upon achieving insight that the world ought not to be, brings itself and the world to an end'.²⁶ How, exactly, the end of the world will be brought about by such a collective consciousness is not entirely clear. However, Hartmann does offer a detailed vision of the necessary steps to reach this insight, arguing that we must pass through three stages of illusion: firstly, the illusion that we can achieve happiness in this lifetime; secondly, that we can achieve happiness in an afterlife; thirdly, that happiness is possible for the human race in the future. In his notes, Laforgue seems to endorse this doctrine of three-fold illusion (see *OC*, III, 1133), but he ridicules the idea of 'l'anéantissement universel' (*OC*, III, 1135) as utterly fantastical, even more impracticable than Schopenhauer's vision of 'la suppression du commerce sexuel dans l'humanité' (*OC*, III, 1135).

This scepticism towards certain aspects of Hartmannian and Schopenhauerian metaphysics is symptomatic of Laforgue's critical attitude towards his philosophical reading. His approach is, indeed, idiosyncratic in some respects. Perhaps most notably, his vision of the Unconscious itself is far from being a dogmatic reflection of Hartmann's work; rather, he extrapolates from his philosophical material in various ways. For Laforgue, the Unconscious is both a force — sometimes blind, irrational and merciless, sometimes divinized as a source of wisdom and providence — and a domain. This domain is essentially utopian, and it is to be found, ultimately, within the self. In this sense, Hiddleston is perhaps right to say that what Laforgue took from Hartmann 'was not so much a philosophical system and a certain vocabulary, but the *idea* of the Unconscious which was to appeal not just to his intellect, but more felicitously to his visual imagination'.²⁷ Hartmann's idea of the Unconscious provided the inspiration for him to survey the 'inner domain [of the self]' and 'gave him the impetus to explore its extraordinary riches'.²⁸ But this exploration was not Hartmann's primary aim in writing *The Philosophy of the Unconscious*; he sought to provide, first and foremost, an account of the workings of the world at large rather than the internal world of the self. For Hartmann, the Unconscious is a metaphysical principle, and the unconscious life of the individual merely a manifestation of this principle. For Laforgue, on the other hand, the individual gains precedence over the metaphysical: he is fascinated, above all, by 'les richesses de tons bizarres changeants qu'on a en fermant les yeux', by 'Les symphonies orageuses, les chœurs d'océans en se bouchant les oreilles' (*OC*, III, 1158). As Hiddleston comments, in Laforgue's work there is often 'the sense of a breach which has been opened up affording a glimpse into another surreal, exotic or frighteningly alien world'²⁹ — although this world is, in fact, more often a source of wonder and yearning than of fear. Laforgue's concern with the individual is also evident in his focus on the ethical doctrines put forward by Schopenhauer and Hartmann. Indeed, it is the ethical dimension of their philosophical systems that Laforgue engages with most intensely, more than metaphysics or (perhaps surprisingly) aesthetics.

Both philosophers' ethics emerge out of their metaphysical visions; both are, moreover, focused on the question of sexuality. Schopenhauer's notion of Will as the fundamental metaphysical principle is premised on his argument concerning the body: he maintains that 'the whole body is nothing but objectified will' (*WWR*, I, 100), that bodily existence consists purely of willing. The corollary of this is the dethroning of reason as humankind's dominant faculty, as the marker of our exceptionalism, an argument that constitutes Schopenhauer's most radical departure from his philosophical predecessors according to Bryan Magee.[30] Humanity's intellectual capacities are merely a function of the will to life: at a certain point in our development, knowledge was required 'for the preservation of the individual and the propagation of the species' (*WWR*, I, 150). But it remains subordinate: 'the intellect is the secondary phenomenon, the organism the primary' (*WWR*, II, 201). His challenge to rationalism is made even more controversial by his assertion that the sexual instinct constitutes the most powerful manifestation of the will to life in our bodies (*WWR*, I, 329). In 'The Metaphysics of Sexual Love', he goes so far as to say that the impulse to sexual gratification represents 'the ultimate goal of almost all human effort' (*WWR*, II, 534). This dictatorial instinct is like 'a malevolent demon, striving to pervert, to confuse, and to overthrow everything' (*WWR*, II, 534), and it exerts such control because what is at stake is 'nothing less than the *composition of the next generation*' (*WWR*, II, 534; author's emphasis). Attraction to a particular person is simply the manifestation of the will to life of the future individual who would be born of that union (*WWR*, II, 535). We are thus slaves to the will of the species; sexual relations do not bring us happiness, and we only believe that they do because nature implants in us 'a certain *delusion*' (*WWR*, II, 538; author's emphasis). The striving for sexual satisfaction, which furthers the species, is 'at the expense of the individual' (*WWR*, II, 540). The proof of this is that after the sexual urge has been satisfied, 'everyone who is in love finds himself duped; for the delusion by means of which the individual was the dupe of the species has disappeared' (*WWR*, II, 540). The will of the species is thus the 'pursuer and enemy' of the individual, in that it is 'always ready ruthlessly to destroy personal happiness in order to carry out its ends' (*WWR*, II, 556). Women are complicit in this ruse: this is the key to Schopenhauer's notorious misogyny.

However, despite this bleak account of sexual love, Schopenhauer does offer some hope. He argues that there is a solution to the suffering caused by desire: the denial of the will to life. He sees this as a kind of pseudo-religious salvation and he 'is keen to link his philosophical discussion with Christianity, Brahmanism, and Buddhism, claiming that the core of all these religions [...] is really the same.'[31] In order to deny the will to life, we must turn against our own bodies and cease to pursue egoistic ends, in particular sexual gratification. Asceticism is thus at the core of Schopenhauer's ethics, primarily in the sense of the denial of sexual desire — the strongest manifestation of the will to life — but also through poverty, fasting and so on. For Schopenhauer, suffering is caused not only by sexual desire, but by all forms of striving (needing, wanting, aiming), since striving for anything implies experiencing deficiency:

> All *willing* springs from lack, from deficiency, and thus from suffering. Fulfilment brings this to an end; yet for one wish that is fulfilled there remain at least ten that are denied. Further, desiring lasts a long time, demands and requests go on to infinity; fulfilment is short and meted out sparingly. (*WWR*, I, 196; author's emphasis)

In short, willing dooms us to suffer:

> so long as our consciousness is filled by our will, so long as we are given up to the throng of desires with its constant hopes and fears, so long as we are the subject of willing, we never obtain lasting happiness or peace. (*WWR*, I, 196)

Even if we find ourselves with nothing to strive for, we are prone to suffering in the form of ennui (*WWR*, I, 312). For the majority of human beings, then, 'life swings like a pendulum to and fro between pain and boredom' (*WWR*, I, 312). But asceticism offers a way out of this predicament, a way to get off the misery-go-round.

Hartmann concurs with many aspects of Schopenhauer's pessimistic vision. In particular, he echoes his cynical view of sexual love. For Hartmann, as for Schopenhauer, the sexual instinct is predominant in human existence, representing the most powerful manifestation of the Unconscious in humankind. He also agrees that sexuality is a pernicious force: 'in love one has not to do with a farce, a romantic drollery, but with a very real power, a demon who ever and again demands his victims'; this is a demon who 'makes the whole world dance on his fool's rope' (*PU*, p. 230). Love is merely an illusion, as demonstrated by its decline after sexual satisfaction: 'No passion of love very long survives enjoyment' (*PU*, p. 231). Again, Hartmann adopts the Schopenhauerian explanation for attraction to a particular person, maintaining that this shows how we are duped by the Unconscious into producing the ideal offspring: 'the dreamed-of bliss in the arms of the beloved one is nothing but the deceptive bait, by means of which the Unconscious deludes conscious *egoism*, and leads to the sacrifice of self-love in favour of the succeeding generation' (*PU*, p. 234; author's emphasis). But at this point Hartmann departs from Schopenhauer's theory of love, instead drawing on Darwinian thought to argue that the delusion of love is, in fact, '*indispensable*' (*PU*, p. 235; author's emphasis) because the 'welfare and most favourable constitution of the next generation' (*PU*, p. 235) is of the utmost importance:

> the *ennoblement of the species* is brought about, in addition to the succumbing of the more unfit specimens of the race through the struggle for existence, by means of a natural *instinct of sexual selection*. Nature knows no higher interests than those of the race, for the race is related to the individual, as the infinite to the finite. (*PU*, p. 234; author's emphasis)

Awareness of this process necessarily raises a conflict with selfish interests, but Hartmann holds that it is possible for conscious thought to 'disengage itself from the point of view of egoism' and even 'be brought by deeper insight passively to permit Nature's ends to be accomplished in preference to its own' (*PU*, p. 235). In other words, Hartmann takes the opposite point of view to Schopenhauer: rather than denying the will to life through sexual abstinence, we should embrace our instinctual urges, and particularly sexuality, since this is essential to the development of the human race towards a state of enlightenment. While love causes suffering and is thus condemnable from the egoistic point of view, 'in the truly philosophical point of view [...] complete devotion to the process and welfare of the universal [...] is presented as first principle of practical philosophy, and thus also all instincts, absurd to conscious egoism but beneficial for the whole, are *fully justified*' (*PU*, p. 241; author's emphasis).

For Laforgue, this ethical dichotomy between Schopenhauer's asceticism and Hartmann's acceptance of sexuality is of central importance. Throughout his career, in both his published and private writings, he returns again and again to the question of whether the sexual instinct should be denied or embraced. Hailed as 'l'Unique Loi' by the male voice in the poetic dialogue of 'Complainte des formalités nuptiales' (*OC*, I, 578), the theme of sexual love dominates Laforgue's mature *œuvre*. It is generally treated with the same cynicism that characterizes both Schopenhauer and Hartmann's theorizations; this cynicism is encapsulated by 'Complainte du soir des Comices agricoles', where the post-coital disillusionment following a frolic in the fields is witheringly expressed: 'Dans les foins | Crèvent deux rêves niais' (*OC*, I, 594). Similarly, in 'Complainte à Notre-Dame des Soirs', the poet impugns 'ces vendanges sexciproques', declaring that 'moi, moi Je m'en moque!' (*OC*, I, 551). But while, for Laforgue, the sexual urge is unquestionably a trap — 'Le but du génie de l'espèce est de nous abuser par l'appât idéal sur les fins qui le servent[;] mieux absolument il nous dupe, mieux nous *aimons*' (*OC*, III, 955; author's emphasis) — the Schopenhauerian solution of self-denial is never wholeheartedly embraced; Laforgue never entirely believes in its practicability or, indeed, its desirability, even if he persistently considers it as a possible ethical path. He is equally ambivalent about Hartmann's call to engage in the life process through procreation, however. While his work registers a yearning for companionship, the domesticity of family life is only intermittently appealing, and is more often portrayed as a blind alley. Laforgue also rejects the fixed gender roles associated with such a life: although his attitudes towards women may seem, on a superficial reading, to be marred by Schopenhauerian misogyny, in fact he laments the way in which patriarchal society has reduced women to sexual objects and reproductive machines.[32] He dreams of making women 'véritablement nos compagnes égales, nos amies intimes, des associés d'ici-bas, les habiller autrement, leur couper les cheveux, leur tout dire' (*OC*, III, 1101). Moreover, he also hints at a vision of sexual relationality that involves mutual pleasure without the burdens of procreation, thus eluding the perils of both Schopenhauer and Hartmann's ethics.

For Schopenhauer, asceticism is not the only means of countering the tyranny of the Will; aesthetic experience also provides an escape, albeit only a temporary one (unlike renunciation, which offers a permanent solution). While reason is subservient to will in 'all animals and *almost* all men' (*WWR*, I, 152; my emphasis), for the select few it is possible for reason to 'withdraw from this subjection, throw off its yoke, and, free from all the aims of the will, exist purely for itself, simply as a clear mirror of the world' (*WWR*, I, 152). This disinterested perception — that is, a form of perception unconditioned by desire for something — is the source of art. In aesthetic experience, we do not see the world in functional terms: 'Raised up by the power of the mind, we relinquish the ordinary way of considering things' (*WWR*, I, 178). If we cease to see an object through the lens of our aims and desires, then 'what is thus known is no longer the individual thing as such, but the *Idea*, the eternal form' (*WWR*, I, 179; author's emphasis). Whether we are creating it or consuming it, art is the 'purest joy' of life; but it only offers a temporary release from willing, 'a fleeting dream' (*WWR*, I, 314). Despite this, aesthetics plays a central role in Schopenhauer's philosophical system. For Hartmann, on the other hand, the creation and contemplation of art are of relatively minor importance. In his chapter on aesthetics, Hartmann's main concern is to draw a distinction between the concept of genius and that of mere talent. He holds that the source of genius is the Unconscious, which bestows the work of art upon the artist in a single stroke; on the other hand, the ordinary artist proceeds in a laboriously piecemeal fashion, merely combining elements of perceptual experience in new ways. The artist of genius receives inspiration from the Unconscious without effort and without any understanding of how it is received, and Hartmann conveys the mysterious nature of this process by describing inspiration as 'a gift of the gods' (*PU*, p. 278).

Hartmann's aesthetics also aims to overcome the dichotomy between idealism and relativism, and in this sense Laforgue wholeheartedly endorses the philosopher's theories: the Unconscious is an ideal, but not a *fixed* ideal. Rather, it is in a perpetual state of flux, producing different forms of creative expression at different times and places. The (Classicist) notion of an eternally unchanging aesthetic ideal is therefore erroneous. However, as I have shown elsewhere,[33] Laforgue departs from Hartmannian aesthetics in at least one key respect: he does not envisage the creative process as involving a single moment of inspiration (as Hartmann does for the work of genius), but as essentially improvisatory. In his brief critical notes on Rimbaud, whose poems he read near the end of his life following their 1886 publication in *La Vogue*, Laforgue makes a statement that applies equally well to his own poetry:

> Une poésie n'est pas un sentiment que l'on communique tel que conçu avant la plume — Avouons le petit bonheur de la rime, et les déviations occasionnées par les trouvailles, la symphonie imprévue vient escorter le *motif*. (*OC*, III, 194; author's emphasis)

Indeed, he uses similar phrasing in an 1885 review of *Les Complaintes* co-written with Charles Henry, remarking on the 'notes voulues ou raccrochées au petit bonheur de la plume' and the 'trouvailles de formules' (*OC*, III, 154) in the collection. Moreover, as Anne Holmes has shown, analysis of Laforgue's manuscripts demonstrates that his creative process was characterized not by spontaneity, but by a laborious process of drafting and redrafting.[34] Laforgue is perhaps closer, then, to Hartmann's picture of the ordinary artist (rather than the artist of genius); the suffering that the ordinary artist undergoes in his efforts to create is certainly foregrounded by Laforgue. In this sense, he also departs from Schopenhauer, who views creative experience as an escape from suffering, not as being inspired by it.

Laforgue's dynamic and, at times, critical engagement with his philosophical sources is largely the product of his own idiosyncratic thinking. But it is also closely connected to the reception of the two philosophers by late nineteenth-century French critics, as well as being embedded in a broader cultural context. For example, Laforgue's focus on Schopenhauer and Hartmann's ethical theories echoes the contemporary critical reception, which tended to emphasize their ethics (especially concerning love, sex and marriage) at the expense of other aspects of their thought. Both philosophers were also viewed as unremitting pessimists (even though both offer solutions to the problem of suffering). Moreover, their pessimism was portrayed as a disease-like force, a miasmatic stench wafting over the Rhine and infecting the minds of the French, especially young men. Schopenhauer's doctrine of chastity was also seen to be corrupting at a time when France's demographic weakness undermined the possibility of avenging its defeat in the Franco-Prussian War. These metaphors of contagion cast German philosophy as fundamentally 'other' to the French body politic.

Ideas of Otherness and the Otherness of Ideas

While the notion of Germany as France's 'other' is established early in the nineteenth century, the idea that it is France's *ennemi héréditaire* only gains prevalence in the wake of the Franco-Prussian War. The contestation of the border between the two nations had been a prominent political issue before, notably during the Rhine Crisis of the 1840s, but it was not until 1871 that the border was actually redrawn with the annexation of Alsace-Lorraine by the newly formed German Empire. In the early Third Republic, nationalism in France took on a particularly patriotic and xenophobic form, replacing the earlier 'humanitarian nationalism' that held up France as the paragon of an egalitarian political order (an idea that emerged after the first Revolution but that persisted well into the nineteenth century).[35] This new right-wing nationalism found its hero in the figure of Georges Ernest Boulanger — 'Général Revanche' — whose popularity in the late 1880s demonstrates the tenacity of irredentist sentiment in France.

But *revanchisme* was not the only ideology to emerge from the French defeat. New theories of nationhood as 'affective community' were put forward in response to German claims that Alsace-Lorraine was culturally and ethnically German, and thus rightfully theirs. In October 1870, Numa Denis Foustel de Coulanges argued that a nation was 'une communauté d'idées, d'intérêts, d'affections, de souvenirs et d'espérances';[36] twelve years later, Ernest Renan's *Qu'est-ce qu'une nation?* (1882) expressed similar ideas:

> Dans le passé, un héritage de gloire et de regrets à partager, dans l'avenir un même programme à réaliser; avoir souffert, joui, espéré ensemble, voilà ce qui vaut mieux que des douanes communes et des frontières conformes aux idées stratégiques; voilà ce qu'on comprend malgré la diversité de race et de langue.[37]

The idea of nation as 'imagined community' thus emerges in prototypical form in the late nineteenth century. But Benedict Anderson's theory is distinct from Renan's in insisting on the importance of print capitalism, and thus language, in the imagining of nationhood. While for Renan linguistic diversity within France shows that language is not essential to national unity, for Anderson the emergence of standard print languages in the nineteenth century was crucial to the rise of the nation-state as the dominant geopolitical form.

The importance of language to the imagined community lies principally in its role in the popular press, which constitutes a vector for 'deep, horizontal comradeship'.[38] But language is also important in the more rarefied sphere of philosophy, where it again plays its part in constructing national identity. From the early eighteenth century, Latin had been in decline as the 'language of philosophy', usurped by French[39] (which also held the status of diplomatic language). But from the late eighteenth century, German philosophers increasingly turned to their mother tongue; Kant, most notably, wrote his later works in German. From the early nineteenth century, then, German and French philosophers were increasingly perceived as belonging to distinct, even competing national philosophical traditions, rather than as a part of a transnational philosophical community. The notion of German philosophy as 'other', as fundamentally opposite to French philosophy, was popularized by Germaine de Staël's *De l'Allemagne*. A product of Enlightenment cosmopolitanism, Staël was nonetheless seminal in constructing German otherness.

While the construction of the 'other' is not central to Anderson's idea of the imagined community, it is implicit in his statement that the nation is 'imagined as both inherently limited and sovereign'.[40] This limitation is crucial because 'even the largest [nation] has finite, if elastic, boundaries, beyond which lie other nations'.[41] The obverse, then, of the imagining of community is the conception of who is *not* part of that national community — the imagining of otherness. This exclusionary thinking is central to Fredrik Barth's theory of the formation of ethnic groups.[42] For Barth, what is fundamental to the constitution of an ethnic group is not 'the cultural characteristics of the members' or 'the organizational form of the group', but rather 'the fact of continuing dichotomization between members and outsiders'.[43] In Daniele Conversi's words, 'Ethnogenesis is not an endogenous process' but rather requires the construction of 'opposition, an external other'.[44] The invention of 'the other' is essential not only to *ethnic* nationalism, but to the imagining of nations in general: nationalism, as Michael Billig points out, 'constructs a constant and politically mobilisable sense of otherness',[45] affirming the self through a negation of what is not-self.[46] Differences between peoples and groups *within* the nation are, meanwhile, relativized and subordinated 'in such a way that it is the symbolic difference between "ourselves" and "foreigners" which wins out and which is lived as irreducible', as Étienne Balibar remarks.[47] The logic of identification is thus circular: membership of the national group is based on perceived similarity; and the perception of similarity is grounded in membership of the national group.

There is also a kind of doublethink at work in the construction of otherness. National 'others' (like Germany) can be subsumed back into a broader sense of self ('the West') in the name of establishing an opposition with a greater 'other' ('the East'). Edward Said hints at this dynamic, multi-layered process in *Orientalism*:

> The construction of identity — for identity, whether of Orient or Occident, France or Britain, while obviously a repository of distinct collective experiences, *is* finally a construction — involves establishing opposites and 'others' whose actuality is always subject to the continuous interpretation and re-interpretation of their differences from 'us'. Each age and society creates its 'Others'. Far from

a static thing then, identity of self or of 'other' is a much worked-over historical, social, intellectual, and political process that takes place as a contest involving individuals and institutions in all societies.[48]

Indeed, a negative approach to the definition of identity — that is, defining 'self' through its opposition to 'other' — is less fraught than a positive approach, particularly for a large, diverse, and rapidly changing society like nineteenth-century France or (to an even greater degree) Europe. The essentialized 'other' serves as a fixed point to which self-identity, with all of its nebulosity and uncertainty, can be anchored: 'the Orient has helped to define Europe (or the West) as its contrasting image, idea, personality, experience.'[49] The Orient represents the 'shadow side' of Western identity, emerging 'according to a detailed logic governed not simply by empirical reality but by a battery of desires, repressions, investments, and projections.'[50] Indeed, projection is crucial both to Orientalist discourse and to the construction of German otherness, the pathologization of German philosophy representing an attempt to disavow the internal factors involved in France's decline.

★ ★ ★ ★ ★

The notion of German philosophy as 'other' has deep roots in the nineteenth century, as Chapter 1 shows. However, after 1870 German philosophical influence, especially that of Schopenhauer and Hartmann, is portrayed as not only alien, but also dangerous, invasive, corrupting. While the pathologization of Schopenhauer and Hartmann's influence is related to the actual invasion of French territory during the 1870–71 Franco-Prussian War, it also expresses broader anxieties about the decline of the French body politic, of which the French defeat is just the most prominent example. Chief among these anxieties was the weakness of demographic growth in France, which prompted deep concern about the fertility of the French populace. For the Decadent movement, however, national decline was a source of creative vitality, and Laforgue — who was sympathetic towards this movement — reconfigures illness and physical debility as aesthetic principles, as we shall see in Chapter 2. His redisposition of the discourse of disease and decline, which is used to demonize the influence of German philosophy, thus constitutes a form of political oppositionality. It also radically subverts the aesthetics of Schopenhauer and Hartmann even as it draws on their pessimistic insistence on suffering, demonstrating the dynamic nature of Laforgue's engagement with his philosophical sources.

The notion of 'oppositionality', as theorized by Ross Chambers, suggests resistance to systems of power from within.[51] In this sense, it is premised on the Foucauldian notion that there is no 'outside', no exteriority, to power — no Archimedean political position from which a regime can be hoisted off its access. In arguing for the importance of ideas of otherness to Laforgue's reception of philosophy, I am not, then, asserting that there is in reality some 'other' that is outside of contemporary discourse; the 'otherness' of Germany and German philosophy is, of course, a socially constructed category. However, Laforgue appealed precisely to the possibility of this 'other' as a means of opposition, and in this sense he was very much typical of his era:

> If the dominant discourse was the speech and writing of a France resolutely middle class, self-absorbed, and certain of its self-sufficiency, then in our period one of the most prominent and most influential of the counter-discourses mobilized to subvert it was what we might term the discourse of *everywhere else* [...].[52]

Richard Terdiman is referring here to 'texts about the imagined or actual trips which would *remove* one from the place where the dominant so effortlessly exercised its domination',[53] and this desire to escape was certainly an important aspect of Laforgue's imagining of otherness. But the idea of German philosophy as 'other' also had a role to play in his critique of the prevailing bourgeois morality *within* France. In this sense, his reception of Schopenhauer and Hartmann conforms to Michel Espagne and Michaël Werner's argument that cultural transfers should always be understood in terms of their role 'à l'intérieur du système de réception';[54] and that within the receiving culture, they serve two functions, 'une fonction de légitimation et une fonction de subversion'.[55] In both cases, 'on cherche une caution extérieure destinée à étayer une argumentation qui n'a sa raison d'être qu'en fonction de la situation intérieure'.[56] While the transgressive qualities of Laforgue's formal experimentation (especially his pioneering *vers libre*) are widely accepted, the subversive nature of his thematics — most notably his treatment of the body and of sexual politics, which rejects contemporary nationalist visions of health and virility as the source of France's renewal — is not always recognized. These thematic concerns are rooted in his reading of philosophy.

Laforgue's engagement with German philosophy is not only based on opposition, but also on a search for a positive alternative, for a more meaningful existence that draws on the *élan vital* of the Unconscious — the ultimate metaphysical principle in Hartmann's philosophy. In the course of this search, Laforgue considers the possibility that other cultures, including Germany, might offer a privileged means of access to the Unconscious. In this sense, Laforgue's reception of German philosophy is informed by positive as well as negative discourses about German otherness, as Chapter 3 shows. He imagines Germany as 'la terre bénie' (*OC*, III, 343) of the Unconscious, thus recapitulating Staël's exoticized vision of Germany as the land of poetry, philosophy and music. But since the Unconscious is the overarching principle of all existence, Germany's closeness to the Unconscious — its 'otherness' to the restrictive Latinate culture of France — can only be contingent. Ultimately, access to the Unconscious must be sought within the self, and more particularly in the deepest, most powerful human instincts. In Laforgue's work, the forest — long associated with myths of German national identity — emerges persistently as the locus where these instincts hold sway. The theme of sexuality is thus crucial to Laforgue's engagement with philosophy. Again, oppositionality is important here, since Laforgue repudiates the *fin-de-siècle* pro-natalist discourse that sees procreative sex as the key to national regeneration. Instead he imagines a liberated form of sexual expression that allows desires to be fulfilled without the burdens of reproductive consequence.

Germany's otherness was reinforced by its perceived association with India, as Chapter 4 shows: German philosophy was seen to be especially susceptible to the influence of Indian thought, which Europe had encountered through Britain's colonial rule and had studied with growing interest since the early years of the nineteenth century. Hartmann and (particularly) Schopenhauer were amongst those associated with Indian religion, especially Buddhism; indeed, both explicitly drew parallels between their ideas and Buddhist doctrine. Laforgue's use of Buddhist terms in his poetry can be traced to his philosophical reading, and his notes demonstrate his fascination with Buddhist ideas. His work also explores how 'Eastern' cultures are related to those of Europe, and in this he again draws on his philosophical sources. Schopenhauer adopted a perennialist standpoint, arguing that there is an eternal source of wisdom that is periodically revealed in certain cultures at certain times: (true) Christianity and Buddhism are thus rooted in the same unchanging source. For Hartmann, by contrast, philosophy and religion — both Eastern and Western — are part of an evolutionary process that culminates in his own philosophy of the Unconscious, and Buddhism is a more advanced form of thought than Christianity, largely because it recognizes the illusory nature of selfhood. Laforgue's early work appears to propound a syncretistic approach to cultural relations that is reminiscent of Schopenhauer. His later work, however, bears the traces of Hartmann's philosophical evolutionism: India and Indian thought are celebrated as both profound and liberating, offering a model for the West.

Laforgue's view of India is thus informed by exoticism, which is also evident in his view of Germany. But while he sometimes indulges in this fetishization of otherness, at other times he undermines exoticist thinking. This is done both explicitly, through the parodying of literary exoticism, and implicitly, through the representation of cultural plurality: in recognizing the diversity of cultural forms, Laforgue moves away from the binary logic intrinsic to 'otherness' (which is one side of the self/other opposition). The celebration of cultural difference, of the multiplicity of cultures and their interrelation, is premised on the notion that the disparities between cultures are not fundamental. This is a kind of cosmopolitanism, understood as entailing 'the positive recognition of difference' and 'a conception of belonging as open'.[57] For Laforgue, this heterogeneity is underwritten by the essential unity of all cultures, since all human civilization is ultimately rooted in the Unconscious, the All-One. The contingent nature of cultural specificity challenges nationalist mythologies; and Laforgue's questioning of the idea that nations constitute distinct entities is part of a broader argument (drawn from Hartmann) that all forms of individuality are fundamentally illusory. This includes the human individual: the multiplicity of quasi-autonomous processes (both physical and mental) within each person implies that the notion of a unitary self is purely arbitrary. Laforgue's reflections on otherness are thus bound up with his thinking on selfhood.

For Laforgue, the multiplicity within the self might permit some sort of tentative harmony, but it might also entail disintegration, dispersal and, finally, dissolution. Chapter 5 shows how Laforgue explores the Buddhist idea of nirvana, which was contemporarily understood as equivalent to nothingness, and more specifically as self-annihilation. Nineteenth-century critics of Buddhism were almost unanimous in seeing it as a religion that worshipped the void, and for some this nihilism implied that there was a fundamental schism in human nature between East and West. At times, Laforgue appears to construct a similar opposition, drawing a dichotomy between 'la vie' and 'le néant' that seems to map onto a West/ East divide. But if in *Les Complaintes* he draws inspiration from 'la vie', which is associated with (sexual) love and with Hartmann's philosophy, in his next collection, *L'Imitation de Notre-Dame la Lune* (1885), he explores ideas associated with 'le néant', namely the obliteration of selfhood and of sexual desire. Semantic nothingness — a void of sense — also haunts his work. Ultimately, though, Laforgue commits to neither of these alternatives: his work is characterized by fluctuation between self-affirmation and self-annihilation, sexual fulfilment and chastity, meaning and nonsense; and, moreover, by *l'entre-deux*, by indefinable or even paradoxical states between such extremes.

Laforgue's treatment of ideas of otherness is complex and, at times, seemingly contradictory. In some of his texts, he seems to adopt an exoticist approach to foreign cultures, celebrating the 'otherness' of Germany and India. But in other texts, he critiques the idealistic pretensions of exoticism. This apparent tension can be at least partly resolved by the notion that the differences between cultures are merely contingent, that there is an underlying unity — a common source and a future reconciliation — to be found in the Unconscious. This notion, which emerges in various forms in Laforgue's writings, suggests that the apparent otherness of other cultures is not essential or eternal, but rather provides a model for the development of French society. Through his idiosyncratic engagement with the ideas of Schopenhauer, Hartmann and Buddhist doctrine, Laforgue thus offers a critique of his own culture, and in particular of the dominant pro-natalist discourse. The suffering body and the desiring body — prevalent in his thematics and crucial as aesthetic principles — have political import too: countering the nationalistic bourgeois morality of his age, Laforgue propounds the release of corporeal energies, both negative (illness and debility) and positive (a liberated, non-reproductive, mutually gratifying (hetero)sexuality).

Laforgue, poète philosophe (et 'dilettante et pierrot')

Laforgue's encounter with other cultures was not solely intellectual; it was also a lived reality, since he spent most of his adult life in Germany working as the French reader to the German Empress Augusta. During this period (November 1881 to September 1886), he was based at the *Prinzessinnenpalais* in Berlin, but also followed the Empress to her various residences in Wiesbaden, Baden-Baden, Koblenz, Hamburg and Babelsberg. His experience of Germany was somewhat limited by the fact that he never learnt German to any degree of proficiency, mainly because the Empress and her entourage were francophone; in a letter to Charles Henry he declares, 'je ne parle que le français ici' (*OC*, I, 758). Nonetheless, his expatriate status was a crucial factor in his approach to ideas of otherness. It was not, however, the sole factor: Laforgue's concern with otherness precedes his departure for Germany. Indeed, it spans his literary career.

This persistent concern goes hand in hand with his enduring interest in philosophy. But in the course of his career, there are numerous shifts in his approach to philosophy, and his interpretation of philosophical ideas. These shifts are evident both in his published work and his private notes, although the difficulty of exactly dating these notes means that a detailed chronology of how his thinking develops is unfeasible. Instead, a broad chronological distinction between the two phases of his career can be drawn, with 1877–81 constituting his early period, and 1882–87 his mature period.

This early period is dominated by his first, unpublished collection *Le Sanglot de la Terre*, his most derivative piece of work. Laforgue ultimately abandoned the collection: his first sign of disillusionment emerges in March 1881, when he states that *Le Sanglot* 'commence à me dégoûter parfois' (*OC*, I, 697). His definitive rejection dates to the early months of 1882, but it is not until May 1883, in a letter to his sister Marie, that he clearly expresses the reasons for this:

> j'ai abandonné mon idéal de la rue Berthollet, mes poèmes philosophiques. Je trouve stupide de faire la grosse voix et de jouer de l'éloquence. Aujourd'hui que je suis plus sceptique et que je m'emballe moins aisément et que d'autre part je possède ma langue d'une façon plus minutieuse, plus clownesque, j'écris de petits poèmes de fantaisie, n'ayant qu'un but: faire de l'original à tout prix. (*OC*, I, 821)

His repudiation of these 'poèmes philosophiques' does not imply that he also repudiates philosophy itself, however. It is, rather, the earnestness, even pomposity ('la grosse voix') of *Le Sanglot* that he has chosen to leave behind. In fact, he explicitly states his attachment to the philosophical aspect of the collection: in a letter to Kahn concerning his new collection *Les Complaintes*, he justifies the inclusion of the poem 'Préludes autobiographiques' (against his friend's advice) precisely because the poem marks his 'philosophical' phase:

> J'ai sacrifié un gros volume de vers philo. d'autrefois parce qu'ils étaient mauvais manifestement, mais enfin ce fut une étape et je tiens à dire [...] qu'avant d'être dilettante et pierrot j'ai séjourné dans le Cosmique. (*OC*, II, 729)

What Laforgue does not state here is that this new, more playful poetic mode ('dilettante et pierrot') is still deeply informed by his engagement with philosophy. Philosophical ideas and images are integrated into his work in a more subtle and ironic fashion, but their underlying importance is — if anything — even greater.

This book does not claim to trace every aspect of Schopenhauer and Hartmann's importance to Laforgue; neither does it seek to inventorize every reference to their work. My concern is, rather, to think in broad terms about how his reading of philosophy is related to contemporary discourses and to his ideas on aesthetics (even if I do also highlight some specific intertextual links, and draw on previous critics' work in this area). Suffering, desire, the fragmented self, the void: these are not only philosophically-inspired themes but also aesthetic principles for Laforgue, alongside the central doctrine of unconscious inspiration that is drawn from Hartmann's work. My focus is, therefore, on poems that might be read as in some sense meta-poetic, poems that constitute significant turning points in his *œuvre* (such as 'Préludes autobiographiques', 'Complainte du Sage de Paris' and 'L'hiver qui vient'). It is in these poems, as well as in his private notes, that we see how deeply ideas of otherness inform his reception of German philosophy, and how tightly they are woven into his poetic project.

Notes to the Introduction

1. Jules Laforgue, *Œuvres complètes*, ed. by Jean-Louis Debauve et al, 3 vols (Lausanne: L'Âge d'Homme, 1986–2000), I, 684. Further references are given in the text as *OC*.
2. Indeed, some critics argue that philosophy 'est moins une pensée, qu'elle n'est pour Laforgue un *registre*' (Philippe Bonnefis, 'Entre Laforgue et Hartmann: le monologue de Salomé', *Lendemains*, 49 (1988), 57–69 (p. 62; author's emphasis); see also Jean-Pierre Bertrand, *Les Complaintes de Jules Laforgue. Ironie et désenchantement* (Paris: Klincksieck, 1997), p. 66).
3. J. A. Hiddleston, 'Laforgue and Hartmann', in *Proceedings of the Xth Congress of the International Comparative Literature Association, 1982*, ed. by Anna Balakian (New York, NY: Garland 1985), pp. 66–72 (p. 68).
4. Madeleine Guy, 'Jules Laforgue, Hartmann and Schopenhauer: From Influence to Rewriting', in *Questions of Influence in Modern French Literature*, ed. by Thomas Baldwin, James Fowler and Ana de Medeiros (Basingstoke; New York, NY: Palgrave Macmillan, 2013), pp. 58–70 (p. 59).
5. See Michèle Hannoosh, *Parody and Decadence: Laforgue's 'Moralités légendaires'* (Columbus: Ohio State University Press, 1989).
6. Ibid., p. 164.
7. Linda Hutcheon, *A Theory of Parody: The Teachings of Twentieth-Century Art Forms* (New York, NY: Methuen, 2000), p. 32.
8. On the role of philosophy in the *Moralités légendaires*, see Guy (2013) and Roger Pearson, 'The Voice of the Unconscious: Laforgue and the Poet as Lawgiver', *Dix-Neuf*, 20, no. 1 (2016), 125–44.
9. Gustave Kahn, *Symbolistes et décadents* (Paris: L'Édition de Paris, 1902; repr. Geneva: Slatkine Reprints, 1977), p. 181.
10. Ibid., p. 181.
11. See Fernand Vial, 'L'Inconscient métaphysique et ses premières expressions littéraires en France: Jules Laforgue', in *Stil- und Formprobleme in der Literatur*, ed. by Paul Böckmann (Heidelberg: Carl Winter, 1959), pp. 358–66 (p. 361); and Graham Dunstan Martin, 'Introduction', in Jules Laforgue, *Selected Poems*, trans. by Graham Dunstan Martin (London: Penguin, 1998), pp. ix-xxxviii (p. xvii).
12. Almost all of Laforgue's critics acknowledge the crucial role played by Hartmann's work (see, inter alia, David Arkell, *Looking for Laforgue: an informal biography* (Manchester: Carcanet, 1979), p. 140; Michael Collie, *Jules Laforgue* (London: The Athlone Press, 1977), p. 11; Médéric Dufour, *Étude sur l'esthétique de Jules Laforgue: une philosophie de l'impressionnisme* (Paris: Vanier, 1904), p. 1; Marie-Jeanne Durry, *Jules Laforgue* (Paris: Seghers, 1966), p. 86; Daniel Grojnowski, *Jules Laforgue, les voix de la Complainte* (La Rochelle: Rumeur des Âges, 2000), p. 21; Hiddleston (1985), p. 66; Pierre Reboul, *Laforgue* (Paris: Hatier, 1960), p. 171; Henri Scepi, *Poétique de Jules Laforgue* (Paris: Presses universitaires de France, 2000), p. 14). Fewer refer to Schopenhauer, but his role in Laforgue's thought is still widely recognized (see, for example, Jeanne Cuisinier, *Jules Laforgue* (Paris: Albert Messein, 1925), p. 115; Edwin Morgan, 'Notes on the Metaphysics of Jules Laforgue', *Poetry*, 69, no. 5 (February 1947), 266–72 (pp. 269–70); T. S. Eliot, *The Varieties of Metaphysical Poetry*, ed. by Ronald Schuhard (London: Faber and Faber, 1993), p. 215; Hannoosh, p. 50).
13. As Warren Ramsey comments, Laforgue's theory of the Unconscious was 'half-borrowed, half-invented' (Warren Ramsey, 'Introduction', in *Jules Laforgue: Essays on a Poet's Life and Work*, ed.

by Warren Ramsey (Carbondale: Southern Illinois University Press, 1969), pp. xii–xxx (p. xx)); for Arkell, it was so unorthodox that 'Hartmann would probably have disowned it' (Arkell, p. 140). Dunstan Martin argues that 'the disrespect with which he treats the great principles of Hartmann's philosophy' means that his approach is a kind of 'blasphemy' (Dunstan Martin, p. xxx). In a similar vein, Bonnefis states that the Unconscious may be 'le Dieu de Laforgue, mais Laforgue n'est pas son prophète' (Philippe Bonnefis, 'Faire parler l'inconscient', *La Quinzaine Littéraire*, 488 (16–30 June 1987), pp. 13–15 (p. 13)).

14. This summary draws on the critical guides of Christopher Janaway (*Schopenhauer* (Oxford: Oxford University Press, 1994)) and Bryan Magee (*The Philosophy of Schopenhauer* (Oxford: Oxford University Press, 1997)) on Schopenhauer, and Dennis N. Kenedy Darnoi (*The Unconscious and Eduard von Hartmann* (The Hague: Martinus Nijhoff, 1967)) on Hartmann, as well as Sebastian Gardner's chapter on Hartmann ('Eduard von Hartmann's Philosophy of the Unconscious', in *Thinking the Unconscious: Nineteenth-Century German Thought*, ed. by Angus Nicholls and Martin Liebscher (Cambridge: Cambridge University Press, 2010), pp. 173–99). For fuller discussions of these philosophers and their thought, see these sources.
15. Ellen Sakari, *Prophète et Pierrot: thèmes et attitudes ironiques dans l'œuvre de Jules Laforgue* (Jyväskylä: University of Jyväskylä, 1974), p. 160; François Ruchon, *Jules Laforgue: sa vie — son œuvre* (Geneva: Éditions Albert Ciana, 1924), p. 146; Pierre-Olivier Walzer, *OC*, II, 584 n. 2.
16. Arthur Schopenhauer, *The World as Will and Representation*, trans. by E. F. J. Payne, 2 vols (New York, NY: Dover Publications, 1966), I, 110. Further references are given in the text as *WWR*.
17. Janaway, p. 29.
18. Ibid., p. 39.
19. Andrew Bowie, *Aesthetics from Kant to Nietzsche* (Manchester: Manchester University Press, 2003), p. 262.
20. As Darnoi notes, Schelling in fact states that he has 'forsaken his earlier pantheistic position in his last or positive philosophy' (Darnoi, p. 18).
21. Darnoi, p. 19.
22. Eduard von Hartmann, *Philosophy of the Unconscious: speculative results according to the inductive method of physical science*, trans. by William Chatterton Coupland, 2nd edn (London: Kegan Paul, 1931). Further references are given in the text as *PU*.
23. Gardner, p. 175; author's emphasis.
24. J. W. Burrow, *The Crisis of Reason: European Thought, 1848–1914* (New Haven, CT: Yale University Press, 2000), p. 64.
25. Gardner, p. 187; author's emphasis.
26. Ibid., p. 187.
27. Hiddleston (1985), p. 71; author's emphasis.
28. Ibid., p. 71.
29. Ibid., p. 71.
30. Magee, p. 158.
31. Janaway, p. 91.
32. See Claire White, 'Laforgue, Beauvoir, and the Second Sex', *Dix-Neuf*, 20, no. 1 (2016), 110–24.
33. Sam Bootle, 'Jules Laforgue and the Illusion of Spontaneity', *Dix-Neuf*, 15, no. 2 (2011), 166–76.
34. Anne Holmes, *Jules Laforgue and Poetic Innovation* (Oxford: Clarendon Press, 1993), pp. 82–86.
35. Raoul Girardet, *Le nationalisme français, 1871–1914* (Paris: Armand Colin, 1966), pp. 13–14.
36. Numa Denis Fustel de Coulanges, *L'Alsace est-elle allemande ou française? Réponse à M. Mommsen, professeur à Berlin* (1870), quoted in Girardet, p. 62.
37. Ernest Renan, *Qu'est-ce qu'une nation?* (1882), quoted in Girardet, p. 66.
38. Benedict Anderson, *Imagined Communities: Reflections on the Origin and Spread of Nationalism*, 2nd edn (London: Verso, 1991), p. 7.
39. Jonathan Israel, *Radical Enlightenment: Philosophy and the Making of Modernity 1650–1750* (Oxford: Oxford University Press, 2001), p. 39.
40. Anderson, p. 6.
41. Ibid., p. 7.

42. Fredrik Barth, 'Introduction', in *Ethnic Groups and Boundaries: The Social Organization of Culture Difference*, ed. by Fredrik Barth (Prospect Heights, IL: Waveland, 1998), pp. 9–38.
43. Ibid., p. 14.
44. Daniele Conversi, 'Reassessing current theories of nationalism: nationalism as boundary maintenance and creation', in *Nationalism: Critical Concepts in Political Science*, ed. by John Hutchinson and Anthony D. Smith (London: Routledge, 2000), pp. 420–33 (p. 427).
45. Michael Billig, 'Socio-psychological aspects of nationalism: imagining ingroups, others and the world of nations', in *Nationalism, Ethnicity and Cultural Identity in Europe*, ed. by Keebet von Benda-Beckmann and Maykel Verkuyten (Utrecht: European Research Centre on Migration and Ethnic Relations, 1995), pp. 89–105 (p. 100).
46. Indeed, the idea of otherness is crucial to the formation of any social group: 'l'altérité est une catégorie fondamentale de la pensée humaine. Aucune collectivité ne se définit jamais comme Une sans immédiatement poser l'Autre en face de soi' (Simone de Beauvoir, *Le deuxième sexe*, 2 vols (Paris: Flammarion, 1973), I, 18).
47. Étienne Balibar, 'The Nation Form: History and Ideology', in Étienne Balibar and Immanuel Wallerstein, *Race, Nation, Class: Ambiguous Identities* (London: Verso, 1991), pp. 86–106 (p. 94).
48. Edward W. Said, *Orientalism: Western Conceptions of the Orient* (London: Routledge and Kegan Paul, 1978; repr. London: Penguin, 2003), p. 332; author's emphasis.
49. Ibid., pp. 1–2.
50. Ibid., p. 8.
51. Ross Chambers, *Room for Maneuver: Reading (the) Oppositional (in) Narrative* (Chicago, IL: University of Chicago Press, 1991), pp. xiv-xv.
52. Richard Terdiman, *Discourse/ Counter-Discourse: the theory and practice of symbolic resistance in nineteenth-century France* (Ithaca, NY: Cornell University Press, 1985), p. 227; author's emphasis.
53. Ibid., p. 227; author's emphasis.
54. Michel Espagne and Michaël Werner, 'La construction d'une référence culturelle allemande en France: genèse et histoire (1750–1914)', *Annales*, 42 (1987), 969–92 (p. 970).
55. Ibid., p. 978.
56. Ibid., p. 978.
57. Gerard Delanty, 'Nationalism and Cosmopolitanism: The Paradox of Modernity', in *The SAGE Handbook of Nations and Nationalism*, ed. by Gerard Delanty and Krishan Kumar (London: Sage, 2006), pp. 357–68 (p. 357).

CHAPTER 1

The Reception of German Philosophy in Nineteenth-Century France

The idea of German philosophy as 'other' was prevalent in France throughout the nineteenth century. Rather than being perceived as merely novel or different, German philosophy was seen as fundamentally alien, as opposed in essence to the French way of thinking, philosophical tradition, and national character. Of course, this view was not unanimously held. But it did have a remarkable currency, both among thinkers who saw themselves as belonging to a transnational intelligentsia or *République des Lettres* and who were thus fascinated by German thought, and among those who condemned the pernicious influence of philosophy from the other side of the Rhine. The imagining of German philosophy's otherness took various forms. For Germaine de Staël, Victor Cousin and other Germanophile intellectuals of the first half of the nineteenth century, there was a fundamental opposition between French materialism (the doctrine that all phenomena are grounded in material causes) and German transcendental idealism (the doctrine that there is a metaphysical principle of some sort beyond mere matter). These intellectuals saw French philosophy as confined to the everyday and the down-to-earth; German philosophy, on the other hand, soared in the rarefied air of loftier spiritual concerns. But for the critics of German philosophy, the opposition was conceived differently, as that of French clarity and German obscurity. This perception was based on style as much as content, the difficulty of German philosophical prose being exacerbated by translations that were often awkward and unclear. Most French intellectuals relied on these translations, since knowledge of German was rare; Laforgue was no exception in this respect.

These conflicting assessments of German philosophy were grounded, partly, in political differences. Hegel, the dominant figure of German philosophy in early nineteenth-century France, appealed to liberally-minded French thinkers in the Restoration because his philosophy of history seemed to promote the idea that the modern liberal state was the apotheosis of political progress. But others argued that the German regime was not as liberal as it might appear; later, with the rise of Prussia's geopolitical influence, warnings about the deleterious effects of German philosophy grew ever louder. After France's defeat in the Franco-Prussian War of 1870–71, they were replaced by vociferous laments for the political naivety of French intellectuals. Moreover, the image of Germany as an idyllic land of philosophy, poetry and music, an image first popularized by Staël, was superseded in the popular imaginary by that of a bellicose, barbarian nation that was France's *ennemi héréditaire*.[1] For some Third-Republic intellectuals, however, the idealized image persisted in spite of the vicissitudes of Franco-German political relations, notably in the form of the Wagnerian movement. The exoticization of Germany had, for Staël, been imbricated with a political critique of Napoleon's regime; but for later French thinkers, the celebration of Germany's supposed otherness was associated primarily with a counter-*cultural* stance, rather than with explicitly *political* opposition.

This defiance of the patriotism that dominated France's late nineteenth-century political landscape manifested itself in an affiliation with the pessimist philosophy of Schopenhauer and Hartmann. Pathologized as a sort of contagion infecting the minds of France's youth, pessimism was cast as fundamentally un-French by many critics. These metaphors of disease were related to a broader medicalized discourse of national decline; the demonization of German thought thus operated according to the logic of projection, anxieties about France's faltering progress being transferred onto a supposedly threatening foreign philosophy. For the Decadent movement, however, notions of decay, decline and degeneration were a source of inspiration, and Schopenhauer was celebrated as a *philosophe maudit*. Unlike Hartmann, whose *Philosophy of the Unconscious* was widely read, having been translated into French in 1877, Schopenhauer was known primarily through critical works (both academic and journalistic), and these works often subjected him to *ad hominem* critiques. A cult of personality thus emerged around Schopenhauer, his detractors condemning him as a misanthropic, almost demonic figure, his supporters revelling in his controversial status. As a result, Schopenhauerians were often portrayed as posers. But interest in his work was not merely attributable to faddish anti-bourgeois posturing: both Schopenhauer and Hartmann were hugely influential on *fin-de-siècle* French literature, particularly in their argument that human existence is driven by the irrational, shadowy forces of the mind, notably that of sexuality. In fact, despite the prominence of German thought in academic circles earlier in the century, Schopenhauer and Hartmann were probably the first German philosophers to have a substantial impact on French literature.

Laforgue was one of the foremost writers to engage with Schopenhauer and Hartmann's thought. As we shall see in the following chapter, his engagement is inseparably related to the discourses surrounding their work, especially that of Schopenhauer. This chapter examines these discourses: first, it situates them within the *longue durée* of French encounters with German philosophy, and shifting perceptions of German otherness; secondly, it explores the critical reception of Schopenhauer and Hartmann, and the disparities in how they were portrayed; finally, it reveals the intersecting corporeal metaphors used to treat their reception, notions of French national decline, and condemnations of *fin-de-siècle* literary culture. In the late nineteenth-century French imaginary, Decadent and Symbolist literature was a vector for the pathogen of German philosophy, for the invasive foreign doctrine of pessimism that threatened to undermine France's progress and international status once and for all: both (home-grown) literature and (imported) philosophy were thus dangerous elements of otherness within the French body politic.

The French Reception of 'la philosophie d'outre-Rhin'

The Decadent movement has been characterized as a transnational aesthetic community,[2] and a similarly border-defying intelligentsia was crucial to the reception of German philosophy in the early nineteenth century too. The key figure of this 'culture humaniste internationale'[3] in France was Germaine de Staël. While in broad terms this culture played an important role in mitigating perceptions of national difference,[4] Staël herself was seminal in constructing the otherness of Germany in general and German philosophy in particular through her work *De l'Allemagne* (1810/13). This perception of otherness became entrenched in an era of growing national consciousness, persisting throughout the century in various forms.

From the opening section of Staël's work, the opposition between France and Germany is made clear: in Latinate civilizations, she states, there is 'moins de penchant pour les idées abstraites que chez les nations germaniques'.[5] Indeed, she argues that French and German epistemologies are completely polarized, since French thinkers consider 'les objets extérieurs comme le mobile de toutes les idées' and German thinkers 'les idées comme le mobile de toutes les impressions'.[6] She thus characterizes French thought as being concerned ultimately with worldly affairs, its empiricist tendency contrasting with German philosophy's propensity for abstraction. The contrast between the two countries is portrayed as fundamental, as rooted in an incommensurable philosophical disparity: for France, Germany is not merely different, it is other. The centrality of abstract ideas to German culture is such that Staël describes Germany as 'la patrie de la pensée',[7] and this became one of her work's most enduring formulations. She even suggests that French culture might benefit from the reinvigorating influence of German thought.[8] It was this overtly expressed desire to imitate Germany that led, ostensibly at least, to the work's banning and its author's exile; as the chief of police, the duc de Rovigo, states in his letter to Staël informing her of these punishments, 'nous n'en sommes pas encore réduits à chercher des modèles dans les peuples que vous admirez'.[9] He goes on to state categorically that 'Votre dernier ouvrage n'est point français'.[10] While Staël views France and Germany as capable of fruitful exchange, the French authorities deem the mere appreciation of other cultures to be tantamount to antipatriotic treachery.

Indeed, the celebration of Germany's supposed liberty in *De l'Allemagne* was intended largely as a critique of the stifling control exercised by the Napoleonic regime.[11] But while the work has been described as 'un panégyrique tendancieux, uni à un dénigrement systématique de la France',[12] its praise for Germany is by no means unmitigated. Its treatment of German philosophy is a case in point: arguing that Germany is 'la nation métaphysique par excellence',[13] Staël defends the intellectual rigour of metaphysical philosophy while criticizing the vagueness of its object of analysis: 'c'est un nuage qu'il faut mesurer avec la même exactitude qu'un terrain'.[14] The connotations of nebulosity and obscurity carried by this image pertain not only to German philosophy's subject matter, but also to its style. Her attitude towards the difficulties of German philosophical prose is, again, ambivalent: on the one hand, she is critical of German philosophers' apparent inability to write clearly and comprehensibly; on the other, she argues that we should not dismiss philosophy that forces us to think deeply. The latter argument extends to a denunciation of those who mock German philosophy, such mockery being rooted (she claims) in intellectual laziness[15] and xenophobia:

> Enfin, si par hasard de tels écrits étaient composés par un Allemand dont le nom ne fût pas français, et qu'on eût autant de peine à prononcer ce nom que celui du baron dans *Candide*, quelle foule de plaisanteries n'en tirerait-on pas?[16]

Her reference to the absurdly alliterative onomastics of the Baron Thunder-ten-Tronckh from *Candide* (1759) is far from casual: Voltaire's lampoon of German philosophy (in the form of Leibnizian optimism) is precisely the sort of idle critique to which she objects.

Staël's discussion of philosophical style rests, once again, on the opposition between France and Germany. The materialist philosophy of France, she writes, values work if its form is 'ingénieuse et lucide', while German idealist philosophy admires work which offers an insight into 'le foyer de l'âme'.[17] Praising the spiritual tendency of German thought, she attempts to justify its obscurity by arguing that such spirituality is necessarily alien to verbal expression: 'les mots ne sont pas propres à ce genre d'idées, et il en résulte que, pour les y faire servir, on répand sur toutes choses l'obscurité qui précéda la création'.[18] Despite this apologia for abstruseness, Staël is also critical of German philosophers' incapacity for clear expression: 'quand il s'agit de faire entrer leurs idées dans la tête des autres, ils en connaissent mal les moyens'.[19] Indeed, she argues that German thinkers too often blur the distinction between metaphysics and poetry in delving into the hidden depths of the soul.[20] For Staël, then, the link between profundity and obscurity is a necessary one, but it does not diminish the murkiness of German philosophy. The myth of 'la clarté française' is the implicit counterpoint here, even if Staël argues that clarity is often the corollary of superficiality. The obscurity of German thought marks it out as fundamentally alien to French culture: as Antoine de Rivarol's famous formulation states, 'Ce qui n'est pas clair n'est pas français.'[21]

While Staël saw the obscurity of German thought as an inevitable if unfortunate result of its profundity, for its critics it was at best obscurantist, at worst deceptive. What it purportedly concealed was a political message — that of German nationalism — and critics from Heinrich Heine and Edgar Quinet in the 1830s to Louis Reynaud and Jean-Marie Carré in the twentieth century all charge Staël with offering an anachronistically idealized vision of the German cultural sphere as uninvolved with contemporary political developments.[22] There was indeed a strongly nationalistic current in German thought in the early nineteenth century, a current that emerged largely in reaction to the Napoleonic occupation of the

German states in 1806–13 and that is perhaps most pronounced in Johann Fichte's *Reden an die deutsche Nation* (*Addresses to the German Nation*) of 1808. It is important to acknowledge that Staël does demonstrate some awareness of the militaristic tendency of German politics (especially in Prussia), even if she insists on the autonomy of the philosophical sphere.[23] However, it is also true that in general she offers a rose-tinted vision of the German people as 'somewhat uncouth but decent, philosophically and artistically talented but incapable of great political action'.[24] This vision was hugely influential. In fact, both Reynaud and Carré argue that *De l'Allemagne* not only inaugurated a perniciously false image that blinded the French to the realities of Prussian ambitions,[25] but also paved the way for Prussian oppression through its 'germanolâtrie':[26]

> la domination intellectuelle d'un peuple sur un autre prépare sa domination politique. Quand l'âme est conquise, le corps ne saurait résister.[27]

These sweepingly negative assessments of German intellectual influence in France are undoubtedly coloured by the recency of the respective World Wars (Reynaud's work having been published in 1922 and Carré's in 1947). In spite of their condemnation of Staël's influence, they are right to insist on the foundational nature of her text, which did indeed inform representations of Germany throughout the nineteenth century.

They are also correct to assert that interest in German thought in the nineteenth century was often associated, in the Staëlian manner, with opposition to French literature (Classicism), philosophy (materialism), politics (monarchism) or religion (Catholicism),[28] even if such oppositionality did not preclude genuine intellectual engagement with German sources. Cousin, the most important figure in the reception of German philosophy in France following Staël's death in 1817, was very much in this mould as a young liberal, seeing German philosophers as 'les promoteurs de la chute finale du despotisme napoléonien'.[29] Even when he became the education minister in the July Monarchy and his Hegelian-inflected Eclecticism established itself as 'the quasi-official philosophy of the state',[30] German philosophy retained its subversive image: Cousin had to conceal the extent of his debt to Hegel since the philosopher was seen as the 'principal apologist of Absolutism'[31] and thus an inappropriate source of inspiration for an ostensibly liberal regime.

Nonetheless, Hegel became the best-known German philosopher in France in the first half of the nineteenth century, principally through secondary sources. Essays in journals such as the *Revue des deux Mondes* and the *Revue germanique* were essential for the dissemination of German idealist thought, since the almost complete absence of German language teaching in early nineteenth-century France[32] meant that few could read original German sources. Even the major works of the most important German philosophers — Kant, Fichte, Schelling, Hegel — remained untranslated in the mid-1830s. Jean-Pierre Lefebvre confirms that German philosophy was generally translated 'peu, tard et mal'[33] and asserts that the first translations only served to contribute to German philosophy's 'réputation d'obscurité et de difficulté'.[34] (This is despite the claims of translators such as Jean Willm, who argued that 'en traduisant les idées germaniques en une langue nette

et aussi claire que la française' he would be doing German philosophy a favour.³⁵)
Obscurity was thus the defining characteristic of German philosophy in the French imagination. This made it an object of ridicule, and as we shall see in the following chapter Laforgue himself indulges in mockery of Teutonic abstruseness in an early poem. But the notion of obscurity also inspired fascination: as Philippe Van Tieghem states, 'Le mystère même d'une pensée difficile à pénétrer, plus difficile encore à assimiler, accroît son prestige'.³⁶

While German philosophy — however poorly understood — had some impact on French thought in the 1830s, there is little evidence to suggest that it had any direct influence on French literature.³⁷ German literature was, by contrast, an important factor in the development of French Romanticism in the 1830s, thanks to Nerval's translations of Goethe's *Faust* (1828) and of German poetry (1830), as well as to translations of E. T. A. Hoffmann's fantastic tales, which influenced Mérimée and Gautier amongst others. The French Romantics were also deeply involved in Franco-German political relations: they played a key role in the Rhine Crisis of 1840, a crisis which saw the French government of Adolphe Thiers belligerently affirm that the nation's borders should be extended to its 'natural frontier', the Rhine.³⁸ Nicolas Becker's 'Rheinlied', with its refrain of indomitable territoriality 'ils ne l'auront pas, le libre Rhin allemand',³⁹ became hugely popular in Germany, and Musset responded with the equally bellicose (and equally popular) 'Le Rhin allemand', which disdainfully proclaimed 'Nous l'avons eu, votre Rhin allemand'.⁴⁰ The other leading Romantics were more conciliatory, however: Lamartine's 'La Marseillaise de la paix' described the Rhine as the 'coupe des nations'⁴¹ and appealed for an end to nationalism ('Déchirez ces drapeaux'),⁴² while Hugo declared that 'La civilisation entière est la Patrie du poète'.⁴³ At the height of Romanticism, then, the notion of a transnational *République des Lettres* was still current, even if more sceptical and patriotic voices were becoming increasingly prominent.

Ultimately, the Rhine Crisis did little to diminish the Germanophilia of many writers. The persistence of Staël's idyllic vision of Germany is demonstrated by Xavier Marmier's 1844 poem 'Soirée allemande', which describes days in Germany spent enveloped in 'ces rêves du Nord' and evenings discussing art and philosophy in a 'chambre tranquille | Pleine de poésie, humble toit, doux asile'.⁴⁴ Later, Flaubert would confirm this cliché of dreaminess in his *Dictionnaire des idées reçues*, describing Germans as a 'Peuple de rêveurs (vieux)'.⁴⁵ The idealization of Germany is also crucial to Laforgue's reception of Hartmann. Despite his awareness of Franco-German political relations, which was due in part to the years he spent in Berlin, Laforgue nonetheless upheld a romanticized image of the 'true' Germany, a Germany that had been partly but not totally stifled by the dominance of the modern, industrialized Prussian state. For Laforgue 'L'Allemagne pure' (*OC*, III, 343) was the chosen land of the Hartmannian Unconscious, and this was manifest in various aspects of German culture, but most notably in its music.

The notion of Germany as the land of music was, of course, a common one. In the latter half of the nineteenth century, German music was embodied by Wagner, who came to prominence in France through the *Tannhaüser* scandal of 1861.

The scandal was perceived by some (notably Gautier) as a reprise of the 'Bataille d'Hernani', and this galvanized support for Wagner in France amongst intellectuals who were on the side of the *romantiques*. His most famous champion was Baudelaire, whose essay 'Richard Wagner et Tannhaüser à Paris' was inspired by Wagner's own essay on aesthetics, 'Lettre sur la musique'.[46] Baudelaire portrays Wagner's music as an expression of the spiritual realm,[47] and this is echoed by Gautier in his 1886 novel *Spirite*, which describes how Wagner's music 'rendait l'au-delà des mots, le non-sorti du verbe humain, ce qui reste d'inédit dans la phrase la mieux faite, le mystérieux, l'intime et le profond des choses....'.[48] While German philosophy's spiritual inclinations are (according to Staël) stymied by the linguistic difficulties of elucidating the hidden depths of the soul, Wagner's music is (for Baudelaire and Gautier) able to side-step this problem. Indeed, Wagner himself argued that music could be understood intuitively, 'malgré l'obscurité de sa langue selon les lois de la logique'.[49] However, Wagner's aesthetic writings — which were in some sense just as important as his music — did invite the charge of obscurity that was so frequently levelled against German philosophy; for example, Charles Vincens, writing shortly after the turn of the twentieth century, dismisses Wagner's theories as 'brumes d'outre-Rhin'.[50] As with German philosophy, problems of clarity were only exacerbated by the 'arcane, if not incomprehensible, style'[51] of French translations. Wagner was, nonetheless, a hugely important figure for many *fin-de-siècle* writers, as attested by the existence of the *Revue wagnérienne* (1885–88). Among these writers was Laforgue, who drew on Wagner's 'Lettre sur la musique' to support his vision of Germany as the land of the Unconscious, as well as transfiguring the composer's opera *Parsifal* in his tale 'Lohengrin, fils de Parsifal' (*Moralités légendaires*).[52]

The reception of Wagner is, in one sense, symptomatic of the French engagement with German thought in the nineteenth century, in that his supporters considered his writings to be spiritually profound while his detractors dismissed them as obscurantist nonsense. However, in another sense he is a case apart: despite the importance of Hegel to French philosophy and political thought, and the engagement of French writers with German literature and Franco-German politics, Wagner represents the first non-literary German thinker to have any significant direct influence on French literature in the nineteenth century. But Schopenhauer's influence followed close on its heels.[53] His work did not begin to attract widespread academic interest until the 1850s, long after the initial publication of *The World as Will and Representation* in 1818, but his fame began to grow after his death in 1860, reaching its zenith in the 1880s. After 1870, Schopenhauer was the best-known and most talked-about German philosopher in France (at least until the breakthrough of Nietzsche's work in the 1890s) and the upsurge in 'le schopenhauerisme' in the 1880s can legitimately be described as a fad.[54] Indeed, interest in the philosopher contained an element of dandyish posturing, as Anne Henry points out: 'tous les snobs blasés peuvent se dire schopenhauériens'.[55] But Schopenhauer's ideas also had a deeper, more substantial influence, an influence that was felt most strongly in French literature rather than French philosophy.[56]

Maupassant, Huysmans, Proust and Gide[57] were among those affected by the broad intellectual sweep of Schopenhauer's thought: 'la dévaluation des idéaux, le règne de l'inconscience, des affects aveugles et des tensions agonistiques, l'appesantissement de déterminations insoulevables, la faiblesse de l'ordre rationnel'.[58] But until 1886, when the first French translation of *The World as Will and Representation* was published,[59] writers' knowledge of Schopenhauer was almost entirely based on critical texts. His reception thus conformed to the pattern established earlier in the century, with secondary works preceding translations, and this served to establish a mythification of both Schopenhauer and his philosophy. In fact, the first widely available translation of his work was published in 1880; but this was a collection of aphorisms (*Pensées, maximes et fragments*, translated by Jean Bourdeau), and it gave very little sense of the systemic nature of Schopenhauer's philosophical enterprise. It drew heavily on Schopenhauer's 1851 publication *Parerga and Paralipomena*, which literally means 'complementary works and matters omitted',[60] and which has been described by Magee as being akin to 'the unused bits of wood in the workshop'.[61] Schopenhauer's dry wit and stylistic elegance lent themselves to aphoristic fragmentation, and this certainly attracted attention to his work, but it did not do justice to the scope of his philosophical system, instead casting him as a purveyor of misanthropic soundbites. By contrast, Hartmann's magnum opus *The Philosophy of the Unconscious* was translated into French only eight years after its 1869 publication in Germany; most *fin-de-siècle* writers, Laforgue included, thus approached Hartmann's work directly rather than through critical sources. But despite this crucial difference in the history of their reception, Schopenhauer and Hartmann were often seen to constitute a unified school of (pessimist) German philosophy,[62] as indicated by Elme-Marie Caro's influential *Le Pessimisme au XIXe siècle* (1878), which was largely devoted to analyses of the two philosophers.

France in the 1870s was certainly ripe for pessimism. The catastrophic defeat in the Franco-Prussian War had prompted a crisis of confidence on a national scale, with widespread anxiety about France's reduced geopolitical status and outdated institutions. It also led many intellectuals to repudiate their Germanophilia. Many of the Parnassian poets who published collections inspired by the war denounced what they saw as the deceptive innocence of German culture,[63] with some, such as Victor de Laprade, alluding to German philosophy specifically:

> Dupes de ces voisins que nous appelions frères,
> De leur jargon obscur naïfs admirateurs
> Nous tendions, par-dessus nos tranquilles frontières,
> Une loyale main à leurs maîtres-chanteurs.[64]

While Laprade does not mention Hegel by name, it is likely that the reference to 'leur jargon obscur' was aimed principally at him. Not only was Hegel the German philosopher most associated with obscurity, he was also held responsible for the development of Germany into a modern, militarized nation-state and was thus 'terriblement dénigré en France'.[65] Schopenhauer and Hartmann's pessimism was also condemned by many critics, but for different reasons: rather than being linked to the Prussian state apparatus, they were seen as exacerbating the decline of French society insidiously. Unlike Hegel, their work gained in popularity in the Third Republic, the French reading public indulging in pessimist ideas despite critics' denunciations of their corrupting influence. But for some intellectuals, it was the notion of corruption itself which was appealing, the perceived otherness of Schopenhauer and Hartmann's thought affording it a certain counter-cultural force.

A Discourse of Disease: the Reception of Schopenhauer and Hartmann in France

In the history of German philosophy's reception in France, the treatment of Hartmann and (especially) Schopenhauer represents a new phase: for the first time, German philosophy was widely portrayed as a threatening, invasive force. This perception of danger fuelled the notoriety of their work, and of the figure of Schopenhauer in particular. Hartmann was not a controversial figure to the same extent as Schopenhauer, around whom myths, rumours and polemic relentlessly swirled; this cult of personality was crucial to the reception of his thought by Laforgue and his contemporaries. But as well as the demonization of Schopenhauer himself, the pessimism, atheism and (supposed) nihilism of his and Hartmann's philosophy were also condemned as diseases infecting the French body politic.

The turning point for Schopenhauer's reputation in France was an article by the Republican journalist and politician Paul Challemel-Lacour published in *La Revue des deux Mondes* on 15 March 1870, some four months before the outbreak of the Franco-Prussian War. Entitled 'Un Bouddhiste contemporain en Allemagne', the article was based on an interview with Schopenhauer that Challemel-Lacour had undertaken a year before the philosopher's death in 1860. It remained well known for many years, as indicated by Maupassant's periphrastic reference to 'l'entrevue du vieux démolisseur avec un politicien français, républicain doctrinaire' in his 1883 *nouvelle* about Schopenhauer, 'Auprès d'un mort'.[66] The tale portrays Schopenhauer as a sinister figure, the metadiegetic narrator even claiming that Challemel-Lacour stated 'J'ai cru passer une heure avec le diable'.[67] This is, in fact, Maupassant's invention. But Challemel-Lacour does depict Schopenhauer as an almost demonic figure who proclaims 'l'absurdité de la vie, l'inanité de toutes les espérances, l'inexorable fatalité du malheur attaché à l'existence humaine'.[68] It is Schopenhauer's views on love that cause his interviewer particular disquiet, however. 'L'amour,' Schopenhauer declares, 'c'est l'ennemi'; it is the tool of 'le Génie de l'espèce', for whom men are 'dupes' and women 'complices'.[69] The only way out of this trap is asceticism, which serves to 'préparer la fin du monde et en indiquer le chemin', since by refraining from sex and thus procreation the ascetic 'sauve de la vie des générations entières'.[70] But this path to redemptive annihilation has been blocked by female treachery:

> Il donne un exemple qui a failli sauver le monde deux ou trois fois. Les femmes ne l'ont pas voulu; c'est pourquoi je les hais.[71]

It is not so much Schopenhauer's misogyny that perturbs Challemel-Lacour, but rather his doctrine of chastity and its logical end-point of human extinction: 'ses paroles [...] me causaient une sorte de malaise, comme si j'eusse senti passer sur moi un souffle glacé à travers la porte entr'ouverte du néant'.[72]

Challemel-Lacour's florid expression of vertiginous philosophical horror drew much attention to this aspect of Schopenhauer's philosophical system. In fact, the eschatological vision that Schopenhauer adumbrates in this interview plays a very minor role in *The World as Will and Representation*; it is only mentioned in passing as the inevitable consequence of his doctrine of chastity: 'if this maxim became universal, the human race would die out' (*WWR*, I, 380). But its prominence in Challemel-Lacour's interview was such that it came to be seen as central to Schopenhauer's doctrine. This distortion was perpetuated by Bourdeau, who, in his introduction to his collection of aphorisms, summarizes *The World as Will and Representation* as 'ce livre fameux qui conduit à l'ascétisme en vue d'amener la fin du monde par la continence absolue des sexes'.[73] Bourdeau also quotes Schopenhauer's (again somewhat incidental) statement in 'The Metaphysics of Sexual Love' that lovers look at each other furtively because they are traitors who secretly strive to 'perpétuer toute la misère et les tourments qui, sans eux, auraient une fin prochaine.'[74] As a result of Challemel-Lacour and Bourdeau's privileging of Schopenhauer's eschatology, pessimism was cast as a kind of apocalyptic nihilism in the popular imaginary. This is illustrated by Zola's *La Joie de vivre* (1884), in which the Schopenhauerian Lazare offers a vision of the end of the world:

> il annonçait le suicide final des peuples, culbutant en masse dans le noir, refusant d'engendrer des générations nouvelles, le jour où leur intelligence développée les convaincrait de la parade imbécile et cruelle qu'une force inconnue leur faisait jouer.[75]

Lazare also recapitulates the misogyny that is evident in Schopenhauer's work, but particularly strongly in Challemel-Lacour's interview:

> Aussi exagérait-il, du matin au soir, son pessimisme sur les femmes et l'amour, dans des boutades féroces. Tout le mal venait des femmes, sottes, légères, éternisant la douleur par le désir, et l'amour n'était qu'une duperie, l'égoïste poussée des générations futures qui voulaient vivre. Schopenhauer entier y passait [...].[76]

Laforgue was one of those influenced by Challemel-Lacour's account of Schopenhauerian thought. His reception of Hartmann was not inflected by contemporary critics in quite the same way: firstly because, as previously noted, Hartmann's work was available in translation not long after its publication; secondly because Hartmann was not subject to the same level of critical attention or controversy. This is despite Hartmann sharing Schopenhauer's cynicism regarding 'le démon de l'amour',[77] and despite offering a far more comprehensive eschatological vision of the total annihilation of the universe.

In fact, in his comparison of Schopenhauer and Hartmann, Caro recognizes that the latter's doctrine of collective salvation is even more far-fetched than the former's: rather than simply preaching the end of the human race, Hartmann envisages 'le suicide cosmique accompli par l'humanité'[78] through a state of universal enlightenment. Caro condemns both philosophers' doctrines, but recognizes that

Schopenhauer's is, at least, potentially practicable, unlike Hartmann's.[79] Paul Janet concurs: 'Vous ne pouvez pas plus anéantir le monde que vous n'avez pu le créer'.[80] But elsewhere in his article, Janet points to the differences in personality of the two philosophers, and it is these differences that explain why Schopenhauer was a far more notorious figure than Hartmann. Hartmann, he states, had 'une nature plus sympathique et plus élevée'.[81] 'Le pessimisme théorique paraît s'unir en lui à des mœurs plus douces. Il n'a point cette misanthropie brutale et cynique qui fait de Schopenhauer un personnage si amusant, mais si insupportable.'[82] While Hartmann led a conventional bourgeois life with his wife and children in accordance with his ethics of social progress through reproduction, Schopenhauer was unmarried and was rumoured to be a womanizer. Indeed, one of the principal arguments levelled against Schopenhauer concerned not his philosophical ideas but his lifestyle, which was deemed to be at odds with his ethics of compassion and chastity. Such *ad hominem* argumentation is suggested in general terms by Bourdeau: 'comme la plupart des moralistes, la vie de Schopenhauer est-elle un commentaire de ses œuvres, souvent un commentaire à rebours: ses actes démentent ce que sa doctrine a d'excessif et d'outré'.[83] His misanthropy is often noted: Caro comments that Schopenhauer's doctrine of pity is incongruous with 'la violence de ses haines'[84] and Théodule Ribot asks how he could have reconciled being both 'un misanthrope farouche et un bouddhiste contemplatif'.[85] His reputed libertinism is also frequently mentioned. Janet quotes Hartmann's critique of Schopenhauer's misogyny, expressed in the form of the circumlocutory retort that those who do not respect women have only met women who do not deserve respect.[86] Ribot, meanwhile, is more direct, referring to 'Les femmes de mœurs faciles qu'il connut à Dresde et en Italie (car il ne paraît pas les avoir toujours détestées, au moins en pratique)...'.[87] Charles de Varigny even goes as far as to allege that Schopenhauer fathered an illegitimate child, who was born — ironically — at the time of the publication of *The World as Will and Representation*, which preached sexual abstinence.[88]

It was these accusations of misanthropy and debauchery, with their concomitant taint of hypocrisy, that created the cult of personality surrounding Schopenhauer. His reputation was even exploited for comic effect. In Maupassant's 'Auprès d'un mort', the *récit emboîté* recounts an eerie and seemingly supernatural occurrence at a vigil over Schopenhauer's corpse: a white object is seen to emerge from the dead philosopher's mouth and scuttle under a chair. However, the story's conclusion reveals this apparition to be none other than his false teeth, forcibly expelled by the effects of posthumous decomposition, and the *nouvelle* can thus be read as mocking rather than endorsing the Mephistophelean image of the philosopher, as playing with the reader's expectations before finally demonstrating their baselessness. Conversely, the physiological explanation for the occurrence might be seen to confirm the frame narrative's view of Schopenhauer as a merciless cynic who would have scorned supernatural explanations:

> Jouisseur désabusé [qui] a renversé les croyances, les espoirs, les poésies, les chimères, détruit les aspirations, ravagé la confiance des âmes, tué l'amour, abattu le culte idéal de la femme, crevé les illusions des cœurs, accompli la plus gigantesque besogne de sceptique qui ait jamais été faite.[89]

By contrast, Félicien Champsaur's *Lulu, pantomime clownesque* (1888) does not portray Schopenhauer as (potentially) diabolical; instead it ridicules him by featuring a clown caricaturing the philosopher.[90]

In his 1888 article 'Clowns et philosophes', the Naturalist writer Henry Céard seeks to defend Schopenhauer against such derision, arguing that 'on attaque Schopenhauer moins sur ses idées que sur sa nationalité'.[91] He maintains that the popular perception of Schopenhauer's thought conforms to the clichés regarding German philosophy that had prevailed since the start of the century:

> Il est Allemand, et [...] on a aveuglément conclu que, semblable à tous les philosophes d'outre-Rhin, il s'était répandu en conceptions nuageuses, aggravant le vague des aperçus par l'obscurité amphigourique du style.[92]

Céard refutes this perception, although in doing so he recapitulates the aforementioned clichés:

> jamais phrase allemande ne fut moins allemande que cette phrase-là; jamais esprit ne fut plus foncièrement français; son mode de penser, son mode d'écrire n'ont rien de commun avec le génie germanique.[93]

Indeed, Schopenhauer's style, with its 'phrase nette, courte, acérée, précise',[94] is reminiscent of the writing of *philosophes* such as Diderot, states Céard. This cultural assimilation of Schopenhauer based on the clarity of his style is a common theme in French criticism of his work. Challemel-Lacour labels him 'un moraliste dans le sens français du mot'[95] and Ribot concurs that 'Il n'est allemand ni par l'esprit ni par le style'.[96] Janet notes that he was brought up in various parts of Europe, including Le Havre, and that this partially French education contributed to his 'goût de la clarté et de la précision'; as a young man, he launched a rebellion 'contre le jargon métaphysique et algébrique, contre le dogmatisme pédantesque et barbare dont l'Allemagne était alors enivrée, et que Hégel [sic] devait porter bientôt jusqu'à une véritable insanité'.[97] This rejection of Germanic obscurity is confirmed by Schopenhauer's own statements, with Bourdeau quoting his assertion that he prefers the French style over the 'lourdeur'[98] of German writing; he also cites the philosopher's declaration of vehement antipathy towards the German nation as a whole: 'je méprise la nation allemande à cause de sa bêtise infinie, et [...] je rougis de lui appartenir'.[99] The fact that Bourdeau places this quotation at the very end of his selection, thereby giving it special prominence, indicates the extent to which he deemed Schopenhauer's abjuration of national identity to be important to a post-1870 French readership.

In addition to its assimilatory function, the perception of Schopenhauer as a *moraliste* also serves to undermine the fundamentally metaphysical basis of his philosophy. Many of the critical works on Schopenhauer downplay the systemic nature of his thought: Ribot's statement that Schopenhauer, despite being both 'un systématique et un moraliste', 'vaut surtout comme moraliste'[100] is typical in this sense. Indeed, in Bourdeau's popular *Pensées, maximes et fragments* it is difficult to discern that there is a system at all. Magee argues that this dismantling of his philosophy into nuggets of worldly wisdom is an unfortunate side-effect of the quality of his prose, which has resulted in 'the living body of his work [being] butchered for aphorisms and epigrams, juicy extracts and dramatic quotations torn out of context'.[101] Bourdeau's collection epitomizes this butchery. As René-Pierre Colin notes, its enormous success was largely founded on 'son caractère de vulgarisation';[102] while acknowledging the metaphysical aspect of Schopenhauer's philosophy, Bourdeau states that he has chosen to emphasize other, less specialized elements of Schopenhauer's work: 'à côté du métaphysicien, on rencontre dans ses écrits un moraliste curieux, un humoriste original et un écrivain clair, accessible à tous, et presque populaire'.[103] Bourdeau argues that in *Parerga and Paralipomena* Schopenhauer himself 'sollicite les suffrages des *honnêtes gens* qui ne se piquent pas de métaphysique',[104] the adaptation of La Rochefoucauld's axiom[105] reinforcing the francization of Schopenhauer's work.

The view of Schopenhauer as a stylist and purveyor of maxims (particularly on love, sex and marriage) does not necessarily preclude *ad hominem* criticism. Janet, for example, argues that Schopenhauer's rejection of earlier German philosophy's obscurity was 'la révolte d'un esprit net et sain [...] contre le mensonge de formules et le despotisme du galimatias',[106] but he offsets his praise of lucidity with the assertion that it is 'uni sans doute à un caractère malade'.[107] This is in keeping with Schopenhauer's Janus-like image as, on the one hand, a Francophile and a master of style and, on the other, a cynical, misogynistic *viveur*. But it also points to the importance of notions of illness to the reception of Schopenhauer's ideas: metaphors of disease and contagion are frequently used to portray his work (and, to a lesser extent, that of Hartmann) as threateningly other. Alexandre Foucher de Careil, for example, uses such a metaphor in relation to Schopenhauer's purported pantheism (a doctrine associated with him because he holds the Will to be ubiquitous), and in doing so he associates him with a specifically Germanic tradition: 'Schopenhauer est un exemple illustre de cette contagion panthéistique qui n'a rien épargné en Allemagne.'[108] While pantheism is deemed to be pathogenic in general terms, Foucher de Careil uses a more specific metaphor to criticize Schopenhauer's endorsement of quietism (the doctrine of passivity and contemplation that was also a seventeenth-century heresy): he describes it as 'un véritable choléra de l'âme'.[109] He also emphasizes French hostility towards this doctrine, which he describes as 'ce procédé mystique de mort anticipée dont nous serions tentés en France de lui faire presque un crime'.[110]

Foucher de Careil uses metaphors of disease, then, to criticize the aspects of Schopenhauer's work associated with religious heterodoxy, and in this he conforms to the view of many Second-Empire thinkers for whom 'l'Allemagne représente [...] la grande menace pour l'Église'.[111] But after 1870, these metaphors are most often used to describe the effects of pessimism. Caro labels pessimism 'une sorte de maladie intellectuelle',[112] a formulation that was quoted by Bourdeau and de Varigny among others.[113] Like Foucher de Careil, Caro also insists on the otherness of German thought, describing pessimism as 'antipathique à l'esprit français'.[114] The Republican *député* Dionys Ordinaire is even more explicit in associating the foreignness of pessimist thought and its contagious effects: 'Il souffle d'Allemagne, depuis quelques années, sur notre jeunesse française, un vent aigre et malsain qui nous apporte une épidémie nouvelle, inconnue à notre vieille Gaule: celle du pessimisme.'[115] While for Caro pessimism is 'une maladie privilégiée, concentrée jusqu'à ce jour dans les sphères de la haute culture',[116] for Ordinaire this is an epidemic that 'infecte une notable partie de notre jeunesse'.[117] It is especially pernicious because it undermines the possibility of avenging the French defeat: 'Pour moi, [...] quand je me sentirais menacé de choir en désespérance, je regarderais, si j'étais jeune comme vous, du côté de l'Allemagne, par la trouée des Vosges, et ce n'est pas Shopenhauer [sic] que je verrais.'[118] Pessimism is thus doubly noxious: in addition to its demoralizing effect on the young — that is, on potential soldiers — it also serves to distract attention from Bismarck, the architect of France's downfall.

Susan Sontag argues that the metaphors of disease traditionally used to suggest intellectual or societal corruption are 'relatively contentless', with little distinction made between particular diseases; by contrast, in the modern use of such metaphors, each disease has its 'own distinctive logic'.[119] Most of the metaphors used to describe Schopenhauer's thought are non-specific ('maladie', 'épidémie', 'contagion') and can thus be categorized as 'traditional' in Sontag's sense; but as we have seen, Foucher de Careil also refers to a specific disease: cholera. Unknown in Europe prior to the nineteenth century, cholera is thought to have originated in India, and it killed hundreds of thousands of Europeans in a series of pandemics throughout the century. Erin O'Connor argues that the disease thus 'provided a figure for the threatening fluidity of cultural and bodily boundaries in an imperialist world economy'.[120] In this sense, it is important to note that Foucher de Careil refers to cholera in relation to quietism, a doctrine associated not only with Christian heresy but also with Eastern thought.[121] But the notion of 'threatening fluidity' is also applicable to the anxieties concerning the porous intellectual border between France and Germany, and the corrupting effects of doctrines circulating transnationally within Europe.

Prior to the discovery of cholera's microbial origin, the two competing etiologies of the disease were those of miasma and contagion. The former deemed local-level insanitary conditions (that is, foul air) to be cholera's cause, thus demanding a response based on hygienism; the latter saw the disease as being passed from person to person, thus demanding quarantinism and border control.[122] In the popular imagination, however, the two theories were conflated into a conception of an airborne menace capable of travelling across borders: in Britain, 'The popular press showed a screeching miasmatic cholera wafting through the air on waves of stench';[123] in France, cholera was depicted as a winged demon.[124] Ordinaire's description of Schopenhauerian pessimism as 'un vent aigre et malsain' blowing into France from Germany conveys a similar impression of ideas being both 'dans l'air du temps' and able to transgress national borders to infect the French. While the 'brumes' of earlier German philosophy were essentially static, being confined to Germany itself or contained within the books and brains of its thinkers, this aeolian image invests pessimist philosophy with a dangerously dynamic power.

These metaphors of contagious disease were crucial to the reception of Schopenhauer in particular and of German pessimism in general. Indeed, the influence of other German thinkers, thinkers not specifically associated with pessimism, was portrayed using the same kind of imagery. Wagner's detractors, for example, referred to the craze for his ideas as '*la wagnériole, la wagnéromanie,* and *la wagnéralgie*'.[125] In the 1890s, Nietzsche's philosophy was similarly pathologized, as Douglas Smith notes: 'At its most extreme, [...] his work is rejected on the grounds that it is not just sick but that the sickness is contagious.'[126] There are, in fact, further parallels between the French reception of Schopenhauer and that of Nietzsche. The latter's work was also subject to a discourse of cultural assimilation, again founded partly on the philosopher's own professed hostility to his homeland; Smith notes 'the tendency to read Nietzsche primarily in terms of his criticism of Germany and his avowed preference for French culture' as a way of naturalizing him 'as a spiritual compatriot'.[127] Moreover, Nietzsche was, like his predecessor, praised for his style, which was seen as especially appealing to the French.[128] Indeed, just as Schopenhauer was described as a 'moraliste', so there was 'a consistent attempt to assimilate Nietzsche to the French tradition of the short essay, the *sentence* and the *maxime,* as represented by writers such as Montaigne, Pascal, La Rochefoucauld'.[129] The French reception of both Schopenhauer and Nietzsche was thus characterized by a kind of doublethink: their work was embraced because of its stylistic similarity to a venerable French tradition of pithy prose; but it was simultaneously rejected on the grounds of its otherness, which threatened to have deleterious effects on French minds. This rejection was by no means universal, however. Counter-culturally-inclined intellectuals saw these dangerous thinkers from across the Rhine as the philosophical equivalents of the *poètes maudits*; indeed, Gilles Deleuze and Colin both use the term 'penseur maudit', for Nietzsche and Schopenhauer respectively.[130]

Such similarities suggest that there are deep cultural issues at stake in the French reception of German philosophy. Smith argues that the Franco-Prussian War provides a context for the reception of Nietzsche, suggesting a 'correlation between this consistent French emphasis on Nietzsche's *Kulturkritik* and a revanchist desire to retaliate in cultural terms for the military defeat at the hands of the Germans in the war of 1870'.[131] The insistence in criticism of Schopenhauer on the philosopher's declarations of aversion towards the German nation can be interpreted in the same way. Indeed, the opposite aspect of his reception in France — the hostility towards his doctrines — might also be read in the light of the Franco-Prussian War: the discourse of invasive disease and of French opposition might be seen as a metaphorical displacement of the actual incursion into France of Prussian troops. This was, argues Claude Digeon, the most traumatic aspect of France's defeat: 'le fait fondamental qui marque la conscience française, c'est bien que la bataille s'est déroulée sur le sol national et qu'elle a revêtu l'aspect d'un envahissement'.[132] It was particularly shocking firstly because no military conflict had taken place on French soil since the end of the Napoleonic Wars some fifty-five years earlier, and secondly because of the swiftness of the defeat, with Prussian troops seizing the French capital in just over six months. The metaphors of contagion that are used in conjunction with philosophical ideas might thus be seen as recapitulating the trauma of foreign troops invading the 'body' of France.

However, this does not entirely explain the use of such metaphors: Foucher de Careil, whose criticism is particularly rich in images of disease, published his work on Schopenhauer eight years before the 1870 War. His use of this discourse in relation to quietist and pantheist ideas suggests that he saw Schopenhauer's philosophy as an attack on the Catholic Church. Indeed, the Vatican itself condemns both quietism and pantheism — alongside rationalism, naturalism, materialism, scientism, positivism, Darwinism, socialism and communism — in the 1864 Syllabus of Errors, a document that conveys its sense of being besieged by contemporary political and scientific doctrines.[133] Opposition to Schopenhauer on religious grounds did not necessarily imply adherence to Papal authority, however. Caro agreed that pessimism undermined Christian faith, but as a champion of Cousinian spiritualism,[134] (a rationalist philosophy that nonetheless proclaimed the existence of God) he did not (like the Vatican) conceive of science and religion as antagonistic. Indeed, he held that Schopenhauer's work threatened both religious belief and the secular cult of progress:

> le pessimisme nous paraît comme le dernier terme d'un mouvement philosophique qui a tout détruit: la réalité de Dieu, la réalité du devoir, la réalité du moi, la moralité de la science, le progrès, et par là l'effort, le travail.'[135]

Given that images of disease are used both before 1870 (by Foucher de Careil) and after it (by Caro and others), and that they are used to condemn perceived attacks on both religious and secular ideals, it is important to situate them within a broader discursive context — that of decline and degeneration.

Defeat and the Downfall of France

The related (but not synonymous) notions of decline, degeneration and decadence had considerable currency in the late nineteenth century, as many critics have noted. The French sense of decline was symptomatic of a pan-European malaise, but France's pessimism also had specifically national origins: it was 'closely related to the feeling that the nation's power and prestige in the world was declining.'[136] Indeed, Max Nordau — whose *Entartung* (*Degeneration*) constituted the most influential analysis of what many perceived to be modernity's ailments — saw the *fin-de-siècle* mood, described as 'the impotent despair of a sick man',[137] as specifically French in origin.[138] He argued that the trauma of the Revolution and the Napoleonic Wars had left the French psyche vulnerable, which exacerbated the impact of the defeat in the Franco-Prussian War:

> Upon this nation, nervously strained and pre-destined to morbid derangement, there broke the awful catastrophe of 1870. It had, with a self-satisfaction which almost attained to megalomania, believed itself the first nation in the world; it now saw itself suddenly humiliated and crushed. All its convictions abruptly crumbled to pieces.[139]

Nordau's account of the French crisis of confidence is undoubtedly hyperbolic. However, Robert Nye confirms that thinkers from across the political spectrum — monarchist, Bonapartist, republican — had all conceived of France as 'la Grande

Nation, the premier military power on the continent and the richest, most populous and economically advanced state in West and Central Europe'.[140] After the French defeat, this view became unsustainable.

The humiliation of defeat prompted a flurry of publications seeking to uncover the roots of French weakness; however, the 1870 War did not mark the origin of discourses of decline, it simply 'made concepts of decline seem credible'.[141] Koenraad Swart argues that the 'decisive turning point in French intellectual history' was in fact the failure of the 1848 revolution, which engendered a profound sense of disillusionment in the idea of social and political progress amongst left-wing intellectuals. In its aftermath, he states, 'the doctrinaire belief in progress began to lose its intellectual respectability'.[142] In fact, there was pessimism across the political spectrum, with one of the first systematic accounts of France's purported decline, *De la Décadence de la France*, being published in 1850 by the conservative Claude Marie Raudot. It indicated a number of deleterious trends, notably the slow growth of the population,[143] Raudot demonstrating that France — formerly the most populous country in Europe — had fallen behind Austria, Russia and Britain in demographic terms.[144] The decline of the birth rate in the Second Empire led some to conclude that 'the future would belong to the more procreative nations of the world.'[145] Not only did this demographic trend continue into the Third Republic, it also became more widely discussed, to the point that it came to occupy a central role in notions of French decadence, even constituting a national 'délire nataliste':[146] 'The decline of the birth rate, more than any other trend in modern France, seemed to indicate that the nation was declining in vitality and might be approaching its downfall.'[147] Post-1870 comparisons between France and Imperial Rome contributed to the idea that the former might, like the latter, end up disappearing altogether.

Comparison with France's chief geopolitical rivals Britain and Germany intensified the sense of anxiety, since both saw annual population increases of around four hundred thousand. The demographic superiority of Germany was particularly troubling, both in its cause and its consequence. Digeon notes that while the German and French populations were roughly equal in 1870, Germany overtook France as a result of the annexation of Alsace and Lorraine, and that by 1880 its population was some eight million ahead of its neighbour's.[148] The fact that Germany became the more populous nation in the decade following its victory meant that the revenge desperately craved by many in France became increasingly unlikely, since the superior German population also gave them a considerable military advantage. This advantage was all the more galling because it resulted from the boost given to the German population by the capture of France's eastern regions.

It was this annexation that constituted the greatest psychological blow to France, argues Reiner Marcowitz: while the payment of five billion francs in reparations was deemed acceptable, the seizure of Alsace-Lorraine 'seemed anachronistic and even barbaric in the age of nation-states and self-determination of peoples'.[149] Indeed, in contemporary accounts France was figured as a body that had been dismembered by the loss of its eastern provinces.[150] Notable among such accounts was that of Jules Michelet, who describes France as the only nation to possess organic unity, both because of its administrative uniformity and because of the fusion of races within the French people. He thus describes the French as 'le peuple le moins démembrable',[151] and condemns Germany's land-grab as an act of Frank-ensteinian transplantation:

> arracher l'Alsace, la Lorraine, d'un corps vivant, de l'unité organique la plus forte qui fut jamais, nous extraire avec un couteau ces viscères pour les fourrer dans un corps comme l'Allemagne qui est en formation, c'est une chirurgie étrange.[152]

Zola uses the same surgical metaphor in his description of Thiers' speech justifying the acceptance of Germany's demand for annexation; however, unlike Michelet, who sees the severance of one part as destroying the whole ('Couper, c'est tuer le tout'[153]), Zola supports Thiers' argument that the loss of Alsace-Lorraine is painful but necessary:

> Sa parole claire, incisive, nette et brillante comme une lame, à chaque réponse opérait pour ainsi dire la malheureuse France couchée sur son lit de douleur. [...] Il me semblait voir dans la main de M. Thiers l'outil du chirurgien qui, au milieu des sanglots, coupe un membre, panse une plaie en faisant appel à toute son énergie.[154]

As Bertrand Taithe points out, Zola portrays Thiers as a 'heroic' surgeon, taking a swift decision to prevent further suffering, unlike the 'conservative' surgeon, who keeps the patient under scrutiny and only amputates if gangrene sets in.[155]

Taithe's argument 'that the defeat of the flesh became the central metaphor of French representations of the war after 1870'[156] is supported by Zola's *La Débâcle* (1892), in which the 'Emperor's increasingly weak body'[157] synecdochically represents the weakness of France as a whole, as Hannah Thompson has shown.[158] But these fleshy images took crucially different forms. Michelet and Zola focus on the consequence of French defeat, equating territorial loss to dismemberment; Arthur de Gobineau, on the other hand, concentrates on the cause of the defeat, which he sees as disease within the French body politic:

> Pour qu'un pays se décompose de la sorte, il faut que le mal le travaille et le perfore par l'intérieur; les blessures infligées par l'assaillant extérieur produisent des entailles, mais non jamais cette liquéfaction purulente de la moelle et du sang.[159]

Gobineau, one of the chief exponents of the theory of French degeneration, saw the debility of the French nation-body as the counterpart to a diminishment in the quality of the actual bodies of the French; the decline in the birth rate was, he argued, attributable to the rise in nervous conditions, hereditary illnesses and diseases of the blood, as well as to 'l'aspect général chétif, pauvre, mesquin'.[160] The metaphors of dismemberment and disease thus reveal themselves to have radically divergent significations: the former is associated with a martyrial vision of France attacked from without, or a heroic conception of the part sacrificed for the whole; the latter, on the other hand, condemns France as rotten from the inside.

The organicist image of the nation-body has a long history,[161] but it was particularly prevalent in late nineteenth-century France, when 'a medical model of cultural crisis developed that exercised a linguistic and cultural imperialism over all other ways of viewing the nation's plight'.[162] As well as its use in sociological and political discourse, the nation-body image also provided a model for literature: in *Le Roman expérimental*, Zola describes the role of the Naturalist novelist as analogous to that of the experimental physician, the Naturalist's task being to study the body politic in order to examine some 'plaie grave qui empoisonne la société'[163] and to discover its cause. Zola argues that 'dans la société comme dans le corps humain, il existe une solidarité qui lie les différents membres, les différents organes entre eux',[164] and Bourget concurs that 'Une société doit être assimilée à un organisme'[165] given the composite nature of both. Each part, states Bourget, has its specific function within the whole, and if any element gains too much autonomy, 'l'anarchie qui s'établit constitue la décadence de l'ensemble'.[166] This law applies to both real bodies and the social body. But while Zola sees literature as standing apart from society in order to diagnose its ills, Bourget argues that literature is subject to the same logic of corporeal disintegration as society itself. This logic is at the root of Decadent style:

> Un style de décadence est celui où l'unité du livre se décompose pour laisser la place à l'indépendance de la page, où la page se décompose pour laisser la place à l'indépendance de la phrase, et la phrase pour laisser la place à l'indépendance du mot.[167]

Moreover, he opens the possibility of revalorizing societal disintegration in terms of the benefits of individualism, especially for the Decadent artist; one might, he argues, reason as follows:

> 'Si les citoyens d'une décadence sont inférieurs comme ouvriers de la grandeur du pays, ne sont-ils pas très supérieurs comme artistes de l'intérieur de leur âme? S'ils sont malhabiles à l'action privée ou publique, n'est-ce point qu'ils sont trop habiles à la pensée solitaire? S'ils sont de mauvais reproducteurs de générations futures, n'est-ce point que l'abondance des sensations fines et l'exquisité des sentiments rares en ont fait des virtuoses stérilisés, mais raffinés, des voluptés et des douleurs?'[168]

The notion of turning inward, away from productive involvement in society, is an extension of conceptions of the Romantic writer;[169] but the medicalized vision of artists as 'mauvais reproducteurs de générations futures' belongs specifically to the late nineteenth-century context of a society concerned above all with demographic weakness.

For Zola, however, the Decadents (and Symbolists) were quite simply 'dégénérés'.[170] In his 1895 essay 'Dépopulation', he argues that the task of overturning France's demographic problems falls not to legislators but 'aux moralistes, aux écrivains, aux poètes';[171] however, in the literature of the Decadent and Symbolist movements, 'nous ne trouvons plus que la guerre à l'amour, à l'amour sain et loyal, qui procrée, et qui s'en vante'.[172] Such works of literature — works which 'exaltent la femme inféconde' and 'méprisent le mâle solide et puissant'[173] — are only contributing to the problems of depopulation.[174] And at the root of this insidiously anti-natalist literature is none other than Schopenhauer and 'sa théorie de la douleur de vivre, sa haine de la vie qu'il poursuit dans la femme et dans l'amour';[175] this doctrine, which has become 'le lieu commun de tous les sots et l'excuse de tous les débauchés',[176] holds that it is a crime to give life to a being doomed to suffer, and that 'le sage est celui qui ne procrée plus, qui rêve de la fin de la vie, par la grève de toutes les forces génératrices'.[177] The influence of Challemel-Lacour is again crucial here.

While Zola condemned the unhealthy content of Decadent and Symbolist literature, others viewed these movements as the result of sickness, or as forms of sickness in themselves. Most famously, Nordau declared that 'symbolic and "decadent" works' were symptomatic of 'two well-defined conditions of disease [...] viz. degeneration (degeneracy) and hysteria'.[178] The medical doctor Émile Laurent, meanwhile, condemned Decadent poetry as a form of 'verbigération',[179] the obsessive repetition of words under the effect of mental illness, and in 1888 Anatole France described contemporary literature as 'une démence et une sorte de manie contagieuse', arguing that it was afflicted with a disease that stymied its development: 'L'esprit de la jeunesse littéraire, l'esprit français dans sa dernière sève, est atteint d'une épidémie qui ne lui permet plus de croître et de fleurir.'[180] Decadent literature was depicted not only as sick, but also as impotent and infertile. For Laurent, Decadent poetry was 'toujours de la maladie, et, par conséquent, une demi impuissance',[181] while Nordau described the Decadents as 'intellectual eunuchs'[182] who were incapable of producing viable textual progeny. Such critiques accuse the Decadent movement of lacking in generative power both biologically and artistically. The confluence of the metaphors used to condemn both *fin-de-siècle* literature and German philosophy is far from coincidental: the degeneracy of the Decadent is also linked to the influence of Schopenhauer and Hartmann. For Nordau, the degenerate was characterized by 'mental weakness and despondency', qualities which were prone to leading to pessimism;[183] he thus declared that 'The degenerate and insane are the predestined disciples of Schopenhauer and Hartmann'.[184]

Decadent writers, meanwhile, openly proclaimed their adherence both to Schopenhauer's ideas and to deviations from a normative physical ideal. In the editorial for the first issue of *Le Décadent*, Anatole Baju declared that the Decadents were 'nés du surblaséisme d'une civilisation schopenhauéresque' and gave a list of the 'prodromes de l'évolution sociale': 'Affinement d'appétits, de sensations, de goûts de luxe, de jouissance, névrose, hystérie, hypnotisme, morphinomanie, charlatanisme scientifique, schopenhauerisme à outrance [...].'[185] The inclusion in this list of 'névrose' and 'hystérie' alongside 'schopenhauerisme' demonstrates the extent of their connection in the contemporary imaginary, as well as confirming the Decadents' celebration of the diseased and degenerate. As Barbara Spackman asserts:

> Decadent writers place themselves on the side of pathology and valorize physiological ills and alteration as the origin of psychic alterity. The decadent rhetoric of sickness embraces and exalts the counternatural as an opening onto the unconscious, an alibi for alterity.[186]

The Decadents were thus drawn to Schopenhauer and Hartmann's work both because of its otherness, and because of the metaphors of disease that were used to express this.

If, as Spackman states, the Decadent text 'hides a diseased, degenerate body',[187] then it is a body infected with the sickness of German pessimist philosophy. Moreover, despite being 'weak and deficient', Decadent literature is also cast, paradoxically, as 'dangerously productive':[188] this is a body that is both infected and infectious, a particularly potent vector of philosophical contagion. In the late nineteenth century, anxieties about French decline are thus projected onto Decadent French literature as well as German pessimism, both being perceived as threatening 'others'. The otherness of Decadence was linked not only to the influence of German philosophy, but to foreign influence more generally: for example, in an 1897 essay on Rivarol, Michel Bréal denounced writers who, 'sous prétexte de progrès, ou par imitation des littératures étrangères, veulent aujourd'hui s'affranchir [des] anciennes règles'[189] of the French language, and he specifically appealed to the myth of 'la clarté française': this myth was 'le drapeau du conservatisme et le repoussoir de la liberté dans l'art'[190] and was frequently deployed to attack the experimentation of *fin-de-siècle* writers, both Symbolist and Decadent.[191] They were, moreover, charged with being jargonistic and wilfully abstruse — Jean de Palacio notes the frequency of 'l'accusation de charabia'[192] — and these arguments of course echo those made against German philosophy. Obscurity was also interpreted as the symptom of mental degeneracy, of a disordered mind: Nordau argues that for the degenerate, 'It is easier [...] to allow his brain-centres to produce semi-lucid, nebulously blurred ideas and inchoate embryonic thoughts, and to surrender himself to the perpetual obfuscation of a boundless, aimless, and shoreless stream of fugitive ideas'.[193]

German philosophy is thus cast as an infectious agent, a miasmatic *vent mortel* gusting across the Rhine; Decadent literature is the host organism that threatens to propagate the infection within France. This vision of pessimism's pathogenic influence combines the rhetorical force of Michelet's metaphor of attack from without and Gobineau's metaphor of decay from within. It challenges Zola's image of France as a body that has had a damaged limb amputated, thus saving it from the gangrenous infection of German occupation and influence; Decadent literature is, precisely, 'un déchaînement des forces anti-vitales' analogous to 'la gangrène', states Vladimir Jankélévitch.[194] It is Zola's application of the body politic metaphor that conforms most closely to its traditional use, which is to suggest 'a naturally bounded and unified space in which the parts come together to form a whole'.[195] But Michelet, too, appeals to this vision of coherence and integrity, even if he recognizes the disruptive effects of the (grotesque and unnatural) German annexation of Alsace-Lorraine. Paradoxically, then, the organicist conception of the French nation-body being threatened by German soldiers and philosophers often represents an attempt to maintain a vision of the nation as 'a self-contained independent unit with fixed boundaries'[196] that is attacked from without but that remains, in essence, internally harmonious — providing literary infection can be isolated and defeated. This vision is doubly denialist: first, in its disavowal of the divisions and tensions internal to France (as exemplified by the Commune) and of the anxieties about French decline, which are projected onto a foreign philosophy; and second, in its conception of nations and bodies as autonomous, self-enclosed systems, a conception that views what is 'other', what is outside of the borders of French territory or tradition, as necessarily dangerous.

Conclusion

As well as anxieties about the collective national body, the othering of German philosophy and Decadent literature also registers a variety of anxieties about the deteriorating quality of individual French bodies, whose weaknesses are reflected in pessimist visions of suffering and Decadent visions of debility. Above all, though, it was the perceived lack of virility and fertility in the French populace that troubled the *fin-de-siècle* imagination; as Nye comments, 'The "master pathology" in the spectrum of pathologies afflicting France was the sluggishly growing population'.[197] This deeply-held fear about France's demographic inferiority provides a crucial context for the reception of Schopenhauer. At the heart of his ethical philosophy was, after all, the idea of chastity, which would only have compounded the decline in the French birth rate. The rumours about his licentiousness sought to undermine this doctrine of asceticism: if the proponent of sexual abstinence could not practise what he preached, why should anyone else? The fact that Schopenhauer belonged — however reluctantly — to the very nation that was the chief source of France's demographic inferiority complex served to exacerbate the antagonism towards his ideas. Of course, the notion that France's demographic problems were due to Schopenhauerian ethics is preposterous. In fact, they were largely attributable to the increasing use of contraception,[198] as Zola himself admits, albeit in condemnatory terms: at the root of France's sluggish birth rate is 'le calcul égoïste des familles limitant le nombre d'enfants pour leur assurer la vie confortable qu'on s'imagine leur devoir'.[199] Schopenhauer is thus a 'bouc émissaire'[200] for French demographic weakness.

For the Decadents, the sexual abstinence promoted by Schopenhauer's theory and the sexual indulgence (allegedly) practised by the philosopher himself were both enticing: both challenged the normative sexual morality that advocated sex within marriage for the purpose of procreation, which itself served the aim of national renewal through demographic growth. In Decadent literature, there is thus fluctuation between 'un idéal de chasteté totale'[201] and an intense eroticism that revels in supposedly deviant forms of sexuality.[202] This dichotomy is of vital importance to Laforgue, as we shall see in the chapters that follow. Drawn to asceticism early in his career, he was critical of Schopenhauer's alleged hypocrisy; ultimately, though, he relinquished his ascetic aspirations, even if the idea of sexual abstinence re-emerges as crucial to the Pierrot figure, one of his most important poetic avatars. His rejection of Schopenhauerian chastity does not imply an acceptance of Hartmann's doctrine of commitment to the world process through procreation, however. Rather, he envisages a form of sexuality that escapes restrictive instrumentalization; indeed, this notion of untamed sexual expression plays a key role in his aesthetic principles.

As well as engaging with the *ad hominem* critique of Schopenhauer, Laforgue's work also draws on many of the discourses of German alterity discussed in this chapter. In his juvenilia, he explicitly invokes the notion of Germanic obscurity, particularly in relation to Hegel. His first known work of literature, a play written in 1877, also recapitulates the idea of pessimism as an illness. This discourse of disease is woven into his mature work too, but now it informs his thinking more deeply. Notions of sickness and physical frailty are, indeed, vital to his aesthetics: as Arthur Symons puts it, 'he sees [...] the possibilities for art which come from the sickly modern being'.[203] Finally, his reception of Hartmann draws on the idealized Staëlian vision of Germany, which is portrayed as the chosen land of the Unconscious. In various ways, then, Laforgue's reception of Schopenhauer and Hartmann is informed by ideas of otherness, which constitute more than a mere filter for philosophical influence: rather, otherness emerges as crucial to the very principles of his literary practice.

Notes to Chapter 1

1. Reiner Marcowitz, 'Attraction and Repulsion: Franco-German Relations in the "Long Nineteenth Century"', in *A History of Franco-German Relations in Europe: From 'Hereditary Enemies' to Partners*, ed. by Carine Germond and Henning Türk (New York, NY: Palgrave Macmillan, 2008), pp. 13–26 (p. 20).
2. Matthew Potolsky, *The Decadent Republic of Letters: Taste, Politics and Cosmopolitan Community from Baudelaire to Beardsley* (Philadelphia: University of Pennsylvania Press, 2013), p. 2.
3. Espagne and Werner, p. 971.
4. Ibid., p. 976.
5. Germaine de Staël, *De l'Allemagne*, 2 vols (Paris: Garnier-Flammarion, 1968), I, 45.
6. Ibid., I, 46.
7. Ibid., I, 47.
8. Ibid., I, 48.
9. Quoted in Staël, I, 39.
10. Quoted in Staël, I, 39.
11. Gerhart Hoffmeister, 'De l'Allemagne', in *The Literary Encyclopedia* (1 November 2005) <http://www.litencyc.com/php/sworks.php?rec=true&UID=5708?> [accessed 24 February 2014].
12. Louis Reynaud, *L'influence allemande en France au XVIIIe et XIXe siècle* (Paris: Hachette, 1922), pp. 137–38.
13. Ibid., II, 141.
14. Ibid., II, 91.
15. Ibid., II, 113–14.
16. Ibid., II, 114.
17. Ibid., II, 159.
18. Ibid., II, 151.
19. Ibid., II, 157.
20. Ibid., II, 157.
21. Antoine de Rivarol, *De l'universalité de la langue française* (Paris: Obsidiane, 1991 [1784]), p. 39.
22. On Heine and Quinet, see Jean-Marie Carré, *Les Écrivains français et le mirage allemand, 1800–1940* (Paris: Boivin, 1947), p. 68; see also Reynaud, p. 160.
23. Staël, I, 63.
24. Marcowitz, p. 14.

25. See Carré, p. 25 and Reynaud, p. 260.
26. Reynaud, p. 160.
27. Ibid., p. 259.
28. See Carré, pp. x-xi and Paul Rowe, *A Mirror on the Rhine? The Nouvelle revue germanique, 1829–1837* (Oxford; Bern: Peter Lang, 2000), p. 224.
29. Philippe van Tieghem, *Les Influences étrangères sur la littérature française (1550–1880)* (Paris: Presses universitaires de France, 1961), p. 152.
30. Rowe, p. 228.
31. Ibid., p. 229.
32. See Paul Lévy, *La Langue allemande en France. Pénétration et diffusion des origines à nos jours*, 2 vols (Lyon: IAC, 1950–52), I, 77; quoted in René-Pierre Colin, *Schopenhauer en France: un mythe naturaliste* (Lyon: Presses universitaires de Lyon, 1979), p. 6.
33. Jean-Pierre Lefebvre, 'L'introduction de la philosophie allemande en France au XIX siècle. La question des traductions', in *Transferts: les Relations interculturelles dans l'espace franco-allemand (XVIIIe et XIXe siècle)*, ed. by Michel Espagne and Michaël Werner (Paris: Éditions Recherche sur les civilisations, 1988), pp. 465–76 (p. 465).
34. Ibid., p. 469.
35. Jean Willm, *Histoire de la philosophie allemande: depuis Kant jusqu'à Hegel*, 4 vols (Paris: Ladrange, 1846–49), I, vii; quoted in Heather Williams, *Mallarmé's Ideas in Language* (Oxford; New York, NY: Peter Lang, 2004), pp. 37–38.
36. Van Tieghem, p. 152.
37. See Carré, p. 48 and Van Tieghem, p. 152. However, in *Subjects of Terror: Nerval, Hegel and the Modern Self* (Stanford, CA: Stanford University Press, 1999), Jonathan Strauss points out that Nerval — a rare example of a Germanophone amongst the French Romantics — makes several references to Hegel, demonstrating some engagement with his philosophy (p. 337, n. 39).
38. As Eric J. Hobsbawm points out, the crisis 'gave universal currency to the theme of the [French] nation's "natural frontiers", a term which, contrary to historical myth, belongs essentially to the nineteenth century' (Eric J. Hobsbawm, *Nations and Nationalism since 1780: Programme, Myth, Reality* (Cambridge: Cambridge University Press, 1990), p. 91, n. 15).
39. Nicolas Becker, 'Le Rhin allemand', trans. by Alfred de Musset, *Poésies complètes*, ed. by Maurice Allem (Paris: Gallimard, 1957), p. 403.
40. Musset, pp. 403–04.
41. Alphonse de Lamartine, *Œuvres poétiques complètes*, ed. by Marius-François Guyard (Paris: Gallimard, 1963), p. 1173.
42. Ibid., p. 1174.
43. Victor Hugo, preface to *Les Burgraves*, in *Théâtre complet*, ed. by J.-J. Thierry and Josette Mélèze, 2 vols (Paris: Gallimard, 1963–64), II, 21.
44. Xavier Marmier, 'Soirée allemande', *Poésies d'un voyageur* (Paris: F. Locquin, 1844). Marmier was 'undoubtedly the best-remembered of the regular contributors to the *Revue germanique* [1829–37] and was probably the best known at the time as well' (Rowe, p. 54).
45. Gustave Flaubert, *Bouvard et Pécuchet: avec un choix des scénarios, du Sottisier, L'Album de la Marquise et Le Dictionnaire des idées reçues*, ed. by Claudine Gothot-Mersch ([Paris]: Gallimard, 1979 [1881]), p. 487.
46. Richard Wagner, *Quatre poèmes d'opéras traduits en prose française, précédés d'une lettre sur la musique* (Paris: Librairie Nouvelle, 1861).
47. 'Cette musique-là exprime avec la voix la plus suave ou la plus stridente tout ce qu'il y a de plus caché dans le cœur de l'homme' (Charles Baudelaire, 'Richard Wagner et Tannhaüser à Paris', in *Œuvres complètes*, ed. by Marcel A. Ruff (Paris: Seuil, 1968), p. 523).
48. Théophile Gautier, *Spirite* (Paris: Nizet, 1970 [1886]), pp. 175–76.
49. Wagner, p. xxxv.
50. Charles Vincens, *Wagner et le wagnérisme au point de vue français* (Paris: Fischbacher, 1902), p. 25; quoted in Elwood Hartman, *French Literary Wagnerism* (New York, NY; London: Garland, 1988), p. 4.
51. Hartman, p. 38.

52. For more on the Wagnerian influence on Laforgue, see Madeleine Guy, 'De la réécriture musicale dans Moralités légendaires', *Dix-Neuf*, 20, no. 1 (2016), 66–80, and Anne Holmes, '"De nouveaux rythmes": The Free Verse of Laforgue's "Solo de Lune"', *French Studies*, 62, no. 2 (2008), 162–72.
53. Wagner was himself influenced by Schopenhauer; but French interest in Wagner does not seem to have played a significant role in the transmission of Schopenhauer's ideas, even if it prepared the ground in a more general sense.
54. Colin, p. 14
55. Anne Henry, 'La réception française de Schopenhauer', in *Schopenhauer et la création littéraire en Europe*, ed. by Anne Henry (Paris: Méridiens Klincksieck, 1989), pp. 32–36 (p. 32).
56. Anne Henry, 'Actualité d'un vieux prophète', in *Schopenhauer et la création littéraire en Europe*, ed. by Anne Henry (Paris: Méridiens Klincksieck, 1989), pp. 11–14 (p. 12); Alexandre Baillot, *Influence de la philosophie de Schopenhauer en France (1860–1900)* (Paris: J. Vrin, 1927), p. i.
57. Anne Henry, 'L'expansion du schopenhauérisme', in *Schopenhauer et la création littéraire en Europe*, ed. by Anne Henry (Paris: Méridiens Klincksieck, 1989), pp. 15–19 (p. 17 and p. 19).
58. Henry, 'Actualité', p. 12.
59. J. A. Cantacuzène, *Le Monde comme volonté et comme représentation* (Leipzig: F. A. Brockhaus, 1886).
60. Janaway, p. 10.
61. Magee, p. 245.
62. Laurent Fédi, 'Le clair-obscur: La philosophie française et l'inconscient', in *Un débat sur l'Inconscient avant Freud: la réception de Eduard von Hartmann chez les psychologues et philosophes français*, ed. by Serge Nicolas and Laurent Fédi (Paris: Harmattan, 2008), pp. 11–56 (p. 34).
63. See, for example, Charles Marie René Leconte de Lisle, *Le Sacre de Paris* (1871), François Coppée, *Lettre d'un mobile breton* (1871), Catulle Mendès, *La Colère d'un franc-tireur* (1870) and Léon Dierx, *Les Paroles du vaincu* (1871) (all mentioned by Carré, p. 95); see also Paul Déroulède, *Chants d'un soldat* (1872), Théodore de Banville, *Idylles prussiennes* (1871) and Paul de Saint-Victor, *Barbares et bandits* (1871) (all mentioned by Reynaud, p. 261 n. 1).
64. Victor de Laprade, 'A la terre de France', *Poèmes civiques* (1873), pp. 54–56; quoted in Girardet, p. 55.
65. Claude Digeon, *La Crise allemande de la pensée française, 1870–1914* (Paris: Presses universitaires de France, 1959), p. 164.
66. Guy de Maupassant, 'Auprès d'un mort', *Contes et nouvelles*, ed. by Louis Forestier, 2 vols (Paris: Gallimard, 1974), I, 728.
67. Ibid., I, 728.
68. Paul Challemel-Lacour, 'Un Bouddhiste Contemporain en Allemagne', in *Revue des deux Mondes*, 86 (March 1870), 296–332 (p. 299).
69. Schopenhauer, quoted in Challemel-Lacour, p. 311.
70. Ibid., p. 312.
71. Ibid., p. 312.
72. Challemel-Lacour, p. 312.
73. Jean Bourdeau, 'Introduction', in Arthur Schopenhauer, *Pensées, maximes et fragments*, ed. and trans. by Jean Bourdeau (Paris: Germer-Baillière, 1880), pp. 1–26 (p. 8).
74. Schopenhauer, trans. by Bourdeau, p. 115.
75. Émile Zola, *Œuvres complètes*, ed. by Henri Mitterand, 21 vols (Paris: Nouveau monde, 2002–10), XII, 71.
76. Ibid., XII, 75.
77. Eduard von Hartmann, *La Philosophie de l'Inconscient*, trans. by D. Nolen, 2 vols (Paris: Germer Baillière, 1877), I, 256. Further references in text as *PI*. All references to Hartmann's work will henceforth be from this French translation, since this was the form in which Laforgue and his contemporaries encountered it.
78. Elme-Marie Caro, *Le Pessimisme au XIXe siècle* (Paris: Hachette, 1878), p. 260.
79. Ibid., p. 260.
80. Paul Janet, 'La Métaphysique en Europe depuis Hegel. III. La Philosophie de la Volonté et la

Philosophie de l'Inconscient', *Revue des deux Mondes*, 21 (June 1877), 614–35 (p. 634).
81. Ibid., pp. 623–24.
82. Ibid., p. 624.
83. Bourdeau, p. 6.
84. Caro, p. 237.
85. Théodule Ribot, *La Philosophie de Schopenhauer* (Paris: Germer Baillière, 1874), p. 176.
86. Janet (June 1877), p. 624.
87. Ribot, p. 12.
88. Charles de Varigny, 'L'Amour, les Femmes et le Mariage d'après Schopenhauer', *La Revue Politique et Littéraire. Revue des cours littéraires (2ᵉ série)*, 18 (January-July 1880), 702–10 (p. 706).
89. Maupassant, p. 728.
90. My thanks to Jennifer Forrest, Texas State University, for this reference.
91. Henry Céard, 'Clowns et philosophes', *Le Siècle*, 19 October 1888, p. 2.
92. Ibid., p. 2.
93. Ibid., p. 2.
94. Ibid., p. 2.
95. Challemel-Lacour, p. 306.
96. Ribot, p. 175.
97. Paul Janet, 'La Métaphysique en Europe depuis Hegel. II. Un philosophe misanthrope', *Revue des deux Mondes*, 21 (May 1877), 269–87 (p. 280).
98. Schopenhauer, trans. by Bourdeau, p. 140.
99. Ibid., p. 166.
100. Ribot, p. 176.
101. Magee, pp. 23–24.
102. Colin, p. 136.
103. Bourdeau, pp. 5–6.
104. Ibid., p. 5; author's emphasis.
105. 'Le vrai honnête homme est celui qui ne se pique de rien' (François de La Rochefoucauld, *Réflexions ou sentences et maximes morales*, ed. by Dominique Secretan (Geneva: Droz, 1967 [1665]), p. 78).
106. Janet (May 1877), p. 280.
107. Ibid., p. 280.
108. Alexandre Foucher de Careil, *Hegel et Schopenhauer* (Paris: Hachette, 1862), p. 318. Schopenhauer does not see the Will as divine, however.
109. Foucher de Careil, p. 300.
110. Ibid., p. 343.
111. Digeon, p. 39.
112. Caro, p. ii.
113. Bourdeau, p. 12; de Varigny, p. 706. As Colin notes (p. 167 and p. 175), Zola invokes the same ideas in his novels *Au Bonheur des Dames* and *La Joie de vivre*. In the former, Octave Mouret dismisses 'les désespérés, les dégoûtés, les pessimistes' as 'tous ces malades de nos sciences commençantes' (Zola, XI, 327). In *La Joie de vivre*, Lazare is diagnosed by Docteur Cazenove as one of the 'jeunes gens d'aujourd'hui, qui ont mordu aux sciences, et qui en sont malades'; pessimism is, he states, 'la maladie de la fin du siècle' (Zola, XII, 144).
114. Caro, p. 94.
115. Dionys Ordinaire, 'La Jeune Génération', *La Revue politique et littéraire. Revue des cours littéraires*, 9 (January-July 1885), 706–10 (p. 706).
116. Caro, pp. ii–iii.
117. Ordinaire, p. 708.
118. Ibid., p. 710.
119. Susan Sontag, *Illness as Metaphor* (New York, NY: Farrar, Strauss and Giroux, 1978; repr. New York, NY: Doubleday, 1990), p. 72.
120. Erin O'Connor, *Raw Material: Producing Pathology in Victorian Culture* (Durham, NC; London: Duke University Press, 2000), p. 10.

121. See Chapter 5.
122. Peter Baldwin, 'Chapter 3: Cholera Comes of Age', in *Contagion and the State in Europe, 1830–1930* (Cambridge: Cambridge University Press, 1999).
123. O'Connor, p. 25.
124. *Le Hanneton*, July 1867; see Patrice Bourdelais and André Dodin, *Visages du choléra* ([Paris?]: Belin, 1987), p. 60 and p. 155.
125. Marcel Schneider, 'L'idée de l'artiste chez Wagner', *Obliques*, 4 (1979); quoted in Hartman, p. 3; author's emphasis.
126. Douglas Smith, *Transvaluations: Nietzsche in France, 1872–1972* (Oxford: Clarendon Press, 1996), p. 43.
127. Smith, p. 36.
128. Ibid., p. 47.
129. Ibid., p. 52.
130. Gilles Deleuze and Michel Foucault, 'Introduction Générale', in Friedrich Nietzsche, *Le Gai Savoir — Fragments posthumes 1881–2*, trans. by Pierre Klossowski (Paris: Gallimard, 1967), pp. i–iv (quoted in Smith, p. 40); Colin, p. 117.
131. Smith, p. 54.
132. Digeon, p. 50.
133. W. F. Hogan, 'Syllabus of Errors', in *New Catholic Encyclopedia*, 15 vols (New York: McGraw-Hill, 1967), XIII, 854–56.
134. Digeon, p. 157.
135. Caro, p. 292.
136. Koenraad W. Swart, *The Sense of Decadence in Nineteenth-Century France* (The Hague: Martinus Nijhoff, 1964), p. xi.
137. Max Nordau, *Degeneration*, trans. by George L. Mosse (Lincoln; London: University of Nebraska Press, 1968 [1895]), p. 3.
138. Nordau, p. 1.
139. Ibid., p. 42.
140. Robert A. Nye, *Crime, Madness, and Politics in Modern France: The Medical Concept of National Decline* (Princeton, NJ: Princeton University Press, 1984), p. 138.
141. Karine Varley, *Under the Shadow of Defeat: the War of 1870–1 in French Memory* (New York, NY: Palgrave Macmillan, 2008), p. 49.
142. Swart, p. 86.
143. Claude Marie Raudot, *De la Décadence de la France* (Paris: Amyot, 1850); see Swart, p. 89. See also Bénédict Morel, *Traité des dégénérescences physiques, intellectuelles et morales de l'espèce humaine et des causes qui produisent ces variétés maladives* (Paris: Baillière, 1857) and Lucien-Anatole Prévost-Paradol, *La France nouvelle* (Paris: Lévy, 1868).
144. Swart, p. 109.
145. Ibid., p. 119.
146. Jean Borie, *Le Célibataire français* (Paris: Sagittaire, 1976), p. 68; quoted in Andrew Counter, 'Zola's fin-de-siècle reproductive politics', *French Studies*, 68, no. 2 (2014), 193–208 (p. 193).
147. Swart, p. 173.
148. Digeon, p. 328. It is to be assumed that Digeon's figure for 1870 refers to the combined total of the German nations, which were not officially united until 1871, following the Franco-Prussian War.
149. Marcowitz, p. 20.
150. Nye, p. 138.
151. Jules Michelet, *La France devant l'Europe*, 2nd edn (Florence; Lyon: Successeurs Le Monnier, 1871), p. 112.
152. Ibid., p. 115.
153. Ibid., p. 113.
154. Zola, IV, 364.
155. Bertrand Taithe, *Defeated Flesh: Welfare, Warfare and the Making of Modern France* (Manchester: Manchester University Press, 1999), p. 189.

156. Ibid., p. 180.
157. Hannah Thompson, 'A Battle in the Feminine? The Gendered Body and the Franco-Prussian War', in *Visions/ Revisions: Essays on Nineteenth-Century French Culture*, ed. by Nigel Harkness et al (New York, NY; Oxford: Peter Lang, 2004), pp. 157–73 (p. 158).
158. On the 'corps social' in Zola's œuvre more generally, see Susan Harrow, 'Chapter 5: Thinking and Visualizing the Social Body', in *Zola, The Body Modern: Pressures and Prospects of Representation* (London: Legenda, 2010), pp. 146–71.
159. Arthur de Gobineau, *Ce qui est arrivé à la France en 1870* (Paris: Klincksieck, 1970 [1870]), p. 73. It is worth noting that Zola offers a similar vision in *Nana*, where — as Charles Bernheimer notes — 'the rotten corpse of Nana is symbolically analogous to the rotten body of Imperial France about to enter the disastrous war against Bismarck's Germany' (*Figures of Ill Repute: Representing Prostitution in Nineteenth-Century France* (Cambridge, MA; London: Harvard University Press, 1989), p. 213).
160. Gobineau, pp. 102–03.
161. As Rasmussen and Brown point out, this history stretches back to Plato's *Republic* and Aristotle's *Politics*, and also encompasses Plutarch, Augustine, Shakespeare, Hobbes and Rousseau (Claire Rasmussen and Michael Brown, 'The Body Politic as Spatial Metaphor', in *Citizenship Studies*, 9, no. 5 (2005), 469–84 (pp. 472–73)). Indeed, the idea of the body-nation was so well established that Flaubert, the master of cliché, has the conseiller Lieuvain make use of it in his speech at the comices agricoles: ' "partout des voies nouvelles de communication, comme autant d'artères nouvelles dans le corps de l'État" ' (Gustave Flaubert, *Madame Bovary* (Paris: Nelson, 1950 [1856]), pp. 203–04).
162. Nye, p. xiii; see also Carroll Smith-Rosenberg, *Disorderly Conduct: Visions of Gender in Victorian America* (Oxford: Oxford University Press, 1985), p. 40.
163. Émile Zola, *Le Roman expérimental* (Paris: Flammarion, 2006), p. 69.
164. Ibid., p. 68.
165. Paul Bourget, *Essais de psychologie contemporaine* ([Paris]: Gallimard, 1993), p. 14.
166. Ibid., p. 14.
167. Ibid., p. 14.
168. Ibid., p. 15.
169. See, for example, Vigny on the figure of the writer in *Chatterton*: 'Il faut qu'il ne fasse rien d'utile et de journalier pour avoir le temps d'écouter les accords qui se forment lentement dans son âme, et que le bruit grossier d'un travail positif et régulier interrompt et fait infailliblement évanouir' (Alfred de Vigny, *Œuvres de A. de Vigny* (Bruxelles: Meline, Cans, 1837), p. 469).
170. Zola, 'Dépopulation' (*Le Figaro*, 23 May 1895), XVII, 431–34 (p. 433).
171. Ibid., XVII, 432.
172. Ibid., XVII, 433.
173. Ibid., XVII, 433.
174. Implicit in this argument is, as Andrew Counter astutely observes, a 'tactical claim [...] for the importance of literary writing'; in condemning the nefarious effects of Decadent and Symbolist works, Zola paradoxically offers 'a profession of faith' in literature as a whole (Counter, p. 198).
175. Zola, XVII, 432.
176. Ibid., XVII, 433.
177. Ibid., XVII, 433.
178. Nordau, p. 15.
179. Émile Laurent, *La Poésie décadente devant la science psychiatrique* (Paris: Maloine, 1897), p. vi; quoted in Jean de Palacio, *La décadence: le mot et la chose* (Paris: Les Belles Lettres, 2011), p. 21.
180. Anatole France, *Le Temps*, 27 October 1888; quoted in Patrick McGuinness, 'Introduction', *Symbolism, Decadence and the Fin de Siècle: French and European Perspectives*, ed. by Patrick McGuinness (Exeter: University of Exeter Press, 2000), pp. 1–15 and 281–84 (p. 282 n. 14).
181. Laurent, p. 83; quoted in Palacio, p. 21.
182. Nordau, p. 31.
183. Ibid., p. 19.
184. Ibid., p. 20.

185. Anatole Baju, *Le Décadent*, 1 (10 April 1886).
186. Barbara Spackman, *Decadent Genealogies: The Rhetoric of Sickness from Baudelaire to D'Annunzio* (Ithaca, NY; London: Cornell University Press, 1989), pp. vii–viii.
187. Ibid., p. 1.
188. Liz Constable, Matthew Potolsky and Dennis Denisoff, 'Introduction', in *Perennial Decay: On the Aesthetics and Politics of Decadence*, ed. by Liz Constable, Matthew Potolsky and Dennis Denisoff (Philadelphia: University of Pennsylvania Press, 1999), pp. 1–34 (p. 6).
189. Michel Bréal, *Essai de sémantique. Science des significations* (Limoges: Lambert-Lucas, 2005 [1897]), p. 156; quoted in Olivier Bivort, 'Obscurité de la langue, clarté de la poésie', in *La Littérature symboliste et la Langue. Actes du colloque organisé à Aoste les 8 et 9 mai 2009*, ed. by Olivier Bivort (Paris: Classiques Garnier, 2012), pp. 75–88 (p. 78).
190. Bivort, p. 88.
191. Paul Verlaine also condemned Symbolism as 'an un-French aberration, thus aligning himself with the critics who believed that the Symbolists had perverted the French mind and polluted the genius of the French tongue' (McGuinness, p. 3). In fact, Verlaine specifically referred to Symbolism as 'un mot allemand' (see Jules Huret, *Enquête sur l'évolution littéraire* (Paris: Corti, 1999 [1891]), p. 109; quoted in McGuinness, p. 3).
192. Palacio, p. 9.
193. Nordau, p. 21.
194. Vladimir Jankélévitch, 'La Décadence', *Revue de Métaphysique et de Morale*, 55, no. 4 (October–December 1950), 337–69 (p. 357).
195. Rasmussen and Brown, p. 473.
196. Emily Martin, 'Toward an Anthropology of Immunology: The Body as Nation State', *Medical Anthropology Quarterly*, New Series, 4, no. 4 (December 1990), 410–26 (p. 420).
197. Nye, p. 140.
198. Allan Mitchell, *A Stranger in Paris: Germany's Role in Republican France, 1870–1940* (New York: Berghahn, 2006), p. 25; Roger Price, *A Social History of Nineteenth-Century France* (London: Hutchison, 1987), p. 73.
199. Zola, XVII, 432.
200. Digeon, p. 339.
201. Jean Pierrot, *L'Imaginaire décadent (1880–1900)* (Paris: Presses universitaires de France, 1977), p. 166.
202. Ibid., p. 168.
203. Arthur Symons, *The Symbolist Movement in Literature* (New York, NY: Dutton, 1919), p. 302.

CHAPTER 2

Otherness and The Suffering Body

Philosophy, for Laforgue, was above all a matter of practical wisdom, a question of finding a way to exist in the here and now. Central to this question was the problem of suffering. Both Schopenhauer and Hartmann see suffering as intrinsic to the human condition, but their solutions to this problem are fundamentally opposed: in Schopenhauer's thought, the dissatisfaction and anguish produced by the Will are only escapable through ascetic practices (or, temporarily, through aesthetic experience); in Hartmann's, suffering must be embraced alongside pleasure as part of the 'world process', a process driven by the Unconscious that will result ultimately in collective enlightenment. For Hartmann, then, asceticism is both selfish and ineffective. This ethical debate between Schopenhauer and Hartmann is played out in Laforgue's work, especially in the first phase of his career (1877–81), when his position on asceticism is subject to a number of shifts. In the unpublished play *Tessa* (1877), his earliest known work of literature, celibacy is condemned; in *Le Sanglot de la Terre*, there is tension between a yearning for monastic self-denial, and a recognition that such rigours are impossible or even misguided; in his philosophical notes, universal chastity is dismissed as impracticable, but renunciation retains some appeal as a solution for the individual. In these same notes, Laforgue expresses his resentment of Schopenhauer's supposed hypocrisy regarding sexual abstinence. The turn away from Schopenhauer in Laforgue's later work is crucially informed by the issue of self-denial, demonstrating the power of the *ad hominem* critiques that sought to undermine the philosopher's personal ethics and thereby inoculate the French against the threat of pessimism. The perceived otherness of Schopenhauerian thought was, in this limited sense, an obstructive element in Laforgue's reception of German philosophy.

But Laforgue did not completely reject Schopenhauer's ideas, some of which re-emerge (albeit sporadically) in his later work. In broad terms, moreover, Laforgue was drawn to German philosophy *because* of its 'otherness'; while his critique of Schopenhauer's ethical failings is a by-product of the hostile discourse of French critics, he did not concur with their demonization of Schopenhauerian thought. In fact, the metaphors of disease that they use to express the dangerous foreignness of pessimism are redisposed by Laforgue, for whom illness, pain and physical weakness are aesthetic principles as well as recurrent thematic concerns. The idea of poetry emerging from the travails of embodied existence reveals the tension at the heart of Laforgue's thinking on suffering: he seeks to escape it, yet knows that art can be made out of it and even, perhaps, relies on it. This conception of creativity is inherently anti-rationalist, and to this extent it draws on his philosophical sources, which assert the dominance of the body's uncontrollable urges over the conscious mind. But Schopenhauer and Hartmann's aesthetic theories themselves are subverted by Laforgue's poetics of suffering: both philosophers view art as opposed to suffering in various ways. Laforgue's concern, both thematic and aesthetic, with the frailties and debilities of the body also signals an oppositional stance towards contemporary nationalist discourses, which conceptualized the individual body as the site of national regeneration. In this sense, Laforgue sets himself against the dominant discourse of physical vigour, health and virility that prevailed in late nineteenth-century France, allying himself — at least tentatively — with the Decadent movement. He thus redeploys the metaphors of illness used to 'other' German philosophy in the service of an opposition to bourgeois values.

Jouer à l'ascète: Suffering, Tragedy, and Self-Denial

Laforgue's first collection of poetry (the unpublished *Le Sanglot de la Terre*) and early philosophical notes reflect Schopenhauer and Hartmann's vision of a Godless universe, as well as being imbued by their pessimism. In fact, given its overriding concern with the representation of suffering (mostly the poet's own), *Le Sanglot* conforms to Schopenhauer's theory of tragedy. But Laforgue goes even further, aiming in his early work to proselytize the philosophers' visions of the end of the world. In his later work, however, he repudiates this grandiose eschatology, instead advocating a more down-to-earth philosophical approach, a shift that is informed by Caro's critiques of the two philosophers' metaphysics. He is concerned ultimately with everyday woes, and with possible answers to the inescapable problem of suffering: these answers include both the renunciation of desire, and faith in a higher power — not God, but the Unconscious.

Suffering is central to *Le Sanglot de la Terre*, the collection of poems that Laforgue describes as his 'vers philo.' (*OC*, II, 729). The central thematic concern of the volume is encapsulated by a line from his earliest surviving philosophical notes, thought to have been written in 1881–82, when he was still working on the collection: 'nous savons que tout est mal sur terre, que l'univers n'a pas de cœur, ni de justice, ni de témoins' (*OC*, III, 1133). Here God's absence and the torments of earthly existence that prove it are presented with philosophical detachment, but in *Le Sanglot* Laforgue rails against this abandonment: 'Nous sommes seuls vous dis-je! | Seuls, perdus sans amour, sans espoir, sans appui' ('Fragments', *OC*, I, 444). This bitterly resented atheism conforms philosophically, if not tonally, with the arguments of both Hartmann and Schopenhauer against the possibility of a divine being.[1] Indeed, the poet expresses a profound sense of regret at the discovery of the philosophical texts that led to his harsh awakening; for example, 'Justice' expresses nostalgia for the 'jours bénis où je croyais encore', before recalling the

> [...] moment fatal, où sans foi, sans doctrines,
> Je me retrouvai seul pleurant sur mes ruines,
> Maudissant les écrits d'enfer que j'avais lus. (*OC*, I, 282)

In 'Lassitude', these philosophical 'écrits d'enfer' are counterpoised by the prelapsarian state in which the poet existed when he still had faith:

> [...] j'étais dans l'Éden, l'arbre de la Science
> Ne m'avait pas encor tenté, j'avais la foi,
> Et ce trésor d'amour, il était tout pour moi,
> Ma force, mon recours, mon but, mon espérance. (*OC*, I, 275)

His loss of faith has left him without a purpose or reason to live:

> Et j'erre à travers tout, sans but et sans envie,
> Fouillant tous les plaisirs, ne pouvant rien aimer,
> N'ayant pas même un dieu tyran à blasphémer,
> Avant d'avoir vécu dégoûté de la vie. (*OC*, I, 276)

'Justice' expresses a similar sense of life's meaninglessness using the same image of aimless wandering: since the 'douces chimères' of his religious beliefs have been swept away by the 'vent du doute et des dogmes contraires', he has been left 'sans but, sans espoir, sans appui', and he resorts to ceaseless, splenetic *flânerie* amongst oblivious Parisian crowds (*OC*, I, 282). Suffering is not only the premise of atheism, but also its result.

This sense of futility is evident both at the level of the individual and on a cosmic scale, since the universe is fundamentally without purpose, a meaningless atomic merry-go-round: 'la nature entière | N'est qu'un perpétuel échange de matière' ('Suis-je?', *OC*, I, 314). While Schopenhauer and Hartmann are both atheist, for the latter the Unconscious nonetheless has a definite aim, namely rationality; for Schopenhauer, on the other hand, the Will is a blind, irrational force. The sense of purposelessness that emerges as central to *Le Sanglot* is thus underpinned by Schopenhauerian thought. 'À quoi bon le Progrès?' asks the poet in 'Lassitude' (*OC*, I, 275), echoing Schopenhauer's statement in the Challemel-Lacour interview that progress is 'le rêve du XIXe siècle',[2] a dream whose preposterousness we will eventually come to recognize. Moreover, Schopenhauer's ideas are crucial to the collection aesthetically as well as thematically. Its underlying principle is related to the theory of tragedy that Schopenhauer summarizes in the following pronouncement, quoted by Ribot: 'le but de la plus haute poésie soit la représentation du côté effrayant de la vie, et [...] là nous soient montrés la douleur sans nom, le soupir de l'humanité'.[3] The expression 'le soupir de l'humanité' is, of course, echoed in the title *Le Sanglot de la Terre*, and the collection also effects the depiction of suffering advocated in this statement. Ribot's quotation is taken from Schopenhauer's chapter on tragedy (*WWR*, I, 252); the reference to 'poésie' is meant in the broadest sense, designating all literary art. Here Schopenhauer argues that tragedy provides insight into 'the real nature of the world' and thereby acts 'as a quieter of the will, produc[ing] resignation, the giving up not merely of life, but of the whole will-to-live itself' (*WWR*, I, 253).

For Schopenhauer, then, tragedy holds a privileged status within artistic production, since it promotes the ultimate ethical solution, the renunciation of willing through asceticism. Aesthetic experience in itself is not, however, a permanent escape from suffering, but rather a temporary release from it. The notion of aesthetics offering a (momentary) respite from Will and its concomitant suffering also features, albeit briefly, in Laforgue's early philosophical notes (which are drawn from Caro,[4] as Hannoosh points out (*OC*, III, 1130 n. 3)):

> Par la contemplation sereine, esthétique ou philosophique/ scientifique (ces deux dernières sont les plus sûres de la quiétude), on échappe à soi, on est affranchi momentanément/ pour un instant du temps, de l'Espace et des nombres, on meurt à la conscience de son individualité, on monte, on atteint à la g[ran]de liberté... sortir de l'Illusoire. (*OC*, III, 1128)

In his later work, the idea that creative experience might provide a release from the strictures of the phenomenal world (time, space, the self) re-emerges, as we shall see in the final section of this chapter. But at this stage it is Schopenhauer's idea of art as a *representation* of suffering, rather than a *release* from it, that predominates in his work. Indeed, it is telling that in these notes, aesthetic contemplation is seen as less effective than 'la contemplation [...] philosophique/ scientifique', these methods being 'les plus sûres de la quiétude'. Similarly, Laforgue's early writing is conceived primarily as a vehicle for philosophical ideas; the act of writing itself remains untheorized.

One of the most important philosophical ideas that *Le Sanglot* seeks to convey is that of the ultimate annihilation of the world. In this, Laforgue draws not only on Schopenhauer's work — or rather on the reception of it in the work of Challemel-Lacour et al — but also on Hartmann's. However, Laforgue revels in the horror of his apocalyptic vision, in contrast to both Schopenhauer (who offers only the briefest of glimpses of an eschatology) and Hartmann (who presents the destruction of the universe as the culmination of rationality). First, an enlightened humankind will turn its back on civilization ('l'Homme alors jusqu'au fond de tout aura creusé, | Désertant les cités, et le crâne rasé'), before the planet itself is annihilated:

> [...] la Terre
> Au lieu du tapis d'or que lui faisaient les blés,
> Ne montrant tour à tour que steppes désolées,
> Que vaste plaine blanche et qu'Océan polaire,
> Sentira tout-à-coup dans la nuit solitaire
> Les suprêmes frissons secouer ses reins gelés.
> ('Pataugement', *OC*, I, 305)

In 'L'Oubli', meanwhile, the poet explicitly dramatizes his role as a prophet of the end times:

> [...] je soufflerai
> La Désillusion dans la cité des hommes,
> Pour que, désespérant de célestes royaumes,
> Tout retourne avec joie au vieux néant sacré!
> ('L'Oubli', *OC*, I, 366)

Le Sanglot was, in fact, intended as the first part of a trilogy of works grounded in pessimist philosophy; the final of these works was to be a 'grand livre de prophète, la Bible nouvelle qui va faire déserter les cités' by preaching 'La vanité de tout, le déchirement de l'Illusion, [...] l'Inutilité de l'Univers' and so on (*OC*, III, 151). The second work was to be a novel entitled *Un raté*. Although the novel was never completed, notes and outlines show how Schopenhauer and Hartmann are — at this point — seamlessly merged in Laforgue's thinking: the artist protagonist, described as a disciple of Schopenhauer, kills himself when he fails to complete a series of works depicting the 'trois stades de l'Illusion de Hartmann' (*OC*, I, 687). At this stage, around 1880–81, Laforgue amalgamates the two philosophers' ideas into a unified pessimistic vision which is summed up by a fragment of dialogue in notes for the novel: 'Le néant est préférable à l'être' (*OC*, III, 880).

Laforgue's self-identification as prophet, which recalls the Romantic model of the poet (as embodied by Hugo, whose book of *Odes* 'manifeste le prophétisme moderne, celui du Poète'[5]), is definitively abandoned in his later work. In March 1882, he writes to Sabine Mültzer of his youthful ambitions:

> Sachez, Madame, qu'à 19 ans j'ai rêvé de m'en aller par le monde, pieds nus, prêchant la bonne loi, la désertion des idées, l'extradition de la vie, etc... (airs connus) —
> Hélas! à la première étape, la gendarmerie m'eût arrêté comme vagabond, — Prophète n'est plus un métier. (*OC*, I, 763)

This self-admonishing realism is echoed in 'Préludes autobiographiques', the first poem of *Les Complaintes*,[6] in which the poet mocks his prophetic aspirations ('fou devant ce ciel qui toujours nous bouda | Je rêvais de prêcher la fin, nom d'un Bouddha!') and states that he has now washed his hands of them, due to 'l'argent, l'art, puis les lois de la France...' (*OC*, I, 548). But it was not merely the pragmatics of legality that led him to repudiate philosophical proselytization: Laforgue's philosophical notes show that he also came to doubt the grandiose ethical and metaphysical visions of Schopenhauer and Hartmann.

These notes bear the imprint of Caro's critiques of the two philosophers, which Laforgue appears to share: he does not challenge Caro's opinions but rather paraphrases and embellishes them.[7] He begins by stating that Schopenhauer's vision of universal chastity is completely unfeasible: 'L'inanition de Schopenhauer est une stupidité. Sa délivrance non seulement de l'homme mais encore de toute vie sur la terre par la suppression du commerce sexuel dans l'humanité est un rêve' (*OC*, III, 1135). Even if humanity did succeed in destroying all life on earth, this would be ineffectual on a cosmic scale given the probable existence of life elsewhere in the universe;[8] in any case, this is a moot point when 'l'humanité n'arrivera jamais à la continence unanime qui serait sa libération' (*OC*, III, 1132). However, this critique of chastity does not imply an endorsement of Hartmann's ethics (which advocate procreation). Indeed, Laforgue is even more critical of Hartmann than he is of Schopenhauer, stating that the Hartmannian notion of annihilation through collective human enlightenment is utterly fantastical: 'Hartmann va plus haut, ses fééries/ fantaisies cosmiques sont encore mille fois moins pratiques que celles de

Schopenhauer' (*OC*, III, 1135). This criticism paraphrases Caro's argument against Hartmannian eschatology. While generally hostile towards the idea of pessimism, Caro reserves particular opprobrium for Hartmann's notion of 'le suicide cosmique accompli par l'humanité':[9] the idea that the obliteration of the entire universe could be provoked by human renunciation of existence is 'de la fantasmagorie pure'.[10]

The key to Laforgue's criticism in this passage of notes is that the idea of salvation on a cosmic scale (through annihilation) is ridiculous; instead we should concentrate on the day-to-day business of earthly existence: 'Il ne faut songer qu'à des remèdes individuels/ terrestres et pratiques, renoncer à amener le Tout à s'anéantir' (*OC*, III, 1135). This shift of focus, from the metaphysical to the terrestrial, is a crucial factor in the abandonment of *Le Sanglot* in favour of the new aesthetic of *Les Complaintes*. It is encapsulated by 'Complainte d'une Convalescence en mai': 'mes grandes angoisses métaphysiques | Sont passées à l'état de chagrins domestiques' (*OC*, I, 616). What the mature Laforgue sought from philosophy was, then, a palliative for our worldly travails, a set of principles for living, or, as he puts it, 'un remède pour cette pauvre humanité qui vient de perdre ses dieux et n'a plus rien' (*OC*, III, 1132). The question of suffering cannot be solved by fantasmagorical visions.

But that is not to say that philosophy has a straightforward answer to this question. In fact, Laforgue seems to replace the 'dieux' that mankind has lost with another god-like force: the Unconscious. In 'Préludes autobiographiques', the poet expresses his acceptance of the pessimistic view of life as 'un épisode qui trouble inutilement la béatitude et le repos du néant', as Schopenhauer puts it,[11] but goes on to place his faith in the Unconscious:

> Je sais! la vie outrecuidante est une trêve
> D'un jour au Bon Repos qui pas plus ne s'achève
> Qu'il n'a commencé. Moi, ma trêve, confiant,
> Je la veux cuver au sein de l'INCONSCIENT. (*OC*, I, 548)

Gone is the 'dérisoire créature' who wrote *Le Sanglot* and who could not accept the 'monstruosités sans but et sans témoin du cher Tout' (*OC*, I, 546); in his place, a poet who trusts in the providential force of this 'cher Tout', the Unconscious: 'Que votre inconsciente Volonté | Soit faite dans l'Éternité!' ('Complainte propitiatoire à l'Inconscient', *OC*, I, 549). The overt parody of the Lord's Prayer in 'Complainte propitiatoire à l'Inconscient', the poem that follows 'Préludes autobiographiques', of course signals a self-conscious elevation of the Unconscious to divine status, one that might be dismissed as ironic or as grounded in nothing more than provocative blasphemy. But Laforgue often uses religious formulations to describe the action of the Unconscious, especially in his texts on his aesthetic principles.[12] For example, the epigraph to his article 'L'Art moderne en Allemagne' (the most important of these texts) is 'L'artiste s'agite, l'Inconscient le mène' (*OC*, III, 337), an adaptation of François Fénelon's dictum 'L'homme s'agite, Dieu le mène'. In the same article, this religiosity is made explicit in Laforgue's description of the Unconscious as

> le dernier divin, le principe mystique universel révélé dans la *Philosophie de l'Inconscient* de Hartmann, le seul divin minutieusement présent et veillant partout, le seul infaillible — de par son inconscience —, le seul vraiment et

sereinement infini, le seul que l'homme n'ait pas créé à son image. (*OC*, III, 339)

Meanwhile, 'Complainte du Sage de Paris', a kind of *ars poetica*, propounds the following principle: 'Rime et sois grand, la Loi reconnaîtra les siens' (*OC*, I, 618); the latter part of this aphorism calques Arnaud Amaury's statement 'Dieu reconnaîtra les siens',[13] with the Unconscious ('la Loi') again standing in for God.

While Hartmann himself insisted that the Unconscious was not a theistic principle, he did often use pseudo-religious language to describe it, notably in his theory of aesthetics.[14] Laforgue's divinization of the Unconscious thus reflects, to a certain extent, his philosophical source. But his faith in the Unconscious is, as Warren Ramsey points out, 'half-borrowed, half-invented';[15] he was far from being a dogmatic follower of Hartmann, as we have seen from his rejection of the philosopher's eschatology. Moreover, it was a doctrine pieced together from various sources. In a letter to his friend Charles Ephrussi dated December 1883, Laforgue describes a night of revelation during which he formulated the aesthetic principles expressed in 'L'Art moderne en Allemagne':

> Je me suis recueilli, et dans une nuit, de 10 du soir à 4 du matin, tel Jésus au Jardin des Oliviers, Saint Jean à Pathmos, Platon au cap Sunium, Bouddha sous le figuier de Gaza, j'ai écrit en dix pages les principes métaphysiques de l'Esthétique nouvelle, une esthétique qui s'accorde avec l'Inconscient de Hartmann, le transformisme de Darwin, les travaux de Helmholtz. (*OC*, I, 850)

Here Hartmann's thought is associated not only with religious epiphany — even if Laforgue's comparison of himself to religious and philosophical figures is undercut by irony, the profusion of these figures serving to mock his own self-aggrandizement — but also with the scientific work of Darwin and Helmholtz. Evolutionary theory is particularly important to Laforgue's aesthetic principles. Opposing the fixed aesthetic ideals of Classicism, he argues that the true ideal is in a state of perpetual becoming: 'une formule esthétique vaste et féconde comme la Loi, ouverte au passé comme aux surprises de l'avenir et aux incohérences du présent [...] ne saurait venir que d'un Idéal placé dans un devenir infini' (*OC*, III, 338). The development of the ideal is determined by a process akin to natural selection: 'la pensée humaine, succession d'œuvres et d'idéaux à l'état de phénomènes en concurrence, exprime l'évolution de l'âme universelle, de la Loi unique' (*OC*, III, 339).

However, one name noticeably absent from this letter is that of Schopenhauer. Indeed, neither his name nor his philosophical ideas feature in 'L'Art moderne en Allemagne' either. Certain Schopenhauerian concepts do re-emerge, occasionally, in Laforgue's mature work; but Schopenhauer is no longer at the centre of Laforgue's philosophical concerns. The reasons for this lie in the discourses surrounding Schopenhauer in late nineteenth-century France, and specifically in the treatment of his doctrine of asceticism.

★ ★ ★ ★ ★

As we have seen, Laforgue is critical of Schopenhauer's ethics of universal chastity, but this does not preclude the possibility of *individual* chastity as a solution to the problem of suffering. Laforgue consistently entertains this possibility in his philosophical notes as well as his literary works, even if his assessment of it fluctuates considerably. In general terms, this focus on Schopenhauer's ethics reflects the contemporary French view of the philosopher as a 'moraliste', and the vicissitudes of Laforgue's reception were also informed by specific aspects of his critical reading. Most importantly, the *ad hominem* critiques of Schopenhauer played a crucial role in determining Laforgue's repudiation of the philosopher.

The idea of sexual abstinence is at the heart of Laforgue's earliest known work of literature, a play entitled *Tessa* that he wrote in 1877 at the age of 17. The play offers a denunciation of Schopenhauer's thought that is influenced by Challemel-Lacour's seminal article 'Un Bouddhiste contemporain en Allemagne'. *Tessa*'s protagonist, a painter called Guido, turns to Schopenhauerian philosophy having been disappointed in love. He becomes misogynistic and resolves to remain celibate. In Act 2, scene vi, the book of philosophy that Guido is reading is quoted; while this is a book purportedly written by Schopenhauer, the quotation is in fact a near-verbatim transcription of the words recorded by Challemel-Lacour in his interview with the philosopher:[16]

> La vie est un mal. La fin du monde sera le salut, la délivrance de l'humanité. Le prix de la continence c'est qu'elle mène à cette délivrance. L'amour est donc l'ennemi. [...] Les femmes sont ses complices. [...] L'ascète sauve de la vie des générations entières. Il donne un exemple qui a failli sauver l'humanité deux ou trois fois. Les femmes ne l'ont pas voulu, c'est pourquoi je les hais. (*OC*, I, 139)

The playwright's rejection of this argument is evident in the play's dénouement: Guido renounces Schopenhauer's philosophy and acknowledges his love for Tessa, his ward, to whom he proposes marriage. Of course, marriage entails procreation, and the idea of offspring is uppermost in Guido's mind when he imagines his life with Tessa: 'd'abord les enfants, rayons des jours moroses' (*OC*, I, 142). Schopenhauerian chastity is thus emphatically denounced. As Olivier Champod notes, *Tessa* problematizes the prevailing view that Laforgue was an adept of Schopenhauer in his early years: 'la référence schopenhauerienne est chez Laforgue, à ses débuts au moins, plus complexe qu'on ne le suppose généralement'.[17]

But as we have seen, Schopenhauerian ideas re-emerge in *Le Sanglot* as well as in the projected novel *Un raté*. Indeed, in notes for the novel the protagonist is described not only as 'un raté de génie' but also as 'vierge' (*OC*, III, 150), suggesting that Laforgue reconsidered the doctrine of chastity after writing *Tessa*. Moreover, an aspiration to asceticism is also sporadically evident in *Le Sanglot*: for example, in 'Trop tard' the poet imagines himself 'Chaste et le front rasé' in a remote monastery, 'Mort à la chair et mort au monde, tout à Dieu' (*OC*, I, 226). In his early philosophical notes, too, Laforgue appears to endorse Schopenhauer's ethics of renunciation as the most viable solution to suffering: 'nous cherchons par amour pour l'humanité à prêcher la résignation et le renoncement que nous regardons comme le seul état heureux auquel l'être puisse prétendre' (*OC*, III, 1133). But it is not merely a matter of preaching self-denial; one must also experience the suffering inherent to earthly existence:

> Avant d'arriver au renoncement il faut souffrir au moins deux ans, jeûner, souffrir de la continence, saigner de pitié et d'amour universel, visiter les hôpitaux, toutes les maladies hideuses ou tristes, toutes les saletés [...] voir toute la douleur de la planète, éphémère et perdu[e] dans l'universel des cieux éternels, inutile, sans but, sans témoin. (*OC*, III, 1129)

The praise for 'renoncement', which is explicitly rejected by Hartmann, shows that these notes are inspired by Schopenhauer's thought, via Caro (see Hannoosh, *OC*, III, 1130–31 n. 5).[18]

While the fragment's use of phrases like 'la douleur de la planète' and 'sans but, sans témoin' is strongly reminiscent of *Le Sanglot*, several poems in the collection cast doubt on the yearning for *askesis* expressed here, as well as in 'Trop tard'. In 'Berceuse', the poet states that he is 'trop lâche [...] pour me faire trappiste' (*OC*, I, 384); in 'L'Oubli', he condemns not his own incapacity for self-denial, but the very practice itself: 'Maudite soit [...] la sérénité des ascètes!' (*OC*, I, 366). In 'Pour le livre d'amour', meanwhile, the poet suggests that he used to practise asceticism, but that he has now renounced this ideal, and he bitterly criticizes his former rejection of love in the name of self-mortification: 'J'ai craché sur l'amour et j'ai tué la chair! | Fou d'orgueil, je me suis roidi contre la vie!' (*OC*, I, 425). Given that the poems of *Le Sanglot* are patently confessional (Laforgue describing the collection as 'l'histoire, le journal d'un parisien de 1880' (*OC*, III, 150)), we can surmise from 'Pour le livre d'amour' that Laforgue himself once adhered to ascetic principles, but later abandoned them. This is confirmed by his correspondence.

In a letter of March 1882 to Sabine Mültzer (with whom he shared a flirtatious epistolary relationship), Laforgue discusses his time in Paris and the period in which he led a life of self-imposed austerity:

> J'étais croyant. Depuis deux ans, je ne crois plus. Je suis un pessimiste mystique. [...] Pendant cinq mois j'ai joué à l'ascète, au petit Bouddha avec deux œufs et un verre d'eau par jour et 6 heures de bibliothèque. J'ai voulu aller pleurer sur le Saint-Sépulcre. Maintenant, dilettante, revenu de tout, j'irais fumer une cigarette sur le Golgotha en contemplant quelque couchant aux tons inédits. (*OC*, I, 763)

Laforgue's declaration that he has abandoned his ascetic ideals and is now 'dilettante, revenu de tout' conforms to a certain extent to the argument of Bourget, his friend and mentor, that 'dilettantism is a pleasurable form of scepticism', as Richard Hibbitt puts it.[19] (Ultimately, though, he goes beyond Bourget's definition, casting dilettantism as 'an ironic, fragmented yet fertile aesthetic'.[20]) Both asceticism and the yearning to return to the Church have now been superseded by a detached, self-gratifying aestheticism. In an earlier letter to Mültzer in which he also asserts his dilettantism ('Maintenant, je suis dilettante en tout'), he states that he 'regarde passer le carnaval de la vie' with amused disinterest; this responds directly to *Le Sanglot*'s expression of 'dégoût' in the face of 'ce carnaval insensé de la vie' ('Fragments', *OC*,

I, 445).²¹ In fact, this detachment is reminiscent of Schopenhauer's description of the serenity attained through self-denial: 'La vie et ses formes flottent désormais devant ses yeux comme une apparition passagère'.²² But for Laforgue, this state of calm contemplation is achieved not through asceticism, but after having rejected it.

In his letter to Mültzer, Laforgue suggests that his asceticism was fundamentally insincere: 'j'ai *joué* à l'ascète' (my emphasis). This echoes the expression used by Guido in *Tessa* to concede the difficulty of maintaining his pessimistic outlook: 'Mais en plein mois de mai jouer le pessimiste!' (*OC*, I, 128). Again, this is a performance, and the ostentatious aspect of Guido's belief is emphasized by the fact that he dresses and paints only in black. The representation of Guido thus conforms to the contemporary notion that all Schopenhauerians were essentially *poseurs*; as Colin states, 'pour la grande presse, il est entendu une fois pour toutes que l'insincérité est le trait dominant des pessimistes'.²³ The notion that asceticism is merely for show is also suggested by 'Pour le livre d'amour', in which Laforgue declares that his self-denial was the result of being 'Fou d'orgueil', echoing Foucher de Careil's statement that asceticism 'n'est souvent qu'un manteau d'orgueil'.²⁴ Guido also admits that his pessimism is the result of being 'un orgueilleux' (*OC*, I, 128). It was not only Schopenhauer's followers who were accused of insincerity, but — as we saw in Chapter 1 — the philosopher himself, since his (alleged) licentiousness made a mockery of his preaching of chastity. These accusations of promiscuity are reflected in Laforgue's early philosophical notes (1881–82). In a fragment that presumably post-dates his expressions of sympathy for Schopenhauerian 'renoncement', Laforgue registers his resentment of the hypocrisy these accusations imply:

> L'égoïste, le dilettante, le misanthrope, le cataph[r]onantrope — rien du Bouddha sublime de la grande mansuétude, de l'ascétisme, — débauché, égoïste, prêche l'inanition, ce bon vivant! et la continence volontaire, ce débauché! (*OC*, III, 1137)²⁵

The repetition and terminal placement of 'débauché' suggest that it is Schopenhauer's sexual indulgence that he finds most abhorrent. Indeed, he also describes Schopenhauer's doctrine of chastity as 'un motif à variations humoristiques dont ce farceur ne croyait pas un mot et pratiquait encore moins' (*OC*, III, 1135).

The difficulty of precisely dating Laforgue's philosophical notes means that it is uncertain whether Laforgue had himself forsaken his ascetic aspirations at the time that this fragment was written. In any case, the key to his vituperative criticism is Schopenhauer's supposed hypocrisy, rather than his *débauche* in itself. The notion that Schopenhauer did not practise what he preached appears to have jarred with the seriousness of Laforgue's philosophical engagement (a seriousness that does not, of course, imply dogmatism). If he turns away from Schopenhauer in his later work, it is largely because of this *ad hominem* critique. It was a critique that sought to immunize the French against the corrupting effects of Schopenhauer's philosophy. In Laforgue's case it had some success, since in his mature work, Schopenhauer is no longer at the heart of his philosophical thinking, as indicated by his letter to Ephrussi of December 1883. Moreover, in his pseudonymously written review of *Les Complaintes* in *La République française* of 21 August 1885, he states that his collection 'renchérit sur le schopenhauerianisme' (*OC*, III, 152) in its adherence to the philosophy of Hartmann, which is 'd'un mysticisme plus large et plus profond et d'un pessimisme moins vulgaire' (*OC*, III, 153). In itself, this attempt to distinguish his work from the contemporaneous fad for Schopenhauer might be dismissed as a self-publicizing ploy; but seen in the context of his philosophical notes (and of the references to 'L'Inconscient' in *Les Complaintes*) it can be taken as essentially sincere.

The repudiation of Schopenhauer and his doctrine of asceticism does not, however, imply that Laforgue reaches a definite conclusion in his ethical reflections. Although he never renews his youthful efforts at concerted self-abnegation, the dilemma between sexual love and celibacy, companionship and solitude, remains central to the thematics of his poetry from *Les Complaintes* to the *Derniers vers*. Indeed, the idea of asceticism itself does not disappear from his work, instead resurfacing in relation to Buddhism and the Pierrot figure (see Chapter 5). His newly detached, dilettantish attitude — evident in the ludic tonality of his mature work — belies a continued engagement with the problem of suffering. While surrendering to the pseudo-divine beneficence of the Unconscious seems to offer a solution to this problem, it is not one that Laforgue can believe in wholeheartedly. In fact, for him the Unconscious is, paradoxically, the source of both salvation and of suffering itself: on the one hand, it represents a sort of guiding wisdom; on the other, it is a purely mechanistic life-force.[26] This life-force creates suffering chiefly through desire, which is 'la ruse | Par qui l'Inconscient à jamais nous abuse' ('Pataugement', *OC*, I, 307). Throughout his *œuvre*, Laforgue is torn between these conflicting visions of the Unconscious, always seeking solace in its providence, yet always equally aware that he must endure the miseries that it provokes in the everyday world.

Decadence and Disease: An Aesthetics of Suffering

The representation of suffering that dominates Laforgue's early work, inspired by Schopenhauer's theory of tragedy, is perpetuated in his mature *œuvre*, albeit with a much more playful tonality. But alongside this a new idea emerges: that the creation of art necessarily *involves* suffering, that the suffering body is, indeed, the very source of creativity. This represents a subversion of the aesthetics of both Schopenhauer and Hartmann. For Schopenhauer, art and suffering are related either through tragedy, or through the idea of a temporary escape from the Will through aesthetic experience. For Hartmann, a creative process based on 'la souffrance, le doute, les tourments de toute sorte' (*PI*, I, 307) characterizes the run-of-the-mill artist rather than the creative genius; the latter is inspired by the pseudo-divine Unconscious.[27] In short, both philosophers conceive of (true) aesthetic experience as in some sense opposed to suffering. While Laforgue does, at times, propound the Hartmannian position that inspiration is 'un don des dieux' (*PI*, I, 307) ('À la Loi inconsciente sera pieusement rapportée cette intervention, illuminisme, génie, éclairs d'inspiration' (*OC*, III, 340)), elsewhere he suggests that the source of creativity might be suffering. This tension is related to his dual conception of the Unconscious. If his aesthetics of suffering represents a subversion of his philosophical reading, then it also constitutes a challenge to contemporary nationalist discourses, which glorified vigorous, virile bodies as the basis of France's future renewal.

In his philosophical notes, Laforgue never explicitly reflects upon his idiosyncratic treatment of Schopenhauer and Hartmann's aesthetic theories. However, his subversion of Schopenhauer's theory is signalled in his use of a particular image, that of the Danaids. In Greek myth, the Danaids were the fifty daughters of Danaus, who were betrothed to the fifty sons of Danaus's twin brother Aegyptus. But Danaus did not want the weddings to go ahead and so instructed his daughters to murder their new husbands on their wedding night. As punishment for their crime, the Danaids were condemned to spend eternity in the underworld trying to fill a bath with water in order to wash away their sins. However, since the bath had a leak (or, in another version of the tale, they were forced to carry the water in leaking vessels), it could never be filled and their task was endless. For Schopenhauer, this image of futile activity and perpetual dissatisfaction is a perfect illustration of the Will: it is analogous to 'the vessel of the Danaids' since 'there is no permanent fulfilment which completely and for ever satisfies its craving' (*WWR*, I, 362). But as Foucher de Careil indicates, art is one way out of this Danaidean bind.[28] For Laforgue, however, the Danaids are used not as an image of the suffering from which art provides relief, but as an image of art itself *as* suffering: in 'Complainte-Litanies de mon Sacré-Cœur', the poet's heart is 'plongé au Styx de nos arts danaïdes' (*OC*, I, 613); in 'Préludes autobiographiques', the poet describes 'la tourbillonnante éternelle agonie | D'un Nirvâna des Danaïdes du génie!' (*OC*, I, 548). In both cases, the use of the Danaids image suggests that creativity ('arts'/ 'génie') is closely related to some form of torment ('Styx'/ 'agonie').

Of course, the notion of the suffering artist has a long history, and was firmly established as a literary *topos* by the Romantics. In the late nineteenth century, however, this familiar conception of art took on a new resonance through the medicalized discourse of national decline examined in Chapter 1. Ideas of physical debility and disease were used to diagnose France's failings, and to demonize German philosophy as a threatening other; the notion of the artist as 'malade' thus assumed a certain anti-nationalistic status. Laforgue's work appears to endorse the (nationalist) discourse of philosophical disease in *Tessa*, in which Guido's pessimism is described as an illness (*OC*, I, 122). But in his later work he engages with it in a different sense, allying himself with the Decadent movement, which revalorized the corporeal vision of French decline. This is a provisional, tentative alliance: as Jean Pierrot points out, we should be wary of labelling Laforgue a Decadent since his literary interests display 'un éclectisme qui doit nous inviter à éviter à son propos tout cloisonnement trop catégorique';[29] more specifically, Clive Scott argues that Laforgue shares the Decadents' preoccupation with 'incurability, hypertrophy, atrophy [...] but not the hereditarily foregone, in its entropic unfolding, in its long-term determinism', nor its fetishistic materialism or its narcissistic self-fashioning.[30] Laforgue's work has even been read as a parody of certain aspects of the Decadent movement.[31] In his pseudonymous review of *Les Complaintes*, moreover, his final statement suggests a certain distance from the movement: he declares that he has contributed to the future development of poetry 'par de nouvelles poésies d'une tenue moins décadente et d'un idéal plus sérieusement moderne' (*OC*, III, 153). But despite this attempt to dissociate himself from the contemporary trend for Decadence, and despite the disparities signalled by Scott, Laforgue's work does display some affinity with that of the Decadents, most prominently in its concern with illness, frailty, and other bodily deficiencies.

His sympathy for the movement is borne out by his correspondence. In a letter to Kahn, Laforgue expresses dismay at not being mentioned in 'un grand article de P[aul] Bourde sur les Décadents' (*OC*, II, 780). He also voices sympathy for the Decadent movement in more substantive terms, notably in a letter of February 1882 to Ephrussi. In it Laforgue teases his friend for his conservative taste in literature by sarcastically endorsing his criticism of Edmond de Goncourt's novel *La Faustin*: 'Cher Monsieur Ephrussi, vous êtes un sage de critiquer ainsi la maladie qui pousse des fleurs du genre de *la Faustin*, vous êtes un sage' (*OC*, I, 751). He goes on, now with complete sincerity, to pity Ephrussi's distaste for Decadence: 'jamais vous ne sentirez le charme de la décadence, je vous plains et assurément, quand je raconterai votre sortie à M. Bernstein, lui qui aime la décadence, il vous plaindra aussi' (*OC*, I, 751). Laforgue begins the letter by addressing Ephrussi as 'homme sain d'esprit, de nerfs et de cœur' (*OC*, I, 751), and again this is intended as gentle mockery: like the Decadents, Laforgue derided the bourgeois obsession with health, informing Kahn in February 1884 that he had 'la santé [...] sans la honte d'en avoir trop' (*OC*, II, 694), as Gérard Briche notes.[32]

Briche argues that Laforgue's sympathy with Decadent ideals is evident in his 'volonté d'exacerber l'acuité des sens par la maladie'.[33] Illness, disease and infirmity certainly haunt Laforgue's poetry, the predominantly spiritual suffering of his early work being accompanied by more bodily pains in his later work. But his references to physical frailty do not always celebrate illness as a catalyst for heightened consciousness or creativity; at times, his affective mode is that of sympathy. He even planned a volume of poetry entitled *De la Pitié, de la Pitié* (which is mentioned as being in preparation on the opening page of *L'Imitation de Notre-Dame la Lune* (*OC*, III, 983 n. 23)). In this sense, Laforgue draws on Schopenhauer's ethics, which advocate pity as a means to overcome the egoism of willing,[34] a doctrine that is also important to his early poetry and philosophical notes ('saigner de pitié et d'amour universel, visiter les hôpitaux, toutes les maladies hideuses ou tristes [...] voir toute la douleur de la planète' (*OC*, III, 1129)). In his mature *œuvre*, such pity is perhaps most overtly expressed in 'Complainte du pauvre corps humain':

> L'Homme et sa compagne sont serfs
> De corps, tourbillonnants cloaques
> Aux mailles de harpes de nerfs
> Serves de tout et que détraque
> Un fier répertoire d'attaques.
> Voyez l'homme, voyez!
> Si ça n'fait pas pitié! (*OC*, I, 591)

The colloquial elision 'n'fait' might suggest an awareness of the potentially maudlin quality of such compassion, but this irony — which is quasi-ubiquitous in Laforgue's mature work — does not entirely undermine the poem's affect. If this poem constitutes a generalized lament for the travails of embodied existence, revealing 'a sickly, weary and pitifully mortal body beneath its Sunday best',[35] then elsewhere it is concern for the health of some individual that predominates. Most often, this individual is the poet's lover: from 'Complainte des formalités nuptiales' ('Allons, vous prendrez froid' (*OC*, I, 577)) to the *Derniers vers* ('Solo de lune', 'Légende', '*Noire bise, averse glapissante*' (*OC*, II, 322, 326 and 337)), the poet's call for his lover to take care of herself is repeated almost obsessively.

In the *Derniers vers*, it is his lover's cough that causes him particular worry, 'Légende' referring to her 'petite toux sèche maligne' and 'Solo de lune' imploring her 'Oh! soigne-toi, je t'en conjure! | Oh! je ne veux plus entendre cette toux!' (*OC*, II, 322). In 'L'hiver qui vient', meanwhile, the spectre of tuberculosis that haunts such references is explicitly invoked ('La phtisie pulmonaire attristant le quartier' (*OC*, II, 298)). In fact, this disease looms over his entire œuvre, from the early novella *Stéphane Vassiliew* to 'Le Miracle des roses' (*Moralités légendaires*). These references have often been interpreted as autobiographical; for example, Marguerite Poulin Caty writes:

> La présence de la maladie parcourt l'œuvre poétique de Laforgue: ce chétif, qui meurt à vingt-sept ans, est obsédé par la douleur physique. Le vent glacial ressemble à la phtisie qui le ronge. Le frisson d'automne lui rappelle qu'il est miné par la tuberculose.[36]

But this interpretation subscribes to a teleological fallacy: while Laforgue did die of tuberculosis, he did not fall ill until the end of 1886, and was not diagnosed with pulmonary illness until May 1887;[37] by this stage, he had written all of his major literary works. References to disease, illness and infirmity in his literary work thus have little to do with his own health, but are, first and foremost, a reflection of his philosophically-inflected pessimism, of his Decadent sympathies, and of the discursive context of corporeal decline on a national level. But while contemporary cultural critics bemoaned the poor quality of French bodies and the consequences of this for France's international status, and while the Decadents revelled in the subversive potential of representing disease, Laforgue's expressions of pity suggest an ethical engagement that calls into question these instrumentalized visions of illness.

Nonetheless, Laforgue does also see 'the possibilities for art which come from the sickly modern being',[38] an aesthetic mode that represents a major departure from Schopenhauer and Hartmann's theories of art, as we have seen, even if it is inspired by their pessimism. In his letter to Mültzer of 5 February 1882, Laforgue conceptualizes his literary creation as emerging from the body, and more specifically as being associated with pain and suffering:

> Au fond, au tréfond[s], quand je me replie sur moi-même, je retrouve mon éternel *cœur* pourri de tristesse, et toute la littérature que je m'arracherai des entrailles pourra se résumer dans ce mot de peine d'enfant, *faire dodo* […]. (*OC*, II, 754; author's emphases)

In addition to his emotional torment ('pourri de tristesse'), he uses images of physical pain ('m'arracherai des entrailles'/ 'ce mot de peine d'enfant') to describe the creative process. Indeed, his conception of himself as the mother of his work implies a double agony: he inflicts pain on himself through his self-midwifery; and the literature that he tears like a child from his 'entrailles' is also in pain, which it attempts to soothe with the cry of '*faire dodo*'. He goes on to quote from a recently composed poem, 'La chanson du petit hypertrophique'. The mother of the 'petit hypertrophique' has died 'd'un' maladie d'cœur' (*OC*, I, 632), with which he too is afflicted, and the doctor has told him 'Que j'irai là-bas, | Fair' dodo z'avec elle' (*OC*, I, 632). With its refrain 'J'entends mon cœur qui bat, | C'est maman qui m'appelle!' (*OC*, I, 632), this poem reveals that the increasingly fragmented prosody of Laforgue's mature work is based on the 'battement, maladif et obstiné' of cardiac arrhythmia, and on the other broken rhythms of the suffering body.[39] Despite inaugurating Laforgue's new aesthetic, the poem was left out of *Les Complaintes*; Jean-Pierre Richard argues that it was omitted precisely because it revealed too openly the collection's bodily principle. The poem is a turning point in another sense too: as Daniel Grojnowski argues, it represents the crucial moment in Laforgue's poetic career when he rejects the lyrical effusion of his early work in favour of a more ludic tonality.[40] But the shift 'du pathétique au parodique'[41] is not entirely clear-cut. The irony of Laforgue's mature work is always Janus-faced: while the poet mocks himself and his own suffering ('Le tourment du Sujet devient objet de dérision de soi par soi'[42]), he also continues to pity himself (as well as mocking his own self-pity and pitying his own self-mockery). As in 'Complainte du pauvre corps humain', the colloquial elisions of 'La chanson du petit hypertrophique' are destabilizing, but not entirely disaffirming.

There is also a double-sidedness to the subject matter of the poem, since the heart of the 'petit hypertrophique' is both swollen and empty, excessive (in its growth) and lacking (in the love of the absent mother).[43] Excess and lack are, as we saw in Chapter 1, intrinsic to Decadence: in its transgression of propriety and moderation, Decadence is always both too much and too little, both rampant and etiolated, over-sexed and sterile.[44] For Laforgue, excess also manifests itself in the overgrowth of selfhood: 'Le débordement hypertrophique [est] indicatif d'une subjectivisation maximale du discours'.[45] But again, lack is inseparable from excess, since this hypertrophic self is also one on the verge of disappearance: the 'petit hypertrophique' will soon 'Fair' dodo' in death. Indeed, the death of the poet is announced in the opening line of *Les Complaintes*, the prefatory 'À Paul Bourget' proclaiming that the poet is 'En deuil d'un Moi-le-Magnifique' (*OC*, I, 545). The meta-poetic 'Complainte des Complaintes' confirms that these poems are the products of 'un défunt Moi' (*OC*, I, 621). In one sense, the poet's registering of his own death enacts an impossibility; we shall return to this paradox — which is closely connected to Hartmann's analysis of mysticism — in Chapter 5. In another sense, though, the poet is simply announcing the death of his old poetic self, of the self-aggrandizing lyrical persona ('Moi-*le-Magnifique*'). As 'Préludes autobiographiques' makes clear, this is not 'la mort mortelle, sans mystère, | Lors quoi l'usage veut qu'on nous cache sous terre' (*OC*, I, 549). But it is, nonetheless, a kind of suicide:

> [...] c'est dans la Sainte Piscine ésotérique
> D'un lucus à huis-clos, sans pape et sans laquais,
> Que J'ouvre ainsi mes riches veines à Jamais. (*OC*, I, 549)

The reference to 'la Sainte Piscine' suggests that this is, in fact, a baptismal suicide, a death that is also a re-birth.

Bleeding not only constitutes a release from the old poetic self of *Le Sanglot*, but also plays a crucial role in Laforgue's new conception of poetic expression.[46] In a later poem from *L'Imitation de Notre-Dame la Lune*, this sanguinary poetics is foregrounded through the term 'cruor', which signifies 'le sang versé, le sang de la violence':[47] 'Ce sont les linges, les linges, | Hôpitaux consacrés aux cruors et aux fanges' ('Les linges, le cygne', *OC*, II, 105). Here, as Jeanne Bem points out, 'Le substrat pulsionnel de l'écriture laforguienne s'y met à nu, le charnel l'emporte sur l'abstrait'.[48] The 'linges' are the pages on which the poet writes, and these are 'linges pollués', 'Linges adolescents, nuptiaux, maternels', 'Linges des grandes maladies' (*OC*, II, 105–06). All conjure up the notion of writing as stain, as smear of bodily fluid: 'l'horreur d'une écriture-souillure'.[49] Laforgue was not only literally tubercular, but also figuratively so, afflicted — in Bourget's phrase — with 'une tuberculose mentale',[50] the words of his poems like the spots of blood on the consumptive's handkerchief.

The image of bleeding dramatizes the shift away from *Le Sanglot* in another sense: in his mature work, this image functions as an important aspect of Laforgue's aesthetics of physical suffering, but in his first collection the same image had an essentially *spiritual* signification. As Richard notes, 'L'image autour de laquelle le *Sanglot* semble construit, est celle d'un Cœur douloureux, qui saigne, qui pleure, le cœur d'un Christ humain et sidéral qui souffre pour la création entière'.[51] This is foregrounded in the poem 'Hypertrophie' (to which 'La chanson du petit hypertrophique' responds):

> Je suis le cœur de tout, et je saigne en démence
> Et déborde d'amour par l'azur constellé,
> Enfin! que tout soit consolé. (*OC*, I, 353)

As Grojnowski points out, the heart of 'Hypertrophie' and of *Le Sanglot* in general is one that draws on the religious paradigm of the Sacred Heart of Christ; that of 'La chanson du petit hypertrophique' and of *Les Complaintes* is, by contrast, physiological.[52] In fact, this shift is hinted at in 'Les linges, le cygne', where the stained sheets are juxtaposed with the 'Nappe qui drape la sainte-table ou l'autel' (*OC*, I, 105). It is made even more evident in 'La Complainte des montres': here, the Sacred Heart becomes a simple ticker, the eponymous watch being described as 'Le sacré cœur d'or revêtu' (*OC*, I, 625). This poem was not included in the final version of *Les Complaintes*, but was adapted and embellished to form 'Complainte des Mounis du Mont-Martre', which again signals, albeit more subtly, the shift away from the idea of 'un divin Cœur' (*OC*, I, 610).

The titular alteration, from 'La Complainte des montres' to 'Complainte des

Mounis du Mont-Martre', is significant, revealing another aspect to Laforgue's use of the heart image. While the ostensible subject of the new poem is also the 'tic-tac froid' (*OC*, I, 610) of pocket watches and other timepieces, the reference to Montmartre in the title, combined with the allusion to the Sacred Heart, suggests the *Basilique du Sacré-Cœur de Montmartre*, which was being built at the time the poem was written. The cathedral was conceived as an expiation for the supposed sins of France (both Imperial and Revolutionary), sins which had culminated in defeat in the Franco-Prussian War, and the Commune.[53] Drawing on the Catholic devotion of the Sacred Heart, the cathedral's construction represented a fusion of religious and nationalist ideologies. Laforgue's rejection of the former thus also implies a rejection of the latter. As 'Complainte-Litanies de mon Sacré-Cœur' (the poem that follows 'Complainte des Mounis de Mont-Martre') makes clear, the heart in Laforgue's mature work is empty, barren, 'un désert altéré', but not only in the sense that it is just a muscular mechanism ('Mon Cœur est une horloge oubliée à demeure, | Qui, me sachant défunt, s'obstine à sonner l'heure!') or in the sense that it symbolizes emotional hollowness ('Mon Cœur [...] | Présente à tout baiser une armure de vide') (*OC*, I, 612–13). It is also lacking as a symbol, having been stripped of its religious and nationalist significations; these significations are alluded to in the poems' titles ('Mont-Martre'/ 'Sacré-Cœur') but refuted or erased in the poems themselves. This erasure or crossing-out of potential symbolic meaning is suggested in 'Complainte-Litanies de mon Sacré-Cœur': 'Mon Cœur est un lexique où cent littératures | Se lardent sans répit de divines ratures' (*OC*, I, 612).

Laforgue's poetics of individual, physical suffering thus represents a rejection not only of narratives of progress and national regeneration, but also of a nationalistic religiosity. The conception of *Les Complaintes* itself is related to this repudiation. Writing to Charles Henry in August 1885, Laforgue states that the idea for his new aesthetic came to him 'à la fête de l'inauguration du lion de Belfort' (*OC*, II, 777) in September 1880, a nationalistic celebration of a new statue commemorating the successful defence of Belfort during its siege by the Prussians in 1870–71. It was predominantly his sense of alienation amidst the drunken revelry of this event that led to his creation of what he calls 'l'esthétique empirique de la complainte' (*OC*, II, 777) — that is, poetry that wryly registers the suffering and depravity of modern life on this 'Drôle de planète' (see his notes on the 'fête', *OC*, I, 650–51) — but his dislocation from the nationalistic pretext for the debauchery may have compounded this feeling of isolation. Many of his poetic avatars are, at least, suspicious of jingoism: Pierrot declares that he hates 'les phrases nationales' (*OC*, II, 88); Salomé is 'fuyeuse de fêtes nationales' (*OC*, II, 445–46); and Hamlet avoids 'les bruits de la ville d'Elseneur' (*OC*, II, 380), noises which might perhaps come from an anachronistic and anatopic *fête nationale*, since the date is recorded as 14 July 1601. Laforgue was no doubt especially sceptical of such displays of patriotic fervour because he lived in an era when they became rife: *le quatorze juillet* was officially instituted in 1880; the Marseillaise (which he parodies in 'Simple agonie': 'Aux armes citoyens! Il n'y a plus de RAISON' (*OC*, II, 319)) was restored as France's national anthem in 1879. For Laforgue, poets should have nothing to do with zealotry, since they are 'd'une autre race que ces porte-drapeaux révolutionnaires, chauvins, foyereux et autres' (*OC*, III, 125–26). Instead, they should be 'anarchistes, nihilistes'; they are 'les seuls êtres qui ne reconnaissent plus aucune discipline ni de conscience ni de santé, ni de société' (*OC*, III, 362). The references to 'discipline' and to 'santé' might, indeed, be understood in the context of another contemporary development: the law of 27 January 1880 saw the integration of gymnastics and military training into the teaching programme, the idea being — as Pierre Arnaud points out — 'to mould each Frenchman into a future soldier, to regenerate the race and make it more virile',[54] all 'in the name of revenge and the recapture of the lost provinces'.[55]

This rejection of a politicized 'santé' is, as we have seen, crucial to Laforgue's poetry. If it deviates from Schopenhauer and Hartmann's aesthetic theories, it does, on the other hand, draw on their pessimistic insistence on the prevalence of human suffering. Moreover, Laforgue directly links his poetics of illness to the Unconscious. In his February 1882 letter to Mültzer, art is conceptualized as a suffering child, with the artist envisaged as its mother; in a later fragment of criticism on Mallarmé, written in 1886, the artist becomes the suffering child himself. In this fragment, Laforgue initially presents his own aesthetic standard: '– l'Inconscient; le principe, après l'effort, l'apothéose de la conscience artistique parnassienne se consolant dans des protestations bouddhiques, — le principe en poésie du bégaiement, de l'en allé' (*OC*, III, 195). He then goes on to state that Mallarmé's method of poetic composition is quite different:

> Chez M. Mallarmé [...], ce n'est pas le bégaiement de l'enfant qui a mal, mais le *Sage qui divague*, — ce n'est jamais une divagation d'images comme dans le rêve et l'extase inconsciente, c'est-à-dire de sentiments exprimés avec l'immédiat de l'enfant qui n'a à sa disposition que le répertoire de ses besoins [...]. (*OC*, III, 195; author's emphasis)

The value of these comments lies less in their analysis of Mallarmé than in what they imply for Laforgue's own aesthetic ideals. Of course, the link drawn between pathology and creativity also points to a broader current in nineteenth-century literature, when artistic ability came to be associated with illness (especially tuberculosis).[56] But while for the Romantics illness was merely the precondition of or analogy for a creative sensibility, for Laforgue (and other post-Romantics) writing itself was infected, was symptomatic: the stuttering of Laforgue's mature verse (its disrupted rhythms, its abrupt tonal shifts) is far removed from Romantic lyricism. The connection drawn between the stuttering of an ill child and 'le rêve et l'extase inconsciente' also suggests Laforgue's affinity with the Decadent movement, which 'valorize[s] physiological ills and alteration as the origin of psychic alterity', that is 'as an opening onto the unconscious'.[57] This connection is reiterated in comments on Verlaine's *Sagesse*, described as 'de la vraie poésie, des vagissements, des balbutiements dans une langue inconsciente ayant tout juste le souci de rimer' (*OC*, I, 845):[58] again stuttering is presented as a vocalic unfettering, a sign of a liberated creative process flowing directly from the Unconscious.

Stuttering also suggests an extension of Bourget's theory of Decadent style: while for Bourget the disintegration effected by 'Un style de décadence' culminates in 'l'indépendance du mot',[59] stuttering implies a breaking-down of the word itself into its constituent syllables. Laforgue's puns — 'sangsuelles', 'sexciproques' (*OC*, I, 555 and 551) — are rooted in this syllabic deconstruction: 'le mot-valise n'apparaît pas comme synthèse de deux en un, mais plutôt comme division d'un mot en deux ou plusieurs, manifestation d'une virtualité de dédoublement dans tout mot commun'.[60] In addition to the aesthetic aspect of Bourget's theory, Laforgue also engages with its social dimensions, endorsing the revalorization of Decadence and the Decadent artist. His critical notes on Hippolyte Taine's neo-Classical aesthetic theories argue that a decadent civilization is just as interesting as 'une civilisation équilibrée'; in fact, 'Les êtres comme les civilisations hypertrophiés sont plus intéressants que les êtres, les civilisations équilibrés' (*OC*, III, 359–60). For Taine, 'le beau c'est la santé' (*OC*, III, 360) and the pinnacle of aesthetic achievement is the nude, with its 'corps parfait et âme parfaite' (*OC*, III, 360), but Laforgue rejects this ideal both for its fixity and for its narrowness. Art should reflect the kaleidoscopic, ever-changing nature of human civilization with all of its apparent flaws; rather than clinging to fixed aesthetic standards, art should be in a state of perpetual becoming driven by the Unconscious:

> La civilisation nous détraque, plus d'équilibre, contre nature soit. Mais cela ne nous regarde pas. L'Inconscient souffle où il veut et comme il veut, laissez le faire et brodons nos arts sur ses étapes. (*OC*, III, 360)

For Taine, moreover, the creative powers of individual artists are in direct correlation with the 'énergies actives de la nation' (Taine, *Philosophie de l'art*, quoted in *OC*, III, 365), an association that Laforgue emphatically refutes with a quotation from Bourget:

> 'Si les citoyens d'une décadence sont inférieurs comme ouvriers de la grandeur d'un pays, ne sont-ils pas très supérieurs comme artistes de l'intérieur de l'âme?' (Bourget, quoted in *OC*, III, 365)

Laforgue thus argues that artists are neither determined by nor determiners of the supposed greatness of a nation. Instead, they are governed by the higher, supranational force of the Unconscious.

In endorsing Bourget's defence of the Decadent artist, Laforgue echoes his own praise of Baudelaire as 'Le premier qui ne soit pas triomphant mais s'accuse, montre ses plaies, sa paresse, son inutilité ennuyée au milieu de ce siècle travailleur et dévoué' (*OC*, III, 162). He relates Bourget's apologia for unproductivity to sexual deficiency: 'Cela est certain,' he writes, referring to Bourget's theory, 'de même que les femmes stériles sont les plus belles, de même que Kant et Newton étaient impuissants' (*OC*, III, 365). As Briche notes, 'cette impuissance que Bourget localise dans le corps social, Laforgue l'étend spontanément, comme si la chose allait de soi, au corps physique'.[61] This connection between impotence and génie is a recapitulation of Baudelaire's 'Plus l'homme cultive les arts, moins il bande, etc'.[62] But Laforgue's treatment of sexuality is ambiguous, since an erotic principle operates on the level of form: the neologistic portmanteaux which are symptomatic of Laforgue's stuttering syllabicity can also be read as sexualized yet unproductive unions of words. In a letter to Kahn of 16 December 1884, Laforgue describes these portmanteaux as based on an 'accouplement de mots qui n'ont qu'une harmonie de rêve mais font dans la réalité des couples impossibles' (*OC*, II, 720), and in the review of *Les Complaintes* that he co-wrote with Henry, he refers to 'quelques néologismes mort-nés pour la plupart' (*OC*, III, 154). We thus return to the notion of unproductivity: while there is a sexual principle at work in Laforgue's neologisms, he is, as Bertrand and Henri Scepi note, resistant to 'la poussée censée ouvrir la voie à la fécondation et à l'engendrement';[63] his couplings do not produce viable progeny.

Notions of sterility and impotence form part of Laforgue's aesthetics of physical debility, which challenge both contemporary nationalist discourses (which focused chiefly on demographic recovery) and neo-Classical associations between beauty and physical perfection. But his notes on Taine, which dismiss the notion of health as aesthetic ideal, present a difficulty for his aesthetics. Laforgue's objection in this instance is based not on the idea that creativity emerges from suffering, but on a questioning of the very notions of health and illness: 'Où prenez-vous la santé?' he asks Taine; 'Apprenez que l'Inconscient ne connaît pas la maladie' (*OC*, III, 360). This is a direct quotation from Hartmann ('L'Inconscient ne connaît pas la maladie' (*PI*, II, 3)). Elsewhere, Hartmann elaborates on this idea:

> l'*Inconscient ne peut ni être malade lui-même, ni causer la maladie de l'organisme qu'il régit*. Toute maladie est la conséquence d'un désordre produit par une action extérieure. (*PI*, I, 183; author's emphasis)

The notion that illness is alien to the Unconscious seems inconsistent with the association that Laforgue draws between suffering and unconscious inspiration, an association that is illustrated by his linking of 'le bégaiement de l'enfant qui a mal' and 'l'extase inconsciente'.

In the above quotation, Hartmann is referring to the *individual* unconscious (the unconscious will that governs physiological processes in all animals), as indicated by the earlier formulation '*le principe psychique du développement organique ne connaît pas la maladie*' (*PI*, I, 182; author's emphasis). But this does not resolve the inconsistency in Laforgue's own thinking, since he seems unaware of this nuance. The tension here is, in fact, indicative of the competing visions of the Unconscious within Laforgue's work: on the one hand, it is a beneficent, pseudo-divine principle or Elysian domain; on the other, a life-force (akin to Schopenhauer's Will) that produces the day-to-day human experiences of illness, suffering and pain. Both, for Laforgue, are sources of creative inspiration. At times, Laforgue seems to offer a reconciliation of these two visions, one which sees suffering as part of the plan of the (divine) Unconscious, and artistic creation as a reflection of this:

> Dans l'émotion artistique il ne faut jamais s'en référer à l'agréable, au pénible etc. — La lutte, l'hésitation, [les] conflits, la déception, la soif — tout ce qui constitue la vie doit constituer la vibration esthétique [...]. Le principe anarchique, concurrence vitale et sélection naturelle, de la Vie-même –. (*OC*, III, 379)

This is not derived from Hartmann's aesthetic theory, but it does reflect, to a certain extent, Hartmann's ethics of commitment to the world process: 'C'est seulement par l'absolu dévouement à la vie et à ses souffrances, non par le lâche renoncement de l'individu qui se retire de la lutte, que le processus du monde peut être efficacement servi' (*PI*, II, 497). But this resolution is only a tentative one, since there persists in Laforgue's work an alternative vision of the Unconscious as a realm that provides solace from suffering.

If the promised land of the Unconscious offers a possible solution to the problem of suffering, then there is also a way out that is derived from Schopenhauer's thought: the idea that aesthetic experience provides a (temporary) release from the torment caused by the Will. In his earliest philosophical notes, Laforgue considers Schopenhauer's theory that through aesthetic contemplation 'on échappe à soi, on est affranchi momentanément/ pour un instant du temps, de l'Espace et des nombres, on meurt à la conscience de son individualité, on monte, on atteint à la g[ran]de liberté... sortir de l'Illusoire' (*OC*, III, 1128).[64] This release from the bonds of selfhood also entails a respite from suffering:

> On tue pour un moment le vouloir individualisé qui est en nous. On meurt au vouloir. Le vouloir est souffrance [...].
> Il n'y a plus de pauvre, ni de riche, de phtisique, ni d'hypertrophique, de soucis, d'estomac, ni d'esclave du génie de l'Espèce [...]. (*OC*, III, 1129)

Laforgue's notes build on Schopenhauer's observation that 'the person who is involved in this [aesthetic] perception is no longer an individual, for in such perception the individual has lost himself; he is *pure* will-less, painless, timeless *subject of knowledge*' (*WWR*, I, 179; author's emphases). In a later fragment of notes, Laforgue returns to the idea of liberation through aesthetic experience, which is now associated specifically with memory and dream:

> Je ne trouverai beau et pur que ce que j'imagine et ce dont je me souviens, — ce qui peut arriver et ce qui a été. Je me sens comme un Ariel au-dessus du Présent — l'odieux et quotidien et importun Présent — ainsi pour la femme et tout — Oh qui jettera un pont entre mon cœur et le Présent? C'est que le souvenir et le rêve sont l'art d'enchâsser les moments, de les prendre en eux ébarbés du moment d'avant et du moment d'après, des regrets et des appréhensions qu'eut aussi ce moment. Aux paysages il enlève le trop froid et le trop chaud et tous les ennuis du corps — l'âme seule est prise — Et ne vivre qu'avec son âme... Ah! ne vivre qu'avec son âme! (*OC*, III, 1093)

Beauty is attained through alternative temporalities ('ce qui peut arriver et ce qui a été'); suffering — both emotional ('regrets'/ 'appréhensions') and physical ('tous les ennuis du corps') — is located in the present moment. Laforgue thus feels a sense of disjunction from 'l'odieux et quotidien et importun Présent', appealing for someone to create 'un pont entre mon cœur et le Présent'. Elsewhere in his later notes he confirms this pessimistic view of present experience: happiness, he writes, can only be tasted in memory and imagination; 'nul n'a jamais pu se dire: le voici, j'en ai, en ce moment dans le présent' (*OC*, III, 950).

The sense of distance from the present that Laforgue feels ('un Ariel au-dessus du Présent') is also, perhaps, experienced during sex, the phrase 'ainsi pour la femme et tout' suggests. This interpretation is reinforced by the poem 'Mettons le doigt sur la plaie', which is closely related to this fragment in its imprecation of 'le cru, quotidien, et trop voyant Présent!' (*OC*, II, 153). Here the poet again describes himself as Ariel: 'Et fol, je me balance | Au-dessus du Présent en Ariel qui a honte' (*OC*, II, 153). The form 'fol', neither masculine nor feminine, suggests an attempt to slip the bonds of gendered existence, while 'honte' might imply the shame of sexual indulgence. Indeed, the title, while ostensibly a proverbial phrase meaning 'to put your finger on a problem', could also be read as a vulgar pun, since 'la plaie' was a contemporary slang term for female genitalia.[65] In any case, the relationship between the present and physical suffering is clear: 'Je fais signe au Présent: "Oh! sois plus diaphane?" | Mais il me bat la charge et mine mes organes!' (*OC*, II, 153). Moreover, in describing his heart as a 'citerne | Des Danaïdes' (*OC*, II, 153), as unsatisfied and unsatisfiable, the poet draws on the same image used by Schopenhauer to describe the torment produced by the Will.

As we have seen, elsewhere in his work Laforgue redisposes this image to suggest that suffering is inherent to art. But in 'Solo de lune', which reworks 'Mettons le doigt sur la plaie' (as well as 'Arabesques de malheur'), he returns to the Schopenhauerian idea that aesthetic experience might provide a release from the Danaidean suffering produced by willing. In the above fragment and in 'Mettons le doigt sur la plaie', the poet bemoans his Ariel-like condition of separation from the present moment, while also recognizing that the present necessarily entails bodily discomfort or pain; in 'Solo de lune', by contrast, the poet notes the suffering of his body but does not dwell on it (initially at least), instead experiencing a sense of joyous liberation from his body *in* the present:

> Je fume, étalé face au ciel,
> Sur l'impériale de la diligence,
> Ma carcasse est cahotée, mon âme danse
> Comme un Ariel;
> Sans miel, sans fiel, ma belle âme danse. (*OC*, II, 320)

The contrast between the harshly plosive alliteration of 'carcasse'/ 'cahotée' and the mellifluous sonority of the following lines, with their liquid and labial consonants and internal rhyme, emphasizes the beatitude of this ecstatic state. Later the poet declares 'je suis Ariel', his desire to 'ne vivre qu'avec son âme' imaginatively realized. This bodiless existence is associated with the beauty of the night-time coach ride: 'La lune se lève | Ô route en grand rêve!...' (*OC*, II, 321). But enduring release is impossible: the poet's ability to portray the night's splendour falters ('Ô solo de lune, | Vous défiez ma plume') and the realities of embodied experience, as well as the anxieties it provokes, surge back into the poem ('Voici qu'il fait très, très-frais', 'Oh! je ne veux plus entendre cette toux' (*OC*, II, 322)). In fact, aesthetic experience might not merely prove to be inadequate, it might lead us directly back into suffering, causing us to neglect our own well-being: 'Elle aura oublié son foulard, | Elle va prendre mal, vu la beauté de l'heure!' (*OC*, II, 322). In one sense, 'Solo de lune' dramatizes Schopenhauer's theory that aesthetic experience can relieve suffering only temporarily; but in another sense, its central themes of loss and regret show that suffering is often itself the source of inspiration.

Conclusion

Laforgue's aesthetics of suffering may subvert the theories of Hartmann and Schopenhauer, but it does draw from the pessimistic current of the philosophers' work. As we saw in Chapter 1, it was pessimism, above all, that was pathologized by French critics as 'other', as an invasive disease infecting the minds of the French; Laforgue's engagement with this discourse is evident in *Tessa*. More broadly, the dominance of illness and physical debility in Laforgue's work — both thematically and as an aesthetic principle — demonstrates his opposition to the contemporary politicization of the healthy body as the locus of national regeneration and revenge against Germany, an opposition that aligns him with the Decadent movement. Like the consumptives of 'Le Miracle des roses', who are 'relégués [...] loin des capitales sérieuses où s'élabore le Progrès' (*OC*, II, 404), Laforgue casts himself as an exile from bourgeois society; this society's glorification of physical vigour is encapsulated in the same tale in the image of young men playing tennis, described as 'une jeunesse en vérité moderne, musclée, douchée et responsable de l'Histoire' (*OC*, II, 403). Indeed, Laforgue describes poetry itself as a tubercular body: 'nous la voyons se mettre à tous les climats, comme un poitrinaire qui ne veut pas mourir' ('Paul Bourget', *OC*, III, 131). Hartmann, too, propounds a kind of literary organicism in his aesthetic theory — only in a very different sense:

> Pour le génie, qui doit ses conceptions à l'Inconscient, tous les éléments de l'œuvre artistique sont si étroitement liés, si bien coordonnés et associés entre eux, que l'unité parfaite de l'œuvre ne permet de la comparer qu'aux organismes de la nature, qui doivent également leur unité à l'Inconscient. (*PI*, I, 308)

For Laforgue, the poetic organism is not one that is characterized by perfect unity or harmony, but by fragmentation, discord, and rupture. The heterometric lines of his free verse suggest the Decadent concern with excess and lack: they are either hypertrophied or atrophied, overgrown or amputated. Form itself thus takes on a certain anti-nationalistic status, defying — in metaphorical terms — contemporary norms of health, just as it flouts *la clarté française* and the rules of French versificatory tradition. Laforgue's aesthetic departs from Hartmann's vision of perfect organic unity in another sense: it is inhabited — infected, even — by other discourses. It is ironic, of course, that philosophy is the most important of these discourses, its very presence within the body of Laforgue's work suggesting both his adherence to philosophical ideas and his subversion of them.

Notes to Chapter 2

1. See, for example, Schopenhauer in Bourdeau: 'La misère qui remplit ce monde proteste trop hautement contre l'hypothèse d'une œuvre parfaite due à un être absolument sage, absolument bon, et avec cela tout puissant' (Schopenhauer, trans. by Bourdeau, p. 43).
2. Schopenhauer, quoted in Challemel-Lacour, p. 312.
3. Schopenhauer, quoted in Ribot, p. 114.
4. Caro, pp. 212–13.
5. Paul Bénichou, *Le Sacre de l'écrivain, 1750–1830* (Paris: Gallimard, 1996), p. 385.
6. Excluding the prefatory 'À Paul Bourget'.

7. As Hannoosh states, these notes 'ne sont pas de simples citations, mais des reformulations synthétiques, des refontes personnelles, des ripostes critiques, des analyses pénétrées de réflexions originales' (Hannoosh, *OC*, III, 1125–26).
8. Janet (June 1877), p. 623.
9. Caro, p. 260.
10. Ibid., p. 265. Laforgue's 'fééries/ fantaisies' transfigures Caro's 'fantasmagorie', as Hannoosh notes (*OC*, III, 1136 n. 4).
11. Schopenhauer, trans. by Bourdeau, p. 40.
12. Bootle (2011), p. 168.
13. The abbot Arnaud Amaury is reported to have ordered his soldiers to kill everyone during the siege of Béziers in the 13th century (part of the crusade against the Catharist heresy), saying 'Dieu reconnaîtra les siens'.
14. Bootle (2011), pp. 167–68.
15. Ramsey, p. xx.
16. Arkell, p. 32.
17. Olivier Champod, '*Tessa*, ou comment brûler Schopenhauer', *Revue de littérature comparée*, 324 (2007), 427–38 (p. 427).
18. At this stage, though, Laforgue does not share Caro's hostility towards Schopenhauer's ethics.
19. Richard Hibbitt, *Dilettantism and its Values: From Weimar Classicism to the fin de siècle* (London: Legenda, 2006), p. 111.
20. Ibid., p. 115.
21. See Hartmann's reference to 'la rage froide qu'inspire le carnaval insensé de la vie' (Hartmann, quoted in Janet (June 1877), p. 635; see also Caro, p. 270).
22. Schopenhauer, trans. by Bourdeau, p. 67.
23. Colin, p. 139.
24. Foucher de Careil, p. 356.
25. The term 'cataphronantrope' features in Janet (May 1877, p. 285), who quotes Wilhelm Gwinner's statement that Schopenhauer 'avait non la haine, mais le mépris des hommes', as Hannoosh notes (*OC*, III, 1137 n. 2). Janet also notes that Schopenhauer 'prêchait l'ascétisme sans le pratiquer' (May 1877, p. 283).
26. J. A. Hiddleston, *Essai sur Laforgue et les 'Derniers vers': suivi de, Laforgue et Baudelaire* (Lexington, KY: French Forum, 1980), pp. 33–34.
27. The creative genius may well be more aware of suffering ('les hommes de génie sont toujours les êtres qui sentent le plus profondément et de la façon la plus incurable le malheur de l'existence' (*PI*, I, 419)), but the process of creation itself is not — for the genius — one that involves suffering, according to Hartmann.
28. Foucher de Careil, p. 248.
29. Jean Pierrot, 'Laforgue, décadent?', in *Laforgue aujourd'hui*, ed. by J. A. Hiddleston ([Paris]: José Corti, 1988), pp. 25–49 (p. 35).
30. Clive Scott, 'The Stuttering Poet: A Deleuzian Reading of a Laforguian Poetics', *Dix-Neuf*, 20, no. 1 (2016), 9–24 (p. 21).
31. Pierrot (1988), p. 36; see also Hannoosh.
32. Gérard Briche, 'Mal de Mère. Portrait de l'artiste en malade: Jules Laforgue', in *Littérature et Pathologie*, ed. by Max Milner (Paris: Presses universitaires de Vincennes, 1989), pp. 205–11 (p. 207).
33. Ibid., p. 206.
34. See, for example, Caro, p. 235. However, Caro also highlights the incongruity of this theory 'avec la violence de ses haines, avec l'injustice et la brutalité savante de ses anathèmes contre ses adversaires' (p. 237).
35. Claire White, *Work and Leisure in Late Nineteenth-Century French Literature and Visual Culture: Time, Politics and Class* (Basingstoke: Palgrave Macmillan, 2014), p. 93.
36. Marguerite Poulin Caty, 'Poétique du spleen dans l'œuvre de Jules Laforgue', *The French Review*, 65, no. 1 (1991), 55–63 (p. 56).
37. See his letter to his sister Marie of 8 May 1887, in which he relates that he has 'un poumon menacé' (*OC*, II, 924; author's emphasis).

38. Symons, p. 302.
39. Jean-Pierre Richard, 'Le sang de la complainte', *Poétique*, 37 (February 1979), 487–95 (p. 488).
40. Daniel Grojnowski, *Jules Laforgue et 'l'Originalité'* (Boudry-Neuchâtel: La Baconnière, 1988), p. 81; see also Grojnowski, *Jules Laforgue, les voix de la Complainte*, p. 25.
41. Grojnowski (1988), p. 81.
42. Ibid., p. 81.
43. Richard (1979), p. 487.
44. Constable et al, pp. 9–10.
45. Henri Scepi, 'La complainte de tous les excès (de l'hypertrophie au fatras)', in *Jules Laforgue: colloque de la Sorbonne: actes de la journée d'agrégation du 18 novembre 2000*, ed. by André Guyaux and Bertrand Marchal (Paris: Presses de l'Université de Paris-Sorbonne, 2000), pp. 27–42 (p. 33).
46. Richard (1979), p. 491.
47. Jeanne Bem, *Le Texte traversé: Corneille, Prévost, Marivaux, Musset, Dumas, Nerval, Baudelaire, Hugo, Flaubert, Verlaine, Laforgue, Proust, Giraudoux, Aragon, Giono* (Paris: Champion, 1991), p. 163.
48. Ibid., p. 159.
49. Ibid., p. 163.
50. Paul Bourget, quoted by L'abbé Mugnier (*Journal*, ([Paris?]: Mercure de France, 1990), p. 360; quoted *OC*, III, 1247).
51. Ruchon, pp. 68–69.
52. Daniel Grojnowski, 'La première des "Complaintes"', in *Jules Laforgue: colloque de la Sorbonne: actes de la journée d'agrégation du 18 novembre 2000*, ed. by André Guyaux and Bertrand Marchal (Paris: Presses de l'Université de Paris-Sorbonne, 2000)), pp. 43–54 (p. 46).
53. Grojnowski, 'La première des "Complaintes"', p. 47.
54. Pierre Arnaud, 'Dividing and uniting: sports societies and nationalism, 1870–1914', in *Nationhood and Nationalism in France from Boulangism to the Great War*, ed. by Robert Tombs (Oxford: Routledge, 1991, repr. 2006), pp. 182–94 (p. 183).
55. Ibid., p. 184.
56. Sontag, p. 32.
57. Spackman, pp. vii-viii.
58. See also Laforgue's comments on Verlaine in his 'Agenda de 1883': 'Quel vrai poète — C'est bien celui dont je me rapproche le plus. Négligence absolue de la forme, plaintes d'enfant –' (*OC*, I, 886).
59. Bourget, p. 14.
60. Yvan Leclerc, '"X en soi": Laforgue et l'identité', *Romantisme*, 19, no. 64 (1989), 29–38 (p. 34).
61. Briche, p. 206.
62. Baudelaire, 'Mon Cœur mis à nu', p. 638.
63. Jean-Pierre Bertrand and Henri Scepi, '"Le rêve d'une langue bornée, mais infinie": Laforgue poète langagier', in *La Littérature symboliste et la Langue. Actes du colloque organisé à Aoste les 8 et 9 mai 2009*, ed. by Olivier Bivort (Paris: Classiques Garnier, 2012), pp. 121–39 (p. 135).
64. These notes are inspired by Caro, pp. 212–13; see Hannoosh, *OC*, III, 1130 n. 3.
65. Pierre Guiraud, *Dictionnaire historique, stylistique, rhétorique, étymologique, de la littérature érotique* (Paris: Payot, 1978), p. 502.

CHAPTER 3

Germany and the Forest as Other

Laforgue's reception of Schopenhauer and Hartmann was informed by the notion of otherness that was expressed through metaphors of disease, but he also engaged more directly with ideas of Germany as other. His experience of living in Germany prompted a series of reflections on this country's culture and its differences from his native France, with two texts in particular offering important insights. In *Berlin, la cour et la ville* (1887), a collection of vignettes on life in the German capital, he paints a somewhat negative picture of German culture as shallow and lacking in vibrancy; but in his article 'L'Art moderne en Allemagne' (1884), he praises Germany's closeness to the Unconscious and condemns the arid, constrictive qualities of (neo-Classical) French culture. This contradiction can be explained partly by the differing circumstances in which the two texts were written, but there is also an important point of similarity between them: in both, Germany is presented as a more primitive society, even if this primitiveness is valorized differently in each. The notion of Germany as the chosen land of the Unconscious is connected to Laforgue's idealized vision of Hartmann's key principle, a vision that co-exists with the more cynical conception of it as a life-force that deals out both pleasure and pain indiscriminately. Laforgue uses the same metaphor for both visions of the Unconscious: that of the forest. The wild forest of Teutonic myth is, for Laforgue, the marker of Germany's otherness, of its fundamental opposition to the over-cultivation of French culture. But the forest also stands for the untamed depths of the self, and principally for the sexual instinct that constitutes the foremost manifestation of the Unconscious as life-force within the individual. In Laforgue's poetry, sexuality has an overshadowing presence. It provides a source of inspiration that draws on the idea of otherness in a different sense: the notion of an unbridled, uninstrumentalized sexual instinct runs counter to contemporary nationalistic visions of regeneration through procreation.

Laforgue in/on Germany

As a (voluntary) exile in Germany for most of his adult life (1881–86), Laforgue had extensive first-hand experience of the country (even if he spent much of his time in the rarefied atmosphere of the German Imperial court): *Berlin, la cour et la ville* and 'L'Art moderne en Allemagne' are the products of this experience, but they also demonstrate the influence of contemporary discourses regarding the German nation. The former draws on elements of the anti-German sentiment that prevailed in France after 1870, whereas the latter offers a romanticized, Staëlian vision of the country, one that presents it as the chosen land of the Hartmannian Unconscious; both, however, are founded on the notion of an opposition between Germany and France. But Laforgue's departure for Berlin in 1881 did not represent his first engagement with discourses of German otherness.

In fact, Laforgue's work registers these discourses from an early age. Although he was only ten at the time of the Franco-Prussian War, one of his earliest poems is grounded in the Germanophobia of the 1870s. 'Ce qu'aime le gros Fritz', published in the short-lived Toulouse journal *La Guêpe* in 1879, is a crude satire of supposedly German tastes, with 'Fritz' portrayed drinking beer and smoking a pipe after his dinner of sauerkraut, accompanied by the 'tic-tac des pendules de France' (*OC*, I, 235); as Pascal Pia notes, 'au lendemain de la guerre de 1870, la rumeur publique accusait les Prussiens d'avoir volé de nombreuses pendules en France dans les maisons dont les habitants s'étaient enfuis au moment de l'invasion.'[1] This example of populist xenophobia in Laforgue's juvenilia demonstrates the impact of 'myths of a glorious defeat and popular *revanchisme*' on Laforgue's generation.[2] The poem also draws on a more deeply rooted *lieu commun* of nineteenth-century French visions of Germany, that of philosophical obscurantism:

> Oui, j'aime à promener ma belle âme allemande
> À travers l'Esthétique et les brouillards d'Hegel;
> Un nuage en bouteille est tout ce que demande
> L'âme éprise de vague et d'immatériel. (*OC*, I, 234)

This disdainful view is repeated elsewhere in Laforgue's œuvre, notably in his condemnation of Hartmann's metaphysics in his early philosophical notes: 'une prodigieuse et vertigineuse fantaisie métaphysique comme il n'en éclot qu'en Allemagne la patrie de Hegel' (*OC*, I, 1135).[3] His condemnation is, as we have seen, inspired by Caro's *Le Pessimisme au XIXe siècle*. But while Caro sardonically wonders whether Wagner will one day create an opera inspired by 'le drame de l'Inconscient'[4] and refers to arguments 'qui ont fortement saisi les imaginations allemandes',[5] these are the only specific references to Germany or German culture in this section. Laforgue's notion of metaphysical absurdity only being possible in 'la patrie de Hegel' is thus his own interpolation; it indicates that he shared the long-established French view of Hegel as a philosophical charlatan, a view that flourished after the war due to the association drawn between Hegel and Prussian belligerence.

Such explicit engagements with anti-German discourses are almost entirely confined to Laforgue's early work. Indeed, given that Laforgue spent most of his adult life in Germany at the heart of the imperial regime, references to Franco-German relations in his literary work, private notes and correspondence are surprisingly scant. But he does occasionally allude to the conflict, perhaps most notably in a letter to his sister Marie from Strasbourg in May 1883. His visit to a city which had become part of the German Empire following the war, and where the militaristic nature of the German presence was apparent in the form of 'des troupiers à lourdes bottes et à casques pointus' (*OC*, I, 823), inspires unusually patriotic sentiments:

> On se croirait en France. — Les enseignes sont en français, etc. On entend partout parler notre douce langue, excepté hélas! par les petits enfants qui reviennent de l'école ou qui jouent dans les ruisseaux, chose qui m'a touché au cœur. (*OC*, I, 823)

He also remarks, with gentle irony, that 'le bon moyen de maintenir le patriotisme dans le cœur des Français est de les faire voyager' (*OC*, I, 823), a statement inspired by hearing a nurse speak to a child in French. Laforgue's (self-conscious and self-mocking) patriotism, then, is based predominantly on his affection for the French *language*, considered, as Eric Hobsbawm points out, the 'soul of a nation' according to the ideologists of nationalism.[6] Indeed, in contemporary patriotic literature, the relinquishment of the French language in Alsace was a key source of pathos, as for example in Alphonse Daudet's 'La dernière classe': a French teacher in a small Alsatian village bids farewell to his pupils, and his valedictory speech focuses heavily on the importance of preserving French, which is praised as 'la plus belle langue du monde, la plus claire, la plus solide'.[7] But Laforgue's work, with its lexical play and formal experimentation, is far removed from this idea of *la clarté française*. His lament for the loss of 'notre douce langue' amongst the children of Alsace should not, therefore, be conflated with this patriotic discourse.

As Raoul Girardet notes, Alsace-Lorraine came to occupy a privileged position in the national mythology of late nineteenth-century France: 'Une innombrable littérature romanesque s'attache à évoquer le drame des provinces perdues, les douleurs de l'exode, les souffrances des réfugiés.'[8] One of the themes that was 'inlassablement repris par l'imagerie et la chanson populaire'[9] was that of families separated by the annexation of Alsace-Lorraine, and Laforgue refers — albeit obliquement — to this topos in 'Complainte des grands Pins dans une villa abandonnée':

> — Et bientôt, seul, je m'en irai,
> À Montmartre, en cinquième classe,
> Loin de père et mère, enterrés
> En Alsace. (*OC*, I, 598)

This is not a biographical reference (even if there is a faint echo of Laforgue's first departure for Germany in 1881 on the day of his father's funeral). It suggests, rather, the poet's sense of solitude, of exile, of rootlessness; but as always, self-pity is undercut by self-mockery. This is evident in the overwrought, almost melodramatic solemnity of the final line, its spurious pathos enhanced by the shift from octosyllables to the trisyllabic coda. Rather than creating a genuinely poignant ending, Laforgue in fact appears to be lampooning a well-trammelled literary cliché. In doing so, he signals a distance between his poetry and sentimentalized nationalistic imagery.

However, even such oblique references to the aftermath of the Franco-Prussian War are rare in Laforgue's literary work and correspondence. In *Berlin, la cour et la ville* too there are only sporadic allusions to this socio-political context; but these references, however sparse, do offer some insight into Laforgue's view of Franco-

German relations. Moreover, the text also hints at a broader vision of German culture: Laforgue consistently points to a certain primitiveness as the defining Teutonic characteristic. This vision is only glimpsed occasionally, since *Berlin*'s main purpose is to offer a portrait of day-to-day life in the German capital, a portrait 'qui tient à la saisie impromptue du pittoresque des choses vues' (Walzer, *OC*, III, 570). The section on 'La Race' is one of those that goes beyond the superficial: here he portrays Germans as generally brutish and unsophisticated, contrasting the raucousness of German children with the refinement of expatriate English girls at a Berlin boarding school. This contrast, he states, illustrates 'l'abîme entre une race qui a des siècles de culture et une race pauvre qui n'est à son aise que depuis une génération' (*OC*, III, 783). (A similar charge is levelled in notes for a planned novella: 'vulgaire, l'Allemagne et ses peuplades de parvenus' (*OC*, III, 918).) The section on 'Politesse' builds on this, suggesting that Germans attempt to conceal their essential primitiveness behind a mask of cultivation: 'L'Allemand est né simple. Sa manie du cérémonieux vient de ce qu'on l'a trop universellement traité de barbare et d'ours' (*OC*, III, 792). Germans' attempts to compensate for this reputation of philistinism result in behaviour that is comically inconsistent; for example, men remove their hats when they enter shops, but carry on smoking their cigars. According to an unnamed source, German women are just as primitive as the men, albeit in a different sense:

> 'l'Allemande est plus naïve que la Française et plus naturelle, par conséquent plus facile et plus animale et plus spontanée. Elle n'a pas comme la Française civilisée ce scepticisme qui fait les trois quarts de la vertu féminine.' (*OC*, III, 784)

This accusation of Teutonic female lasciviousness fits neatly into the paradigm of a race that cannot quite disguise its atavistic barbarism.

Laforgue suggests that in some instances Germans actively endorse their association with barbarian ancestry: 'L'Allemand idéal: le type des guerriers modernes dans les bas-reliefs de la dernière guerre en opposition au latin. Pas de prétention au distingué, pas même la peur d'être traité de Goth, de Visigoth, Ostrogoth' (*OC*, III, 784). Laforgue thus argues that Germans themselves are complicit in constructing the same opposition between French civilization and Germany barbarity that was pervasive in France following the 1870 War. However, his account of the Germanic idealization of bellicosity is bathetically counterpoised by a portrayal of the typical German male: 'Type tout opposé et bien allemand: constitution grêle, barbe rousse irrégulière, cheveux plantés très bas sur le front, lunettes' (*OC*, III, 784). This scornful caricature serves to undermine the pretension to belligerent masculinity that is evident in German art. Laforgue thus suggests that Germans do not fulfil the extremes of their own paradoxical aspirations: they are neither fearsome barbarian warriors nor — as 'La Race' suggests — modern sophisticates. Instead, they are merely gauche, uncultured and coarse.

Berlin undoubtedly has a satirical aspect, but it is not an overtly political text: its references to the 1870 War are largely restricted to remarks on artistic representations of it, as above. In a similar vein, Laforgue describes a ball held by the

Emperor in his palace, where guests, including Prussian officers, congregate in the 'salle des Tableaux'; Laforgue notes the evident disquiet of one of the French military attachés, a former artilleryman, in having to pass in front of paintings that offer triumphalist representations of the recent German victory, as well as between 'deux haies d'officiers prussiens étalant leur morgue, malgré eux' (*OC*, III, 728). Laforgue's own feelings on this scene remain uncertain, but he does hint at a certain sympathy with the attaché.[10] In other passages, his resentment of German jingoism is obvious. There is bitter sarcasm in his comment on a poster advertising a 'Fête dans un vaste jardin à bière. *Le bombardement de Strasbourg*, en deux parties': 'Voilà qui doit attirer les Alsaciens de Berlin' (*OC*, III, 758). But such remarks on the tangible reminders of France's humiliating defeat are infrequent, and they do not suggest that he is pandering to *revanchiste* sentiment, but merely that he resents the bellicose nationalism that is sometimes evident in contemporary Germany. He is equally sceptical of French nationalism, despite expressing his affection for the French language in his letter from Strasbourg. Moreover, his mockery of German boorishness should perhaps be taken with a pinch of salt, since the circumstances of the text's composition undoubtedly influenced its tone. Laforgue wrote it in the final months of 1886 when, having resigned his position in the German court, he found himself with the prospect of a wife to support, a home to establish, and no regular source of income.[11] The decision to use the notes he had taken during his time in Germany as the basis for a journalistic work was no doubt motivated largely by this financial imperative: several works on Germany had been published in the 1870s and 1880s, and some had met with great commercial success. As Walzer notes, the tone of these works was largely critical, in order to appeal to the prevailing anti-German feeling (*OC*, III, 565). While Laforgue's critiques are generally mild, and wry rather than rancorous, his vignettes do sometimes verge on crowd-pleasing derision.[12] Nonetheless, in its allegation of Germanic primitiveness, *Berlin* adumbrates a vision of German otherness that is taken up by the article 'L'Art moderne en Allemagne'. This article constitutes a crucial exposition of his aesthetic theories, one which shows the importance of the 'German other' to his reception of Hartmann's work.

Written in 1883–84, 'L'Art moderne en Allemagne' presents an idealized vision of Germany that is at odds with the somewhat cynical, even disdainful view of *Berlin*. Laforgue had already lived in Germany for more than two years when he began writing 'L'Art moderne...', so it cannot be dismissed as the utopian fantasy of a *nouvel arrivé*. Indeed, in a fragment from his philosophical notes that explains the process of writing 'L'Art moderne...', he insists on the empirical nature of the article: 'Une observation quotidienne et réaliste immédiate de la vie germanique, sans parti-pris (principe) philosophique m'a amené à certaines conclusions naturelles, indépendantes' (*OC*, III, 1149). These conclusions conformed perfectly to the philosophy of the Unconscious: 'En réunissant ces conclusions et en en cherchant le pourquoi, je vois qu'elles s'adaptent absolument, comme si elles en découlaient, au principe philosophique qui était déjà ma religion' (*OC*, III, 1149). If both texts are ostensibly based on everyday observation, why do they present such divergent visions of Germany? The answer may lie partly in the financial motivations for *Berlin*. But it is also related to the work of Caro, who put forward a dualistic model of national identity. While condemning the modern, Hegel-influenced Germany, Caro sought simultaneously to maintain a more positive view of it:

> On pourrait même dire qu'il y a deux Allemagnes: l'une idéaliste et rêveuse, l'autre pratique à l'excès sur la scène du monde, utilitaire à outrance, âpre à la curée.[13]

Digeon glosses this distinction as being between 'l'Allemagne de Kant (et de Mme de Staël) et l'Allemagne de Hegel et de Bismarck',[14] between 'l'ancienne voisine faible, pacifique et fraternelle' and the 'nation moderne, puissante, guerrière et ambitieuse de conquêtes'.[15] Laforgue's two works on Germany correspond to 'les deux Allemagnes',[16] with *Berlin* treating the capital of the new, imperial Germany, and 'L'Art moderne en Allemagne' focusing on the old, peaceful land portrayed by de Staël.

Laforgue's endorsement of Caro's theory is made clear in 'L'Art moderne...', in which he uses the term 'l'Allemagne pure' to refer to the old Germany, in opposition to the new, Prussian-dominated German Empire. While the former is characterized by 'Le vaste génie méditatif et prolifique', Prussia 'n'a jamais rien eu à voir avec la grande sensibilité artistique ou spéculative' (*OC*, III, 345). His view of the old Germany is very much in the Staëlian vein, but it connects this romanticized vision to Hartmann's thought:

> L'Allemagne pure est, avant tout, la terre bénie de ce que nous avons appelé les préoccupations immédiates de la Loi, mysticisme, religion, science, rêveries sociales et du seul art qui y confine jusqu'à s'y confondre, la musique. (*OC*, III, 343)

It is Germany's cultural production, from mysticism to music, that shows that this is the chosen land of the Unconscious ('la Loi'). But as well as culture, nature is also crucial to Laforgue's argument: 'L'Allemagne pure est à tous égards, en effet, la fille immédiate de la Nature, de cet inconscient soupçonné par tous les penseurs ses vrais fils et révélé chez elle' (*OC*, III, 343). This suggestion that Germany is the land of the Unconscious because of its closeness to nature constitutes a revalorization of *Berlin*'s argument for Germanic primitiveness.

It is significant that Laforgue places 'mysticisme' at the head of this list of German talents, since Hartmann himself sees mysticism as essential to the German character:

> C'est grâce aux influences mystiques que le génie du peuple allemand, que les héros de la poésie et de la philosophie de l'Allemagne moderne nous ont préservés des sables mouvants, sous lesquels le matérialisme de la France menaçait, au siècle précédent, de nous engloutir complètement. (*PI*, I, 394)

The opposition drawn by Hartmann here between Germany and France is also crucial to 'L'Art moderne en Allemagne'. If Germany is the land of the Unconscious, then France is a nation dominated by rationalism. This contrast is played out through the association of each nation with a different ancient culture: Germany is compared to Vedic India, while France is compared to the world of Classical antiquity. More specifically, it is Germany's 'forêt panthéiste' which is described as the 'Vraie terre de Védas du Nord' (*OC*, III, 343). Laforgue did not invent this correlation between Germany and India; as we shall see in Chapter 4, the strong German interest in Indological study led to frequent remarks by French commentators on the affinity between the two cultures. Of course, the view of France as the heir to Classical culture was also common, and was implicit in the notion of Decadence, which compared France (and Paris in particular) to the Roman Empire in its dying days.

Since the first part of 'L'Art moderne en Allemagne' consists principally in a critique of neo-Classical aesthetics, it is no surprise that Laforgue portrays Classical (and hence French) civilization with some degree of scorn. Despite achieving high levels of logical and rhetorical sophistication, it is essentially artificial and insincere, since it is cut off from the source of creativity, the Unconscious:

> L'Hellène [...] — et par suite le Français, fils aîné du monde gréco-romain, de ce monde sophiste, diplomate et mathématicien d'une part, soldat et légiste de l'autre, qui lui a fait mettre en coupe réglée, selon Malherbe, ses forêts druidiques, jusqu'au romantisme revenu du Nord, — l'Hellène dilettante, subtil rhéteur, euphuiste, poli, brillant, sobre, comédien, menteur, est né démailloté de la vie inconsciente. (*OC*, III, 344)

The forest thus emerges as a crucial image of national identity. While German forests are 'les vrais tropiques de l'Europe, mais tropiques du Nord' (*OC*, III, 343), a description that suggests abundant, uncontrolled growth, France's 'forêts druidiques' are subject to a 'coupe réglée'. This regime is the product of a society which is 'sophiste, diplomate et mathématicien d'une part, soldat et légiste de l'autre'; that is, highly organized and highly rational, and apparently pragmatic in its view of nature. Robert Pogue Harrison argues that this utilitarian standpoint is a corollary of humanism, for which the forest is not 'a consecrated place of oracular disclosures; [...] a place of strange or monstrous or enchanting epiphanies; [...] the imaginary site of lyric nostalgias and erotic errancy'[17] but merely a natural resource to be managed. The 'coupe réglée' alludes to this notion of utility, but it also refers to the formalization of French verse propounded by Malherbe (and dismissed by Théodore de Banville with the withering lines 'Malherbe vint, et [...] la Poésie | En le voyant arriver, s'en alla'[18]). Uniformity of metre, line length and stanzas are paramount in the poetic rules of Classicism, and Laforgue compares these characteristics, albeit tacitly, to the regular felling and spacing of trees. Of course, a 'coupe' is also the rhythmic break in a line of verse: the rhythmic experimentation of Laforgue's mature poetry, in particular the *Derniers vers*, thus represents a rejection of Malherbian versification in favour of a less regulated approach.

Laforgue consistently uses the forest metaphor to establish the opposition between Germanic and Latinate cultures: 'si le Latin est de ceux que, selon le proverbe allemand, l'arbre empêche de voir la forêt, l'Allemand avouera que la forêt l'a toujours empêché de voir l'arbre' (*OC*, III, 345). This opposition can be glossed as that of analysis and synthesis, materialist and metaphysical philosophy, Classicism and Romanticism. Indeed, Laforgue invokes three of the most prominent cultural figures of French Classicism (as well as a forebear from Antiquity) to illustrate his point: 'Longtemps, certes, le Latin, le Français n'a pas vu la forêt, tyrannisé qu'il était par l'arbre idéal selon Cicéron et Boileau, Poussin et Lenôtre, par l'arbre-canon mesurant la forêt' (*OC*, III, 345). The reference to Le Nôtre (misspelt as Lenôtre) is particularly significant: as the pre-eminent garden designer of the seventeenth century, responsible for the geometric layouts of gardens such as Versailles, he personifies the control of nature that Laforgue associates with France. What is lacking from the Classical French view of nature, Laforgue suggests, is a sense of its atmosphere, its spirit. It is in (Romantic) Germany that this spirit is to be found. The notion of Germany as the 'other' of France is central to 'L'Art moderne en Allemagne'; of course, the use of the forest image to illustrate this opposition is grounded in the cultural mythology of German nationalism, which casts forests as 'sanctuaries of origins, race, community'.[19]

The wild Teutonic forest is thus emblematic of Germany's closeness to the state of nature. But if the forest's relationship to civilization is one of antithesis, it is also one of precedence: 'We gather from mythology that their vast and sombre wilderness was there before, like a precondition or matrix of civilization, or that [...] the forests were *first*.'[20] The opening sentence of Staël's *De l'Allemagne* draws on this mythology, noting that 'La multitude et l'étendue des forêts indiquent une civilisation encore nouvelle':[21] this is a culture that has barely emerged from the wilderness. Laforgue's insistence on Germanic primitiveness in *Berlin* recapitulates this point. But since forests precede *all* civilizations, France arose out of this same wilderness: indeed, this is implicit in Laforgue's comment on the French 'forêts druidiques', which were controlled by Classicism, 'jusqu'au romantisme *r*evenu du Nord' (my emphasis). The advent of Romanticism in France was not so much an arrival as a return, a force that untamed the forests of French literature, that released latent, suppressed energies. This suggests that, for Laforgue, the otherness of Germany is not an essential, transhistorical truth; rather, there is only a *contingent* opposition between France and Germany. The same conclusion is suggested by Laforgue's article on Impressionism, which makes reference to Wagner's 'Lettre sur la musique' (1861). Wagner draws an analogy between the sounds that a solitary walker might hear in a forest at sunset, and the music he aspires to create: from the sonic diversity of the forest, these 'voix d'une variété infinie', there eventually arises 'la grande, l'unique mélodie de la forêt'.[22] For Laforgue, pointillism produces the same effect, the individual brushstrokes resolving into a synthetic whole:

> Plus de mélodie isolée, le tout est une symphonie qui est la vie vivante et variante, comme 'les voix de la forêt' des théories de Wagner en concurrence vitale pour la grande voix de la forêt, comme l'Inconscient, loi du monde, est la grande voix mélodique, résultante de la symphonie des consciences de races et d'individus. (*OC*, III, 331)

Just as the apparently disparate sounds or brushstrokes reveal their overarching unity, so ostensibly distinct races and nations are in fact elements of the All-One, the Unconscious. National or cultural otherness is, in this sense, fundamentally illusory.

In 'L'Art moderne en Allemagne', Laforgue again turns to Wagner, but now to make a very different point about national identity. Here he refers to 'la forêt sacrée des théories nationales de Wagner [...] peuplée de cette mythologie fantasque et fuyante d'un Songe d'une nuit d'automne ou de Noël, spectres du Brocken, sapins, clairs de lune, willis de Novalis, etc.' (*OC*, III, 343). He thus associates the Wagnerian forest not with the supranational Unconscious, but with a specifically Germanic folklore. This transfigures not only the use of Wagner in 'L'Impressionisme', but also the composer's own arguments: for Wagner, the sounds of the forest provide an analogy for music, and music is the universal language, 'une langue également intelligible à tous les hommes, [...] la puissance conciliatrice'.[23] It is the realization of Romanticism's search for 'une forme idéale, purement humaine, affranchie de toute entrave de mœurs nationales, appelée par conséquent à transformer ces mœurs nationales en mœurs purement humaines'.[24] But the tension between 'L'Impressionnisme', which promotes this idea of transcending national boundaries, and 'L'Art moderne...', which puts forward an exoticizing vision of Germany, is not insuperable. As Laforgue suggests elsewhere in 'L'Art moderne...', the otherness of Germany is not necessarily timeless or essential. Rather, the exotic qualities of Germany — its mysticism, its wildness, its rich mythology — are representative of a culture that is closer to the Unconscious than is France, a culture that offers privileged access to the Unconscious; but they are not indefinitely restricted to Germany. There is no reason that France, too, cannot open itself up to the revivifying powers of the Unconscious.

'[L]es forêts vierges de la vie': the Forest as 'Other' in Laforgue's Poetry

For Laforgue, the forest is not merely associated with the national folklore of Germany; he also draws on an even more deep-seated cultural mythology according to which the forest is the antithesis of civilization itself.[25] As Harrison argues, forests have throughout history presented a challenge to humanity's legal institutions: 'Be it religious, political, psychological, or even logical law, the forests, it seems, unsettle its stability. Forests lie 'beyond' the law, or better, they figure as places of outlaw.'[26] The forest does not merely constitute an extra-legal domain, but also represents the 'other' or shadow side of legality, of civilization: in forests 'we see a strange reflection of the order to which they remained external.'[27] In psychoanalytical terms, this is a process of projection:

> In the history of Western civilization forests represent an outlying realm of opacity which has allowed that civilization to estrange itself, enchant itself, terrify itself, ironize itself, in short to project into the forest's shadows its secret and innermost anxieties.[28]

It is not merely anxieties that are projected into the forest, however, but also desires. Forests 'encouraged dispersion, independence, lawlessness, polygamy',[29] with the regulation of sexual desire through matrimony being challenged by the seclusion of the forests, which enabled sexual freedom. Of course, the notion of the forest as a place of erotic adventure is commonplace, from *A Midsummer Night's Dream* to Rodolphe's seduction of Emma in *Madame Bovary*,[30] and this topos also features in Laforgue's work (see, for example, the 'ballets corrosifs' (*OC*, I, 560) of a sexual encounter in the woods in 'Complainte de l'Orgue de Barbarie'). But this use of the forest motif is just part of a broader vision that is allied with the cultural mythology described by Harrison. For Laforgue, the forest figures as the other of consciousness, the dark, turbulent realm of the mind where our instinctual drives hold sway: this is not the Unconscious as utopia or pseudo-divine principle, but the manifestation in the individual of the Unconscious as all-powerful life-force.

Laforgue's reference to this other use of the forest image also features in 'L'Art moderne...', although it is ostensibly unrelated to the idea of the Germanic forest: 'Il est un domaine qui, on le sait, vient d'ouvrir à la science les forêts vierges de la vie, c'est l'atmosphère occulte de l'être, l'inconscience' (*OC*, III, 339). It is perhaps significant that 'inconscience' is uncapitalized here, since it refers to the unconscious level of the *individual* mind, rather than (directly) to 'l'Inconscient' as metaphysical principle. Given the dominance of sexuality in this substratum of the self, it is ironic that Laforgue refers to 'les forêts *vierges* de la vie' (my emphasis), even if the surface meaning is clear: this is an unexplored and uncultivated domain.

This new terrain required a new form. Consequently, in *Derniers vers* Laforgue emphatically rejects the 'coupe réglée' of traditional versification in favour of a looser, liberated metricity. The collection is thus grounded formally in Laforgue's vision of the Unconscious as an untamed wilderness, constituting a kind of poetic re-wilding. While traces of traditional forms remain visible, they are overrun by heterometric lines and erratic rhyme schemes. In 'L'hiver qui vient', we see this process in action: the second stanza is an almost completely regular quatrain of alexandrines in *rimes croisées*, and it is followed by a rhyming couplet again in alexandrines; but the pattern is broken by the trisyllabic 'Il bruine' (*OC*, II, 297), and this rupture is dramatized by the lines that follow:

> Dans la forêt mouillée, les toiles d'araignées
> Ploient sous les gouttes d'eau, et c'est leur ruine. (*OC*, II, 297)

The regular rhyme scheme is broken by 'araignées' (the internal rhyme with 'mouillée' replacing it); and the hendecasyllabic line that follows disrupts regular metricity, as though the rain has enacted the 'ruine' of the alexandrine as well as the spider webs. Alexandrines do re-emerge in the rest of the poem, but they are sporadic and rarely subscribe to the 'coupe réglée' of the traditional caesura. In fact, this disruption is already foreshadowed in the almost-regular second stanza, the final line of which — 'Et tant les cors ont fait ton ton, ont fait ton taine!...' (*OC*, II, 297) — deviates from the 'coupe centrale' in its 8/4 pattern. Of course, its onomatopoeia also represents a disturbance of lyrical diction, the raucous hunting horn usurping the delicate lyre.

In this poem, and indeed throughout the *Derniers vers*, the 'cors' also stand for 'corps':[31] the disruption of Classical versification is performed not only through sound, but also through the body. If the Classical veneration of the healthy body as the apotheosis of beauty (an ideal that Laforgue explicitly opposes in his notes on Taine)[32] is reflected in the control, harmony and regularity of the alexandrine, then free verse represents an unfettering of the body's energies (both positive and negative). This liberated prosody 'articulat[es] the intermittences of breathing or the heartbeat';[33] moreover, the frequent use of 'Ah' and 'Oh' in the *Derniers vers* reaffirms the presence 'du corps respirant, soupirant, expirant'.[34] This is not the regular breath or pulse of a healthy body, but the irregular rhythms of sexual excitement, illness and so on. The disorder of the body is, moreover, a reflection of psychological disturbance, of inner torments and desires. Free verse, then, is a 'highly subjective, psychologically motivated rhythm' that registers 'the oscillations of the emotions and the intellect directly'.[35] If, according to his contemporary Camille Mauclair, Laforgue sought to 'modeler plus exactement et en liberté les mots sur la fantaisie de la pensée',[36] then he was not alone in this aspiration:

> The *verslibristes* of the late nineteenth century envisaged a verse in which every modulation in the poet's psychic and organic condition, every creative impulse, conscious and unconscious, by definition unique and unrepeatable, would find its corresponding realisation in a perfectly adapted line of verse, itself necessarily unique and unrepeatable.[37]

But Laforgue was particularly attuned to the psychological potentialities of free verse, unlike others of his generation, who were more focused on the musicality of this new form: 'tandis que je parlais expression musicale, Laforgue répondait expression psychologique', states another contemporary, Édouard Dujardin, relating their conversation about free verse in March 1886.[38] Indeed, in early 1882 Laforgue was already imagining 'une poésie qui serait de la psychologie dans une forme de rêve' (*OC*, I, 757).

The 're-wilding' enacted by *vers libre* is thus an expression of both psychological concerns and the liberation of bodily desires. Accordingly, in *Derniers vers* the forest provides a locus for (imagined) sexual adventure (see 'Solo de lune'); but the more troubling and disruptive aspects of sexual desire also feature in the forest setting (see 'L'hiver qui vient' and 'Ô géraniums diaphanes'). This portrayal of sexuality as an overwhelmingly powerful and destructive force reflects the vision of Schopenhauer and Hartmann, even if the latter argues that we should accept the sexual instinct in the name of progress despite its detrimental effects. But the poems of *Derniers vers* also problematize philosophical accounts of sexual desire, offering alternative visions of erotic relations, rather than simply decrying the exploitation of human desire for the purposes of the species (as does Schopenhauer) or accepting it (as does Hartmann).

Similarly, 'Pan et la syrinx' from *Moralités légendaires* raises doubts about Hartmann's ethics, even while seemingly propounding a Hartmannian position. Indeed, the philosophical source is made explicit here: as Pearson points out, Pan 'tries to explain to Syrinx that he is himself the embodiment of the Unconscious in its teleology of sexual desire and reproduction',[39] using the term 'Tout' (to designate the Unconscious) when he importunes Syrinx: '"La journée s'avance et je n'ai jamais aimé. Voulez-vous laisser être tout pour moi, au nom de Tout?"' (*OC*, II, 457). Despite its ridiculous nature, 'Pan's ardent protestation of love is pure Hartmann'.[40] His pursuit of her, once she has bridled at his proposition and fled, is also emblematic of the disturbingly violent nature of sexual desire according to Schopenhauer and Hartmann: 'Oh, je t'aurai!' Pan tells himself, 'je te tordrai les poignets, je te broierai tes petits os de chatte, je t'apprendrai!...' (*OC*, II, 458). The chase takes place in a primal wilderness of prairies and woods: 'On traverse de grands bois de pins en solitudes kilométriquement claustrales où il fait sombre depuis le commencement du monde' (*OC*, II, 460). Moreover, the Dionysian element of Pan's desires[41] is echoed in the opening stanza of '*Ô géraniums diaphanes*', where references to 'thyrses' and 'dévergondages' (*OC*, II, 330) conjure up visions of bacchanalian orgies in forest clearings.

Even prior to Syrinx's appearance, Pan imagines — in poetic form — a sexual encounter in the depths of the woods:

> Oh! ce sera tant toi!
> Ingénieusement je t'emmènerai
> Au plus profond des bois,
> Là où il fait le plus frais;
> Et puis tu pourras t'étirer sur le gazon
> Après tant d'après-midi virginales,
> Et t'abandonner à la bonne saison
> Dans l'assourdissement des cigales. (*OC*, II, 453)

In one sense, her arrival merely provides the opportunity for him to fulfil his lust ('elle est née pour en venir là, elle est outillée pour en venir là' (*OC*, II, 454)[42]). Pan, to this extent, represents the modern view of sexual desire, as put forward by Hartmann: for him, 'the "ideal" is simply the teleology of the Unconscious, the fulfilment of the life-process through sexual reproduction, in which Syrinx is at once an end and a means'.[43] While Pan stands for this materialist, Hartmannian (and 'post-Darwinian'[44]) view of sex, Syrinx is 'spiritualiste', representing 'the kind of idealism that Hartmann identifies as "illusion"'.[45] To a certain extent, the 'spiritual and religious dimension to which [Syrinx] aspires [...] represents an obsolete way of thinking about the human condition'[46] for Laforgue. But Pan's approach to the Hartmannian Unconscious reveals the perils of philosophy, showing that Laforgue has not entirely accepted the materialist point of view or repudiated the spiritualist one.

The paradox of Pan's conduct is that his very awareness of his philosophical goal is what prevents him from realizing it. Believing his conquest of the Syrinx to be predestined, he does not act but defers to the Unconscious, using his recurrent expression of fatalism 'tout est dans Tout':

> Il relève les yeux: elle le regarde de toute sa beauté qui semble décidément sans but. — S'il se jetait immortellement à ses pieds pour l'étourdir! — Mais il se contient. Arrivera ce qui doit arriver; tout est dans Tout. (*OC*, II, 455)

It is significant that her beauty is 'sans but', since earlier Pan has made a philosophically-informed translinguistic pun linking 'aime' to the English 'aim', in order to illustrate the idea that love is the ultimate goal. But rather than reacting spontaneously to her beauty, he plays a tune on his 'galoubet' and sings a song — one that proclaims in a decidedly unmaterialist manner that 'Ce n'est pas sa chair qui me serait tout' (*OC*, II, 455) — and then finds that she is still looking at him admiringly: 'Pan relève la tête. Elle est là, à sourire, comme désarmée par ce grand enfant et un peu aussi grâce à la beauté exceptionnelle de cette matinée' (*OC*, II, 456). Again, instead of responding in kind, as the narrator suggests he should — 'Pan n'aurait qu'à répondre par un brave sourire!' (*OC*, II, 456) — Pan shrugs his shoulders and engages her in conversation. He laments his substandard instrument ('Si, du moins, j'avais un instrument plus riche que ce galoubet! je vous chanterais tout ce que je suis! Oh! Je chanterais fantastiquement!' (*OC*, II, 456)) despite her having appreciated his songs: her first words are 'C'est très joli, ce que vous jouiez là' (*OC*, II, 454). The irony of the tale, then, is that his pursuit of her, which is precipitated by his overly blunt philosophico-sexual proposition ('Voulez-vous être tout pour moi, au nom de Tout?'), leads to his gaining a superior instrument (the panpipes of the original myth) through her disappearance, an instrument that allows him to express the spirituality that he has previously dismissed due to his philosophical outlook; but had he not challenged her spiritualist vision so bluntly, he might in fact have ended up achieving his (sexual) goal. In short, to be the best servant of the Unconscious, it is perhaps better not to be an overly conscious one.

Pearson argues that the lesson of 'Pan et la syrinx' is perhaps the following: 'as much as we may intellectually subscribe to the new thinking of Darwin and Hartmann, human beings will always find it difficult to dismiss sentiment as mere illusion in the service of the reproductive cycle'.[47] Or, indeed, that sentiment *should* not be dismissed. After all, before his violent expression of lust ('Oh, je t'aurai! je te tordrai les poignets') Pan imagined a less exclusively carnal relationship ('ce n'est pas sa chair qui me serait tout'). Crucially, the same or similar lines are used in 'Dimanches (*Bref, j'allais me donner...*)' from *Derniers vers*, but now in the reverse order:

> Ah, que je te les tordrais avec plaisir,
> Ce corps bijou, ce cœur à ténor,
> Et te dirais leur fait, et puis encore
> La manière de s'en servir
> De s'en servir à deux,
> Si tu voulais seulement m'approfondir ensuite un peu!
>
> Non, non! C'est sucer la chair d'un cœur élu,
> Adorer d'incurables organes
> S'entrevoir avant que les tissus se fanent
> En monomanes, en reclus!
>
> Et ce n'est pas sa chair qui me serait tout,
> Et je ne serais pas qu'un grand cœur pour elle. (*OC*, II, 307)

Here, pure sexual desire is superseded by a vision of a relationship based on a balance of the spiritual and physical. As Hiddleston points out, 'Il convient pourtant de distinguer cet état d'un abandon à la loi de l'Inconscient, car il semble doublé d'une sorte d'amour platonique, union des âmes et non seulement des corps.'[48]

Similarly, in 'Solo de lune', the poet presents a sexual encounter that is characterized not by brute instinct but by mutual pleasure:

> Dans ces bois de pins où depuis
> Le commencement du monde

> Il fait toujours nuit,
> Que de chambres propres et profondes!
> Oh! pour un soir d'enlèvements!
> Et je les peuple et je m'y vois,
> Et c'est un beau couple d'amants,
> Qui gesticulent hors la loi. (OC, II, 321)

This scene seems to respond to 'Pan et la syrinx', since there are two important intertextual links between the poem and the tale: first, Pan is described as playing his pipe 'dans la vallée inondée d'un mémorable solo de lune' (OC, II, 451); secondly, a near-identical expression is used to describe the woods ('de grands bois de pins [...] où il fait sombre depuis le commencement du monde' (OC, II, 460)). In 'Solo de lune', the forest becomes an eroticized *locus amoenus*, the stage for a fantasized sexual encounter, but not one based on violence; the term 'enlèvements' suggests not abduction, but an idiosyncratic derivation of the verb 'enlever' in its literary sense of 'ravir, transporter'.[49] This is a specifically sexual rapture — see 'chambres' and 'amants', but also 'gesticuler', a contemporary slang term for sexual intercourse[50] — and the phrase 'hors la loi' suggests the lovers' unmarried status: this is not sex for procreation (whether that aims at national regeneration or planetary annihilation) but for pleasure. As Hiddleston points out, the term 'noce' also implies a sexual relationship, but this is different from the 'noces de sexes livrés à la grosse' of 'Pétition' (OC, II, 313), 'grosse' alluding to the brute functionality of sex through both 'grossesse' and 'grossier':[51] in 'Solo de lune', 'c'est donc l'extase sans peine, la noce sans la grossièreté'.[52] In Laforgue's work, then, the forest is imagined as the 'other' of bourgeois society not only because it represents a domain where the sexual instinct is given free rein; it is also a place where sexuality is uninstrumentalized, where it exists purely for pleasure's sake.

* * * * *

Laforgue's poetry challenges normative sexual morality not only through visions of untamed sexual expression, but also through ideas of sexual disappointment and failure: through both excess and lack. It is in the first of the *Derniers vers*, 'L'hiver qui vient', that thwarted desire and sexual failure come to the fore most prominently. Here, notions of physical debility are intertwined with motifs suggesting national decline. But the poem ultimately turns away from politicized visions of the body, dramatizing a return to the individual.

In 'L'hiver qui vient', the poet looks back on his failed final rendezvous with his lover: physical intimacy has been scuppered by the rain, which has left all the benches wet, thus preventing them from sitting side by side. Emotional intimacy is also threatened, as signalled by the opening line's invocation of a 'Blocus sentimental' (a pun on the 'blocus continental' imposed on Britain by Napoleon) and by the image of the 'fils télégraphiques' (OC, II, 298) being gnawed by rust. Since this is their 'dernier dimanche', they must face a winter — perhaps longer — apart. The poem's lament for winter's arrival is accompanied by an elegy for the summer: 'Adieu vendanges, et adieu tous les paniers, | Tous les paniers Watteau des bourrées sous les marronniers' (*OC*, II, 298). As Hiddleston notes, the term 'vendanges' has a sexual connotation in Laforgue's work, most ostensibly in the image of the 'vendanges sexciproques' (*OC*, I, 551) from 'Complainte à Notre-Dame des Soirs' and the 'spasme universel des uniques vendanges' (*OC*, I, 316) of 'Fantaisie', from *Le Sanglot de la Terre*. The joyous sensual liberation suggested by Watteau's paintings has departed with the summer sun, the harvest superseded by the more primal and violent hunt.

But while in 'Pan et la syrinx' it is the male Pan who is 'en chasse' (*OC*, II, 458) in his pursuit of Syrinx, in 'L'hiver qui vient' the male appears to be the quarry. Specifically, it is the sun who is hunted. Traditionally male in Classical mythology, the sun is also portrayed as masculine by Laforgue, who describes it as a 'Bellâtre' (*OC*, II, 71) in 'Un mot au Soleil pour commencer'. More broadly, the sun is an image of 'the generative drive'[53] in Laforgue's work, an association that is supported by (if not derived from) Ribot's comparison of Schopenhauer's Will to 'le soleil'.[54] But while the Laforguian sun is, in Edwin Morgan's phrase, 'an accursed fecundating star',[55] in 'L'hiver qui vient' the sexual potency of the solar lothario is undermined. Indeed, the poem's evocation of the sun's fading powers offers an extended metaphor for the weaknesses of the male body. Initially, however, he is presented as powerful and industrious, as the 'Grand Dynamique' ('Au large', *OC*, II, 76):

> Soleils plénipotentiaires des travaux en blonds Pactoles
> Des spectacles agricoles. (*OC*, II, 297)

The summer sun is fully potent ('plénipotentiaires'), and associated with work and productivity ('travaux'), wealth ('Pactoles') and fertility ('agricoles'), the recurrent plosives [p], [k] and [t] reinforcing phonetically the sun's masculine strength. But these aestival manifestations of the sun are conspicuously absent in the poetic present: 'où êtes-vous ensevelis?' (*OC*, II, 297), the poet asks. Instead, it is a weakened, wintry sun that appears in the poem, its feebleness indicated by the dominance of the soft sibilant fricative [ʒ] ('gît', 'jaunes genêts'), in stark contrast to the prior succession of plosives. The sun is lying down, exhausted: 'un soleil fichu gît au haut du coteau' (*OC*, II, 297). He is ill, perhaps anaemic: 'blanc comme un crachat d'estaminet' (*OC*, II, 297). The simile suggests degradation, both moral and physical, this mighty source of energy — the pride of the summer's agricultural shows — now reduced to comparison with a gobbet of spit on the floor of a tavern.

A corollary of the sun's ill health and exhaustion is, the poem suggests, sexual failure. While he is lying 'sur son manteau' in the woods, this is not the premise for a sexual encounter but rather for exhausted recumbence. Likewise, the 'litière' may suggest a bed, but it is actually a scene of abjection not eroticism, since it refers to the tavern's saw-dust floor where the sun lies like spit, as well as conjuring up the scatological image of an animal's litter (and thereby recalling the 'berceaux fienteux' of 'Complainte de l'Orgue de Barbarie' (*OC*, I, 560)). The image of spit also subverts notions of sexual prowess in that it serves as an ironic substitute for semen. Indeed, in the late nineteenth century, spitting was irrevocably associated with tuberculosis,[56] which was often characterized as a disease resulting from the repression of sexual desire;[57] in the early twentieth century, the pioneer of psychosomatic medicine Georg Groddeck argued that tuberculosis was caused by libidinal deficiency, referring to 'the guilt of the ever-repeated symbolic dissipation of semen in the sputum'.[58] A more extreme form of emasculation is suggested by the subtext of castration in the image of the sun as 'une glande arrachée' (*OC*, II, 298), even if the ostensible referent is a throat gland ('dans un cou') rather than a testicle.

The sun is thus weak and ill, his masculinity threatened. He is even close to death ('gît', 'ensevelis'). But the hunting horns' cry of 'Taïaut! Taïaut! et hallali!' (*OC*, II, 298) implies a desire not for the sun's demise, but, ironically, for his revival: 'les cors lui sonnent [...] | Qu'il revienne à lui!' (*OC*, II, 297). Given that there is often, in Laforgue's work, 'une équivalence entre les fanfares des cors et la violence de l'acte sexuel'[59] (see, for example, 'Complainte du soir des Comices agricoles' (*OC*, II, 593–94)), the horns seem to be calling for a revitalization of the sun in order that they (or the hunters) might be sexually gratified. This association between love and the hunt is made even more explicit in 'Le mystère des trois cors' (the poem that follows 'L'hiver qui vient'), as Hiddleston points out:[60] '– Taïaut! Taïaut! Je t'aime! | Hallali!' (*OC*, II, 303). This exclamation is made by the 'cor dans la plaine' (*OC*, II, 303), which is evidently female;[61] the use of the same phrasing by the horns in 'L'hiver qui vient' suggests that they might also be female (or blown by female hunters). The aggression of the hunt and the shift of power from sun to hunters, from male to female, is evident in the line announcing the horns, which is composed of monosyllables and end-stopped by an exclamation mark. Its vigorous staccato contrasts starkly with the flaccid repetition of the preceding five-line sentence describing the sun, the anadiplosis of which parodies Léon Dierx's 'Soir d'octobre'[62] and, by extension, the overly sentimental pastoral poetry of the 1880s in general.[63] Moreover, the plosives [k] and [t] of the stanza's first two lines (used to describe the summer sun) are recapitulated in 'cors' and 'Taïaut'. The [p], meanwhile, is notably absent both from the soundscape of this part of the stanza, and from the 'cors' that stand for the female 'corps'.[64] But this does not signal a lack of power; rather, by excizing the silent 'p' of 'corps', the 'cors' show that the apparent potency of the male body (signalled by the ostentatious consonance of the 'Soleils plénipotentiaires') was always already illusory.

Despite the presence of the 'cors', there are no explicit representations of the female body in the poem. Not only is the body of the poet's lover excluded, she is not referred to directly in any way, even as 'elle', the only ostensible reference to her being in the indirect object pronoun 'nous' ('Vous nous avez gâté notre dernier dimanche'). But the spectral presence that is created through the heterographic 'cors' is thickened by other indirect portrayals of her body. Hiddleston points out the double meaning of 'paniers', which signifies both baskets and the underwiring of skirts; the latter meaning echoes Laforgue's use of the image of a skirt to refer to women throughout his work.[65] In fact, there is another stage to this fetishistic abstraction of female corporeality, since in contemporary slang 'panier' was also a euphemism for the vagina.[66] Likewise, 'jardinets' also alludes to female genitalia, the term 'jardin' being used in the Song of Solomon for the female body in general and the pudenda in particular.[67] The poem thus suggests an unsuccessful attempt to expunge any female bodily presence, a process dramatized within the poem itself: the sound of the 'cors' is carried away by the north wind, but lingers on in the form of 'd'échos', itself a quasi-homophonic echo of 'des corps'. Similarly, the reference to Little Red Riding Hood exposes the erasure of female physicality:

> Oh! les tournants des grandes routes,
> Et sans petit Chaperon Rouge qui chemine!... (*OC*, II, 298)

The line parodies Dierx's farewell to 'les vierges, le long du sentier qui chemine',[68] and the replacement of virgins by (the also virginal) 'petit Chaperon Rouge' is far from innocuous. In Charles Perrault's eighteenth-century version of this tale (the version that was current in Laforgue's era), the 'moralité' makes clear that her journey through the words is an allegory of a girl's passage to womanhood:[69] her absence from the 'routes' thus implies an attempt to disavow female sexual maturation. But the return of repressed sexuality is evident in the following stanza, where the poet's lament for the destruction of the 'modestes jardinets' by the wind implies a reluctant acknowledgement of the inevitable despoliation of sexual innocence.

In 'L'hiver qui vient', the forest topos is thus dominated by the fear of sexuality: fear of the rapacity of female desire (represented by the horns), fear of an inability to fulfil this desire (represented by the feebleness of the sun). But also — and perhaps even more deeply — fear of his *own* desire: the wolf (who stands for the dangerous sexual predator in Perrault's version) is absent not only from the *histoire*, but also from the *récit* itself; the poet's own sexuality is the inassimilable, unspeakable kernel of the poem. In this sense, the triviality of an unsuccessful rendezvous conceals 'the greater tragedy, that desire is both inescapable and unacceptable, (self-)destructive even'.[70]

★ ★ ★ ★ ★

If 'L'hiver qui vient' implicitly challenges nationalistic discourses of corporeal normativity through its representations of illness and sexual desire, it also draws on ideas of national decline more directly. Indeed, the poem's vision of a waning sun alludes to decline on a global level, tapping into late nineteenth-century anxieties about the demise of the earth itself: the second law of thermodynamics (which was first formulated in the 1850s) 'seemed to predict the inexorable approach of a steady-state solar system, a dead world and an extinguished sun'.[71] This entropic vision is reflected in Laforgue's 'Pâle soleil d'hiver' from *Le Sanglot*, which proclaims 'tu mourras, ô vieille lampe usée, | Soleil jaune et poussif, pâle soleil d'hiver' (*OC*, I, 382), as well as in the 'soleil mort' of 'Complainte de l'Automne monotone' (*OC*, I, 570) and in 'L'hiver qui vient' itself. But in addition to this apocalyptic vision — an alternative, dehumanized route to the eschatology of Schopenhauer and Hartmann, perhaps — the dying sun of 'L'hiver qui vient' also alludes to fears that the French nation might itself disappear.[72] The notion of France as 'la nation-soleil', the luminous centre of a planetary system of nations, was widespread in post-Revolutionary France. This idea is recapitulated in a related stellar metaphor in Whitman's poem 'O Star of France', which apostrophizes France and praises 'Le rayonnement de ta foi, de ta puissance, de ta gloire' (*OC*, II, 353), as Laforgue translates it. But these are former glories: 'O Star of France' laments the ravaged state of 'la grande nation' in 1870–71, and 'L'hiver qui vient' likewise alludes to France's defeat in the image of 'les patrouilles des nuées en déroute' (*OC*, II, 298).

Unlike Whitman, though, Laforgue is not so much mourning the defeat as parodying the 'intense exaltation militaire'[73] of the 1870s and 1880s: in describing the cart-ruts routing the clouds as 'don quichottesques' (*OC*, II, 298), he exposes nationalistic fantasies of military prowess as fundamentally chimerical.[74] Similarly, the poem parodies Vigny's 'Le Cor',[75] which links the poignancy of 'le son du Cor, le soir, au fond des bois'[76] to *La Chanson de Roland*, a text that was positioned 'as foundational in an aesthetic and ideological account of Frenchness'[77] in the late nineteenth century (especially after 1870) because of its glorification of the courage of the Franks, the supposed ancestors of the French. The parody is made more explicit in 'Le mystère des trois cors', where the hunting cry of 'Hallali!' is accompanied by 'Roncevaux!' (*OC*, II, 303). Moreover, rather than a tale of heroism, the poem relates the 'mystère très-immoral' (*OC*, II, 304) of a *ménage à trois*, the three 'cors' resolving their love triangle by repairing to a hotel together (before being found dead in the morning). This burlesque element is absent from 'L'hiver qui vient', but it too subverts Vigny's poem in its focus on the forest as a topos of raw sexual energy rather than sentimental nationalism.

The sexualized reading of the sun image in 'L'hiver qui vient' coheres with the view of it as a representation of national decline: France's demographic problems, one of the main sources of contemporary anxieties, were often attributed to a lack of virility. If the 'Soleils plénipotentiaires' might thus be read in terms of France's former greatness, then the 'soleil fichu' signals that the France of the poetic present is in decline. In this sense, the ill health that is suggested by the description 'blanc comme un crachat d'estaminet' (*OC*, II, 297) takes on renewed significance: it points toward the discourse of disease and degeneration that was used to describe the 'body' of France. This corporeal vision of the nation is suggested, albeit subtly, by Laforgue's translation of 'O Star of France', where Whitman's description of France as 'a mastless hulk' (*OC*, II, 352) is translated by Laforgue as 'une carcasse démâtée' (*OC*, II, 353): although this is ostensibly a direct translation, 'carcasse' of course carries the secondary meaning of 'body'.

But in general Laforgue's work is concerned primarily with the suffering of the individual body, not the collective (national) body. Consequently, the metaphorical illness of the sun is superseded by references to actual respiratory disease:

> C'est la toux dans les dortoirs du lycée qui rentre,
> [...]
> La phtisie pulmonaire attristant le quartier,
> Et toute la misère des grands centres. (*OC*, II, 298)

The Schopenhauerian sympathy of 'Complainte du pauvre corps humain' is again evident here. But this reference to disease in general is itself superseded by an image of the poet's own suffering, which is both physical and spiritual, his palliatives including 'lainages, caoutchoucs, pharmacie, rêve' (*OC*, II, 299). This shift is foreshadowed in the opening line of the poem, which expresses the poet's difficulties of communication with his lover using the punning 'Blocus sentimental!': the national is transfigured as the personal. Indeed, in an earlier version, the poet's final declaration that he will 'donner la note' of this season was appended with 'Pour mes compatriotes' (*OC*, II, 301); the exclusion of this phrase reinforces the notion that the poem's movement is away from the national and towards the individual. Just as Laforgue is sceptical of Schopenhauer and Hartmann's grandiose visions of universal annihilation, so ideas of national redemption are also suspect. All we can hope for are 'des remèdes individuels/ terrestres et pratiques' (*OC*, III, 1135).

The return to the individual does not imply a resurgence of the stable lyrical self. Rather, in 'L'hiver qui vient' we hear a poetry born of 'échos', a poetry sung 'en chœur': that is, poetry that emerges not from the lyrical self but from the echolalia of other discourses, and from the tentative polyphony of the multiple voices within a non-unitary self. If Laforgue's free verse is intended to represent the unconscious, then this is not the unconscious as deeper, originary self, but as something other, something fragmented.

Conclusion

In much of Laforgue's writing on Germany, the country where he spent most of his adult years is viewed through an exoticizing lens. In *Berlin*, Laforgue derides the citizens of the Imperial German capital for their gaucheness, lack of cultivation, and even primitiveness. The German nation, Laforgue suggests, is closer to the state of nature, its barbarism only imperfectly concealed by a veneer of modernity. In 'L'Art moderne en Allemagne', however, this naturalness is valorized positively: here, Germany is portrayed as the chosen land of the Unconscious, the 'other' to France's restrictively Classical culture. This utopian vision recapitulates Staël's idealization of Germany, but with a Hartmannian inflection. But Laforgue also experienced the day-to-day realities of life in Germany, and, as his letters show, it was not a life characterized by creative fervour but by boredom, frustration, and homesickness. The vision of Germany in 'L'Art moderne en Allemagne' thus belongs essentially to the realm of myth, and its reference to the forest motif perhaps represents an implicit acknowledgement of this fact.

Ultimately, the forest (as symbol of the Unconscious) is not confined to Germany, even if German culture offers privileged access to this realm: the Unconscious is a supranational force that cannot be restricted by arbitrary borders. It resides within each of us as the 'atmosphère occulte de l'être', the hidden domain of the self where repressed desires and anxieties reside. In Laforgue's poetry, the shadow side of the human mind finds free rein, not only thematically through the representation of sexual desire, but also formally, with free verse making manifest the disruptive elements of the unconscious. This disturbance of Classical versification challenges French literary tradition, just as the sexual themes of Laforgue's work defy contemporary bourgeois morality. Moreover, in representing both the excess of desire and its lack, both sexual liberation and sexual failure, Laforgue undermines the nationalist discourses that glorified procreation as the key to restoring France's power and status.

Notes to Chapter 3

1. Pascal Pia, 'Notes et variantes', in Jules Laforgue, *Les Complaintes: suivies des Premiers poèmes*, ed. by Pascal Pia (Paris: Gallimard, 1979), pp. 338–438 (p. 366).
2. Varley, p. 51. Varley is referring here to Maurice Barrès, born in 1862 (two years after Laforgue).
3. See also an early version of the poem 'Marche funèbre pour la mort de la Terre' which refers to the 'Cerveau fou de Hegel' (*OC*, I, 345).
4. Caro, p. 115.
5. Ibid., p. 117.
6. Hobsbawm, p. 95.
7. Alphonse Daudet, *Contes du lundi* (Paris: Lemerre, 1873); quoted in Girardet, p. 44.
8. Girardet, p. 38.
9. Ibid., p. 38.
10. See also Laforgue's article on the 'Exposition du centenaire de l'académie royale des arts de Berlin', where he bemoans the triumphalism of German painters' representations of the war (*OC*, III, 312).
11. See Jean-Jacques Lefrère, *Jules Laforgue* ([Paris]: Fayard, 2005), p. 532. As Lefrère notes, Laforgue had received a generous salary in Germany, but had no savings at the time of his return.
12. Despite this, *Berlin* remained unpublished as a complete text until after his death, though some chapters were published in the literary supplement of *Le Figaro* in the first months of 1887.
13. Elme-Marie Caro, *Les Jours d'épreuve* (Paris: Hachette, 1872), pp. 52–53; quoted in Digeon, p. 160.
14. Digeon, p. 162.
15. Ibid., p. 164.
16. Caro, p. xx.
17. Robert Pogue Harrison, *Forests: The Shadow of Civilisation* (Chicago, IL: University of Chicago Press, 1992), p. 121.
18. Théodore de Banville, 'Enfin Malherbe vint...', *Œuvres de Théodore de Banville; Les Cariatides; Roses de Noël* (Paris: Lemerre, 1889), p. 253.
19. Harrison, p. 164.
20. Ibid., p. 1; author's emphasis.
21. Staël, I, 51.
22. Wagner, p. lxv.
23. Ibid., p. xii.
24. Ibid., p. xi.
25. Harrison, p. 2.
26. Ibid., p. 63.
27. Ibid., p. 63.
28. Ibid., p. xi.
29. Ibid., p. 6.
30. Flaubert, *Madame Bovary*, p. 228.
31. Significantly, the two terms never appear in the same poem.
32. See p. 68.
33. Peter Collier, 'Poetry and Cliché: Laforgue's "L'Hiver qui vient"', in *Nineteenth-century French poetry: Introductions to close reading*, ed. by Christopher Prendergast (Cambridge: Cambridge University Press, 1990), pp. 199–224 (p. 214).
34. Bem, p. 161.

35. Collier, p. 214.
36. Camille Mauclair, *Jules Laforgue, Essai* (Paris: Mercure de France, 1896), p. 46.
37. Clive Scott, *A Question of Syllables: Essays in Nineteenth-Century French Verse* (Cambridge: Cambridge University Press, 1986), p. 157.
38. Édouard Dujardin, *Les Premiers Poètes du vers libre* (Paris: Mercure de France, 1922), p. 58.
39. Pearson, p. 137.
40. Ibid., p. 138.
41. See his references to 'les enivrants récits que me faisait Bacchus de sa conquête d'Inde' and to 'Thyrses, et chevelures emmêlées!' (*OC*, II, 462).
42. Pearson, p. 137. The expression 'en venir là' means 'to have sex' (*OC*, II, 518 n. 1).
43. Ibid., p. 138.
44. Ibid., p. 138.
45. Ibid., p. 138.
46. Ibid., p. 138.
47. Ibid., p. 141.
48. Hiddleston (1980), p. 52.
49. *Le Nouveau Petit Robert* (1994), I.2, p. 768.
50. Guiraud, p. 364.
51. Hiddleston (1980), p. 64.
52. Ibid., p. 65.
53. Peter Dale, *Poems of Jules Laforgue* (London: Anvil Press Poetry, 2001), p. 456; see also Hiddleston (1980), p. 40.
54. Ribot, p. 71.
55. Morgan, p. 269.
56. David S. Barnes, *The Making of a Social Disease: Tuberculosis in Nineteenth-Century France* (Berkeley and Los Angeles, CA: University of California Press, 1995), p. 77 and p. 83.
57. Sontag, p. 25.
58. Georg Groddeck, quoted in Sontag, p. 24.
59. Hiddleston (1980), p. 45; see also Lawrence Watson, *Jules Laforgue: Poet of His Age* (Mahwah, NJ: Office of Communication Services, Ramapo College of New Jersey, 1980), p. 36.
60. Hiddleston (1980), p. 47.
61. Ibid., p. 45.
62. Armelle Leclercq, 'Jules Laforgue à la lisière des langages: Fonctions subversives du jeu intertextuel', in *(Ab)Normalities*, ed. by Catherine Dousteyssier-Khoze and Paul Scott (Durham: Durham Modern Languages Series, 2001), pp. 139–50 (pp. 146–47).
63. Lawrence Watson, ' "L'Hiver qui vient": Poème-Manifeste', in *Laforgue aujourd'hui*, ed. by J. A. Hiddleston ([Paris]: José Corti, 1988), pp. 135–53 (p. 141).
64. Collier, p. 219.
65. See in particular 'Complainte du pauvre Chevalier-Errant' (*OC*, I, 575), 'Complainte du roi de Thulé' (*OC*, I, 592) and 'Complainte du Sage de Paris' (*OC*, I, 617).
66. Guiraud, p. 475.
67. Cantique des cantiques 4:16. Both terms are used in 'Complainte du Sage de Paris', which refers to 'ces jupes éphémères' and 'leurs jardins d'un jour' (*OC*, I, 617).
68. Léon Dierx, 'Soir d'octobre', in *Les Lèvres closes* (Paris: Lemerre, 1868), p. 89.
69. See Charles Perrault, *Contes*, ed. by Marc Soriano (Paris: Flammarion, 1989), p. 256.
70. Collier, p. 218.
71. Burrow, p. 50.
72. See, for example, Gobineau, p. 82.
73. Girardet, p. 14.
74. This refers to the scene in which Don Quixote sees clouds of dust arising from two herds of sheep on a road and mistakes them for two armies about to enter battle, prompting him to join the 'fray' and kill several sheep.
75. Hiddleston (1980), p. 86.
76. Alfred de Vigny, 'Le Cor', *Poèmes antiques et modernes* (Paris: Canel, 1826), p. 83.

77. Simon Gaunt, 'The Chanson de Roland and the Invention of France', in *Rethinking Heritage: Cultures and Politics in Europe*, ed. by Robert Shannan Peckham (London: Tauris, 2003), pp. 90–101 (p. 97).

CHAPTER 4

The Eastern Other (1): Multiplicity

The idea of otherness was associated with Schopenhauer and Hartmann's philosophy not only because of its 'German-ness', but also because of their use of Eastern thought, especially Buddhism. Laforgue's work draws on this aspect of his philosophical reading in two key senses: first, Buddhist ideas as filtered through Schopenhauer, Hartmann, and their French critics play an important role in his thought; second, his work explores the differing conceptions of the East-West relationship espoused in these sources. Most important to Laforgue is Buddhism's challenge to the idea of stable, coherent selfhood. This is evident both in his notion of the self as multiple or fragmented — a notion that is enacted as well as depicted in his poetry — and in his idea that there is a 'oneness' underlying all phenomena which entails that individuality is essentially illusory. These apparently contradictory ideas find resolution in Hartmann's theory of individual identity.

The multiplicity of selfhood is related to the use of diverse cultural referents — amongst which is, of course, Buddhism — in a de-hierarchized model of intercultural relations, a model that favours the pluralism of 'cultural difference' over the binarism of 'cultural otherness'. But there is a tension in Laforgue's thinking about foreign cultures: at certain key moments, he recuperates an 'othering' view of the East, one that exoticizes India as a source of spiritual renewal and sensual fulfilment. (In this sense, his perceptions of India and of Germany overlap; indeed, this association was well-established in late nineteenth-century French culture, as we shall see shortly.) This chapter explores this tension, thinking through the ways in which Laforgue figures the relationship between different cultures and how these figurations relate to his conception of the self. In doing so, it draws connections between two important but apparently distinct images in Laforgue's *œuvre*, images which are crucial to his thinking on selfhood: the bibelot and the underwater world.

Germany, the India of the North

'"Grattez un Allemand, vous verrez reparaître l'antique sectateur de Bouddha"':[1] this declaration by an expatriate Italian in Germany, reported by Foucher de Careil, demonstrates the extent to which Germany was associated with Indian thought and religion (especially Buddhism) in the popular imaginary of the late nineteenth century. In fact, the association dates back at least as far as Staël. She argues that there is a climatic basis for the philosophical differences between the Mediterranean and northern nations of Europe: while the warmth of the southern lands makes their inhabitants more susceptible to sensory pleasure (and thus materialist philosophy), in nations like Germany 'la rigueur du climat' prevents the enjoyment of 'les délices de la nature' and thus necessitates recourse to 'les plaisirs de l'âme';[2] in this, Germans are similar to the peoples of the East, where the extreme climate (in this case, an 'excès de la chaleur'[3]) also engenders a contemplative mind-set. 'La philosophie des Indiens ne peut être bien comprise que par des idéalistes allemands,' she concludes.[4] This argument for an Indo-Germanic affinity is recapitulated by thinkers like Michelet, who describes Germany as 'l'Inde de l'Europe',[5] and Jean Raynaud, for whom Germany is an 'Orient moderne qui [...] germe du sein des cendres inanimées de l'antique Orient' and which is exoticized as having 'merveilleuses richesses et [...] pensées profondes qu'elle dérobe à nos regards dans le mystère de son langage'.[6]

While Foucher de Careil concurs with this account of Germany's 'Oriental' mysticism, his valorization of it is entirely different. He insists on the philosophical divide between Latinate culture and Germanic culture, the rational character of the former proving resistant to supposedly esoteric Eastern ideas, in contrast to the more mystical inclination of the latter. France is thus portrayed as a bastion against 'le nihilisme oriental', while Germany (naively) 'a cru trouver dans l'Inde le dernier de la sagesse antique et toute une renaissance philosophique et religieuse'.[7] In this sense, Foucher de Careil (writing in 1862) pre-empts the more critical assessments of the German affinity with Indian thought that emerged after the Franco-Prussian War. In *L'Année terrible*, Hugo emphasizes the phantasmic element of Germany's 'exotic' lustre, asserting that Germanophiles in France saw their neighbour as comparable to 'l'Inde aux aspects fabuleux'.[8] Caro, meanwhile, attempts to account for the supposed German predilection for Indian thought, and especially Buddhism. Marvelling at 'le lien mystérieux'[9] between Eastern thought and contemporary German philosophy, he comments that it is strange enough that millions of Asians 'boivent à longs traits l'opium de ces fatales doctrines qui énervent et endorment la volonté', but it is even stranger that the Germanic race — 'une race énergique, disciplinée, si fortement constituée pour la science et pour l'action'[10] — should have accepted them. He explains this acceptance of 'la philosophie du nirvâna' in Germany by drawing on Staël's vision of Germanic placidity; the yearning for Buddhistic serenity is, he argues, a reaction against militarism on the part of 'un peuple qui n'est pas belliqueux par nature [...] qui à travers son triomphe a des visions de sa vie tranquille d'autrefois et comme la nostalgie du repos'.[11] This vision is connected to Caro's theory of 'les deux Allemagnes', a theory that Laforgue himself endorses (as we saw in the previous chapter). Laforgue also explicitly draws on the discourse linking Germany and India. In 'L'Art moderne en Allemagne', he describes Germany's 'forêt panthéiste' as the 'Vraie terre de Védas du Nord' and as 'les vrais tropiques de l'Europe, mais tropiques du Nord' (*OC*, III, 343); the Ganges, meanwhile, is labelled the 'Rhin oriental' (*OC*, III, 343). Germans themselves are 'Des bouddhistes — mais qui ont dans l'ascendance de leur race tout un terrible et maigre moyen âge chrétien' ('Notes sur l'Allemagne', *OC*, III, 819). If this reinforces the argument that his view of Germany conforms in certain respects to the logic of exoticism, it is also indicative of his profound interest in Indian religion, especially Buddhism; this interest was inspired by his reading of Schopenhauer and Hartmann, and crucially inflected by their interpretations of Buddhist doctrine.

Both philosophers draw on Buddhism to support their ideas. The first of Buddhism's Four Noble Truths — the doctrinal core of the religion in most Buddhist traditions — asserts the prevalence of suffering in human life, and both Schopenhauer and Hartmann compare this doctrine to their pessimistic vision of existence (*WWR*, II, 623; *PI*, II, 439). The second Truth explains that this suffering is caused by craving and desire. This idea is central to Schopenhauer's doctrine: the Will manifests itself in human existence as a near-ceaseless striving, chiefly for sexual gratification but also for other forms of physical satisfaction, social fulfilment and so on; and since this striving can never be completely satisfied, it produces suffering. Both philosophers also refer to the Vedanta school of Hindu philosophy to support their monist metaphysics. Schopenhauer frequently makes reference to the concept of Maya, or illusion — a concept found in both Hinduism and Buddhism — to refer to the fact that our knowledge of the world is restricted to 'its phenomena as separated, detached, innumerable' and that we are denied immediate insight into 'the inner nature of things, which is one' (*WWR*, I, 352). But Schopenhauer's limited understanding of Indian religion is evident in his conflation of Hindu and Buddhist thought: he states that 'Brahmanism and Buddhism [...] teach man to regard himself as Brahman, as the original being himself' (*WWR*, II, 463) when in fact the concept of Brahman is exclusive to Hinduism (Brahmanism). Buddhism, by contrast, teaches that the underlying reality is emptiness, rather than the 'world soul' designated by the term Brahman. For Hartmann, this world soul is analogous to the Unconscious, and he praises the philosophy of the Vedanta for 'une pénétration et une netteté qu'ont à peine égalées les plus récents parmi les penseurs européens' (*PI*, I, 35–36). He also praises Buddhism for having uncovered the illusion of selfhood: just as Buddhism propounds the idea that reality is fundamentally empty, so it also declares that human beings have no (fixed or enduring) self. Hartmann does not refer directly to this doctrine of 'no-self' (a doctrine that is fundamental to Buddhist thought), but he does cite Buddhism's dismissal of the idea of 'l'immortalité individuelle' in support of his claim for the illusoriness of individuality (*PI*, II, 440).

Despite their shared interest in Indian philosophy and religion, Schopenhauer and Hartmann offer different views of the relationship between Eastern and Western cultures, and these differences are of vital importance to Laforgue's own conception of cross-cultural relations. Schopenhauer's viewpoint is that of perennialism: he argues that Buddhism, Hinduism and Christianity belong to an eternal source of wisdom that periodically yields the same insights across different eras and cultures. This is illustrated by his references to the Indian concept of 'Maya', which consistently compare it to Kant's 'phenomenon' and to the shadows in Plato's cave (*WWR*, I, 8, 253, 274 and 419). He also asserts that the ethical core of Buddhism and (true) Christianity is the same (*WWR*, II, 604). But he does not believe that *all* cultures are connected to this source; in fact, one of Schopenhauer's key concerns in asserting Eastern analogies for Christianity is to separate it from the other Abrahamic religions. As well as being an anti-Semite, Schopenhauer was also critical of Islam, arguing that the origins of European civilization lie not in the Near East but in India and in Classical antiquity. This distinction is paradigmatic of nineteenth-century Orientalism: drawing on philology's discovery that languages belong to families and that European languages are not part of the Semitic family but the Indo-European, Orientalism constructed an opposition between two kinds of Orient:

> Language and race seemed inextricably tied, and the 'good' Orient was invariably a classical period somewhere in long-gone India, whereas the 'bad' Orient lingered in present-day Asia, parts of North Africa, and Islam everywhere.[12]

But while philology also represented a challenge to Christian doctrine since it dispelled the Biblical notion that language was bestowed by God, Schopenhauer sought to draw comparisons between Christianity and Buddhism, one of the religions of this 'good' Orient.

Hartmann does not draw the same distinction between different Eastern religions, even if his conception of Eastern thought is typical of Orientalism's essentialist vision:

> Il est dans la nature des Orientaux de se montrer moins systématiques que nous dans le développement de leurs idées, mais d'être plus ouverts aux pressentiments des vérités les plus cachées, aux mystérieuses suggestions du génie. (*PI*, I, 34)

This condescending portrayal of the 'irrational' and 'mystical' qualities of Eastern peoples is linked to his view that Buddhism has a privileged (and presumably intuitive) insight into the real nature of the world: he rejects Schopenhauer's theory that Buddhism belongs to the same universal, unchanging source of wisdom as Christianity. Both religions propound 'le mépris du monde, associé à la vie transcendante de l'esprit', but Buddhism's promise of an eternal state of bliss does not entail 'l'immortalité individuelle'; Christianity, on the other hand, appeals to 'l'égoïsme de l'homme' in its doctrine of eternal life for the individual soul (*PI*, II, 440). Hartmann argues that Christianity's promise of individual immortality is illusory since individuality itself is merely a phenomenon that disappears upon death, the only true, persistent entity being the Unconscious. For Hartmann, then, Buddhism is characteristic of a more advanced state of consciousness than Christianity, since it recognizes that selfhood is fundamentally chimerical. But he sees his own philosophy of the Unconscious as superseding both Eastern and Western faiths.

These differences between Schopenhauer and Hartmann are grounded in their theories of history. For Hartmann, all cultures are involved in an ongoing process of historical development, one that has led to his philosophy of the Unconscious and that will lead in the future to collective human enlightenment. This view might be characterized as a kind of philosophical evolutionism. For Schopenhauer, on the other hand, history is just an endlessly repeated cycle, and so there is nothing new under the sun: rather, there is an unchanging core of philosophical truth that is manifested at certain times and in certain cultures. His perennialism was part of a current of nineteenth-century thought that also included the comparativism of Max Müller,[13] the universalism of the Parliament of Religions[14] and the syncretism of the Theosophical Society.[15]

While perennialism saw Buddhism and Christianity as belonging to a common source, there also existed a Christianizing view of Buddhism, which held that Buddhist doctrine was merely a 'hidden' or corrupt variety of the Gospel; this theory was widespread in the Early Modern period, when the first encounters with Buddhism took place.[16] In the nineteenth century, the explicitly Christianizing view of Buddhism became discredited as more came to be known about the religion. But in certain ways it persisted. Firstly, the very notion of Buddhism as a singular 'world religion' was premised largely on the Christian paradigm. Prior to the nineteenth century, Western scholars were largely unaware of the connections between the religious practices they encountered in Sri Lanka, Nepal, Japan and so on, all of which derived from the teachings of the Buddha.[17] Indeed, the various Buddhist cultures themselves had little sense of belonging to a unified tradition.[18] The notion of Buddhism as a singular 'world religion' was essentially an invention of Western scholarship (even if, as Donald Lopez points out, this vision was re-appropriated by Buddhists in a kind of strategic essentialism: 'During the nineteenth century, monks from a variety of traditions came to speak of a single pan-Asian Buddhism in an attempt to counter the attacks of Christian missionaries and colonial officials.'[19]) This process of invention functioned according to an assimilatory logic that sought to recast Buddhism within the mould of the Abrahamic tradition: rather than examining the diversity of Buddhist practices, nineteenth-century Western scholars focused on the figure of the Buddha and on Buddhist texts, thus privileging the elements — founder and textual doctrine — deemed obligatory for the constitution of a 'world' religion.[20]

The Christianizing view of Buddhism was also evident outside the academic sphere. The growth of popular interest in Buddhism in the nineteenth century was based partly on accounts of the life of the Buddha that compared him — explicitly or implicitly — to Christ.[21] The comparison was often drawn on the basis of his self-sacrifice: according to the standard biography of the Buddha, the Prince Siddhārtha Gautama, also known as Sākyamuni ('sage of the Sakya clan'), renounced his life of luxury at the age of twenty-nine having witnessed various forms of suffering in the city outside his palace, and spent many years as a wandering ascetic (within the Brahmanic tradition). But he later repudiated this way of life, instead sitting in meditation at the foot of a tree and remaining there until he achieved enlightenment (nirvana); he then preached his first sermon, before going forth to spread his new doctrine. Even those who were critical of Buddhism, such as the Orientalist Jules Barthélemy-Saint-Hilaire — 'the doyen of Buddhism's critics'[22] in the words of Philip Almond — praised the Buddha for 'une grandeur d'âme peu commune; une pureté morale presque accomplie; une charité sans bornes; une vie héroïque qui ne se dément pas un seul instant'.[23] Tacitly comparing him to Christ, Barthélemy-

Saint-Hilaire states that the Buddha 'n'est venu en ce monde que pour sauver les êtres';[24] he also makes this comparison explicit, arguing that 'sauf le Christ tout seul, il n'est point, parmi les fondateurs de religion, de figure plus pure ni plus touchante que celle du Bouddha'.[25]

This interreligious comparison, as well as the other forms of relation between religions evident in the work of Schopenhauer, Hartmann, and their French critics (perennialism, syncretism, evolutionism), are reflected in Laforgue's *œuvre* in various ways. His reading of German philosophy both provoked his interest in Buddhist ideas, and prompted a series of reflections on how the thought of Eastern cultures was related to that of the West.

Laforgue, 'bouddhiste dilettante'

Laforgue's conception of interreligious and intercultural relations is subject to a significant shift. While his early work propounds a reluctant atheism, it also suggests a residual adherence to religious syncretism that shows the influence of Schopenhauer. In his mature work, however, he follows Hartmann in detaching Christianity and Buddhism, distancing himself from the former while exploring the latter in more depth. He thus rejects *Le Sanglot*'s synthesis of religions; he also repudiates its fusion of cultures. In *Les Complaintes*, by contrast, his use of cultural references is characterized by a playful, dilettantish eclecticism that is emblematized by the figure of the bibelot. This ludicity in fact conceals two serious philosophical points: the diversity of cultural references implies a rejection of Eurocentric hierarchies of cultural value; and it also has profound implications for poetic selfhood, serving to enact the disintegration of the poetic self. Buddhism thus occupies a privileged role within this heterogeneous cultural landscape, since its doctrine of no-self is analogous to what is at stake in this heterogeneity: the repudiation of the lyrical self.

In the 'vers philo.' (*OC*, II, 729) of *Le Sanglot*, the recurrent juxtaposition of references to the Buddha and Christ suggests something akin to Schopenhauerian perennialism, which draws comparisons between Buddhism and Christianity. However, both are presented as sources of wisdom that have ultimately proved inadequate: the poet of *Le Sanglot* has, reluctantly, abjured his religious beliefs. In 'Pataugement', for example, the poet lists eminent religious and philosophical figures who believed in life after death, a list headed by the Buddha and Jesus — 'Bouddha méditant sous le figuier mystique, | Jésus criant vers Dieu son sublime abandon' (*OC*, I, 304) — before offering a vision of the apocalypse and dismissing hope of an afterlife. Later in the poem, 'Cakya' and 'Jésus' are again invoked (alongside 'Rembrandt, Beethoven et Shakespeare' (*OC*, I, 306)) in a final celebration of humanity's achievements before the world is destroyed. The same collocation of the founders of Buddhism and Christianity is evident in other poems, and here too admiration is mixed with despair in religious belief. This despair is most often expressed through a sense of abandonment, as for example in 'Marche funèbre pour la mort de la terre':

> Où donc est Çakya, cœur immense et sublime,
> Qui saigna pour tout être et dit la Bonne loi?
> Où Jésus triste et doux qui douta de la foi
> Dont il avait vécu, dont il mourait victime? (*OC*, I, 343)

'Cauchemar' is more succinct, its melancholic, Baudelairean scene of Parisian gloom being punctuated by the cry 'Et Jésus et Bouddha sont partis!' (*OC*, I, 330). This association between the Christ and the Buddha is redolent of contemporary comparisons between the two figures, as well as echoing Schopenhauer's perennialism. However, in repeatedly asserting their absence, the poet seems to proclaim his disillusionment with all religion.

Despite this, the repeated references to religious figures in *Le Sanglot* suggest a residual attachment to some kind of syncretistic faith. Religion may ultimately be abandoned, but it is at least taken seriously. In *Les Complaintes*, by contrast, there is a playfully random melange of cultural references that includes terms taken from the lexicons of Christianity and Buddhism. Indeed, the poet openly mocks his former syncretism in 'Préludes autobiographiques':

> Puis, fou devant ce ciel qui toujours nous bouda,
> Je rêvais de prêcher la fin, nom d'un Bouddha!
> [...]
> Mener ces chers bourgeois, fouettés d'alléluias,
> Au Saint-Sépulcre maternel du Nirvâna! (*OC*, I, 548)

The homophonic rhyme 'bouda'/ 'Bouddha' serves to accentuate the scorn with which the poet now treats his prophetic pretensions, while the *rime pauvre* of 'alléluias' and 'Nirvâna' indicates that the target of his ridicule is not Buddhism as such, but his own naïve melding of Buddhism and Christianity. The syncretistic aspect of his religious yearnings is also lampooned by the deliberately convoluted image of the 'Saint-Sépulcre maternel du Nirvâna'; the self-mockery is reinforced by the eradication of the caesura, which creates an effusive, dodecasyllabic merge of the two religions, eschewing both hemistichal division and hemispheric difference. The adjective 'maternel' seems to acknowledge that the poet's religious feelings stemmed from a regressive desire for motherly comfort, and its position at the midpoint of the line emphasizes that it was this emotional need that formed the fusional element in the poet's now-denounced syncretism. If the repudiation of religious belief in *Le Sanglot* implies an intellectual, if not emotional, acceptance of Hartmann's position that the philosophy of the Unconscious has superseded religion, then in 'Préludes autobiographiques' the poet openly declares his adherence to Hartmannism, stating that he wants to spend his life 'au sein de l'INCONSCIENT' (*OC*, I, 548). The next poem in the collection is, moreover, 'Complainte propitiatoire à l'Inconscient', which enacts the overwriting of Christian faith in its parody of the Lord's Prayer. Regret at the loss of faith seems to have given way to a derisive detachment from religion, mirroring Laforgue's declaration that he is 'dilettante, revenu de tout' in his letter to Mültzer.[26]

But in fact, Laforgue does not dissociate himself from religion as such; rather, he repudiates his Christian faith, while deepening his interest in Buddhism. This distinction is rooted in Hartmann's treatment of the two religions. In particular, Hartmann's discussion of the differences between the Buddhist and Christian conceptions of the human individual is vital to Laforgue. The shift in Laforgue's understanding of selfhood and its importance to the new aesthetic of *Les Complaintes* are signalled by the opening line of the collection, where the poet declares himself 'En deuil d'un Moi-le-Magnifique' ('À Paul Bourget', *OC*, I, 545). And the role played by Buddhism in this shift is hinted at in the poet's self-description as a 'brâve bouddhiste' (*OC*, I, 545) in the same poem. Indeed, in a letter to Kahn, Laforgue links Buddhism and dilettantism, problematizing the notion that being 'dilettante' implies a rejection of all religious doctrine, as the letter to Mültzer seems to suggest (see above). In this letter to Kahn, written in September 1882 — six months after the one to Mültzer — Laforgue describes the shift that has taken place in his outlook since his rejection of *Le Sanglot*: 'Maintenant ma grande envie est de voyager, de voir, de *jouir* des choses. Avant j'étais bouddhiste tragique et maintenant je suis bouddhiste dilettante' (*OC*, I, 800; author's emphasis). In the letter to Mültzer, Laforgue declares himself a 'dilettante' on the basis that he has renounced both Christian belief and Buddhistic asceticism ('j'ai joué au petit Bouddha'); in the later letter to Kahn, however, dilettantism is *connected* to the idea of being 'bouddhiste'. To be a dilettante is not, then, to reject Buddhism as such, but only to reject self-denial: in its contemporary usage, dilettantism connoted (amongst other things) sensual pleasure. For Bourget, dilettantism was 'une disposition de l'esprit, très intelligente à la fois et très voluptueuse',[27] and Laforgue's own references to the term imply that he followed Bourget's definition. Indeed, he associates dilettantism with specifically sexual pleasure: in his article on Bourget, he states that the dilettante is one who believes that 'la suprême poésie est dans l'extase spasmodique de la Communion' (*OC*, III, 132), the sexualized blasphemy encapsulating the shift away from Christian faith towards the pleasures of the flesh. In his letter to Kahn, moreover, he emphasizes that he now wants to '*jouir* des choses', with all of its sexual connotations.

But the idea of being a dilettante did not only imply sexual liberation. It also represented, in Hibbitt's words, the 'desire for a multi-faceted soul'.[28] This idea of multiplicity is crucial to Hartmann's conception of selfhood too, the individual being constituted by a provisional assemblage, rather than any fixed, enduring essence:

> *Je* suis un phénomène semblable à l'arc-en-ciel dans les nuages. Comme lui, *je* ne suis qu'un ensemble de rapports; *je* change à chaque seconde comme ces rapports eux-mêmes, et m'évanouirai avec eux. (*PI*, II, 213–14; author's emphases)

It is in this sense that Hartmann views Buddhism as a doctrine that is closer than Christianity to his philosophy of the Unconscious, since it too sees the self as ephemeral, as ungrounded in any permanent reality. The idea of being a 'bouddhiste dilettante' is not, therefore, oxymoronic, since both terms imply a rejection of the idea of a stable, unchanging self. Laforgue may not have been a Buddhist in any formal sense, but this declaration is not entirely tongue-in-cheek: the aesthetic inaugurated by *Les Complaintes* is premised precisely on such a conception of fluid selfhood. This is made manifest in the multiple personae of the collection: Pierrot, the poet's foetus, Paris, a fig tree, the King of Thule, and so on.

The splintering of the unitary lyrical self is accompanied by a poetics of cultural eclecticism, the collection's lexical field including terms from the Bible, Classical mythology, Buddhism, Hinduism, and (of course) German philosophy, as well as French folklore, literature, and popular song. The desire to travel that is linked to dilettantism ('ma grande envie est de voyager') is thus fulfilled poetically in *Les Complaintes*, even as the collection laments the impossibility of actual travel ('Je n'aurai jamais d'aventures' ('Complainte sur certains temps déplacés', OC, I, 598)). In this sense, 'Complainte des pubertés difficiles' performs a meta-poetic function: it comments on (as well as enacting) both the anarchic combination of cultural referents, and their claustration within the poetic scene, a domestic interior. The poem portrays a bourgeois drawing room in which a jade elephant (described as a 'Bon boudha d'exilé') is juxtaposed with a Sèvres vase depicting a scene from a fable by Florian and an earthenware figurine of 'Un gros petit dieu Pan' made in Tanagra, Greece (OC, I, 564): this miscellany of cultures and mythologies acts as a *mise en abyme* of *Les Complaintes* as a whole. It also appears to suggest that the collection's cultural references are mere lexical trinkets. As Jean-Pierre Bertrand states, the poem both depicts and enacts 'une poétique du bibelot',[29] and the defining feature of the bibelot is, in Janell Watson's words, 'Superfluousness, or the absence of use-value'.[30] The bibelot is thus the embodiment of aestheticism, of art for art's sake; it is also associated with dilettantism, since the dabbling *bibelotiste* collects a variety of objects for display without necessarily knowing much about them. Bourget, indeed, argues that the bibelot is the embodiment of 'cet esprit de dilettantisme et de critique' that dominates the nineteenth century.[31] Nordau concurs, although he condemns this trend, asserting that the late nineteenth-century abundance of bibelots is symptomatic of the degeneration of modern culture. Indeed, in his critique of the eclectic *fin-de-siècle* interior he lists a series of objects that are remarkably similar to those described in 'Complainte des pubertés difficiles':

> a figure of Tanagra near a broken jade snuff-box, a Limoges plate beside a long-necked Persian waterpot of brass [...]. In a corner a sort of temple is erected to a squatting or a standing Buddha.[32]

He attributes 'The present rage for collecting, the piling up, in dwellings, of aimless bric-à-brac' to 'an irresistible desire among the degenerate to accumulate useless trifles'.[33] This uselessness is crucial to the 'poétique du bibelot' that is evident in Laforgue's work: not only are objects foregrounded, rather than the poet's emotions, but words seem to become *like* bibelots — decorative but without use, sonorous but semantically null.

However, the very uselessness of these lexical baubles is what constitutes — paradoxically — their deeper significance: since they do not (necessarily) serve as symbols of the poet's emotions but are, in a sense, self-standing entities, they perform Laforgue's rejection of the lyrical self. To this extent, Laforgue builds on the anti-lyricism of post-Romantic poetry. It was Baudelaire, argues Theodor Adorno, who first registered the precarity of lyricism, understood as a reaction against 'the domination of human beings by commodities that has developed since the beginning of the modern era';[34] Baudelaire's work made manifest the effect of this domination on literature, since 'it did not stop with the sufferings of the individual but chose the modern itself, as the antilyrical pure and simple, for its theme'.[35] Laforgue's work goes one step further in this sense, not only turning the poetic gaze towards the material clutter of the *fin-de-siècle*, but also placing these objects at the focal point of the poem. The bourgeois drawing room of 'Complainte des pubertés difficiles' is thus analogous to the curiosity shop in Balzac's *La Peau de chagrin*, which 'made each object a poetic element';[36] as Rancière points out, this is literature as the 'self-poeticization of life, converting any scrap of everyday life into a sign of history and any sign of history into a poetical element.'[37] But since Laforgue's chosen form is not the novel but lyrical poetry — a form that traditionally places the poet at the centre of the work — his use of such scraps has another, equally radical consequence: as well as constituting a source of creative expression, this clutter also becomes a cipher for liberation from the bounds of lyrical selfhood.

This liberation is explicitly dramatized in the final stanza of the poem, which rejects the egocentricity of *Le Sanglot*, deriding its self-aggrandizement and self-pity:

> Mais lui, cabré devant ces soirs accoutumés,
> Où montait la gaîté des enfants de son âge,
> Seul au balcon, disait, les yeux brûlés de rages:
> 'J'ai du génie, enfin: nulle ne veut m'aimer!' (*OC*, I, 565)

The final line parodies two poems from *Le Sanglot*, 'Éclair de gouffre' (*OC*, I, 325) and 'Les Boulevards' (*OC*, I, 327), both of which declare 'j'ai du génie'. Moreover, the position of the poet's former self ('lui') on the balcony implies that he has his back turned to the room, renouncing its bourgeois banality, as also suggested by the notion that he is 'cabré devant ces soirs accoutumés'. By contrast, the poet of *Les Complaintes* has turned *toward* the cultural muddle of the room (and of modernity), accepting the inevitability of these 'soirs accoutumés' and indeed making poetry out of them. This shift is, of course, enacted by 'Complainte des pubertés difficiles' itself, the first four stanzas of the poem being devoted entirely to describing the room, with no references to 'lui' or 'je'. The poem's rejection of *Le Sanglot*'s lyrical selfhood is also, by implication, a repudiation of its traditional conception of 'génie' as emerging from some originary source within the individual. In *Les Complaintes*, by contrast, the poet inscribes his own schizogony, his fracturing into multiple selves. While for Mallarmé the 'Aboli bibelot d'inanité sonore' is implicated in the poet's 'disparition élocutoire' — 'Car le Maître est allé puiser des pleurs au Styx | Avec ce seul objet dont le Néant s'honore'[38] —, for Laforgue the array of bibelots or avatars is constitutive of a '*fragmentation* élocutoire'. The elephant is one such avatar. Indeed, this 'Bon boudha d'exilé' plays a privileged role in the poem, since the Laforguian challenge to stable selfhood is inspired, in part, by the Buddhist idea of no-self that Hartmann draws on in his work. In another sense, though, Laforgue departs from Hartmannian thought: for Hartmann, the *bricolage* that characterizes *Les Complaintes* is associated with the run-of-the-mill artist, rather than the genius (who receives the work of art as a whole in a moment of inspiration). The poet's mockery of his own former claims to genius in 'Complainte des pubertés difficiles' does not necessarily suggest that he sees himself as a mere hack, but it does reinforce his problematization of Hartmann's aesthetics.

As well as its implications for poetic selfhood, the poem's disparate jumble of artefacts is also metonymic of the model of intercultural relations in the poet's mature work. The syncretism that is mourned in *Le Sanglot* is replaced by an eclectic, even disjunctive relationship between cultures. As Bertrand indicates,[39] there is no communication between the objects in the room. The jade elephant's trunk is 'sans flair', so it cannot smell the flowers painted on the Sèvres vase; meanwhile, the figurine of Pan reaches out to the vase's painted figures, but its arms are 'tout inconscients'. This symbolizes separation between the cultures represented by these objects: the jade elephant is a figure from the Far East (probably China), the vase from France, and Pan from Greece, as the phrase 'venu de Tanagra' highlights; moreover, the origin of all of these objects is emphasized by the terminal positioning of 'Orient', 'Sèvres' and 'Tanagra'. The poem thus foregrounds cultural difference, rejecting the naïve cultural fusion of the poet's earlier work. But if, within the poem-world, there is disjunction between these cultural artefacts, the text itself brings them together through the rhyme scheme, which reaches across stanzaic borders and thereby links 'Orient' and 'Florian', 'jade' and 'pommade'. This is not, however, the syncretistic logic mocked in 'Préludes autobiographiques' by the *rime plate* of 'alléluias' and 'Nirvâna', a rhyme that derides the forced attempt to fuse ideas from different cultures (a derision enhanced by the poverty of the rhyme). Here, the use of *rimes mêlées* suggests a much looser association, a model of intercultural relations that revels in diverseness while repudiating hierarchy ('The mixture of the curiosity shop made all objects and images equal'[40]). Eclecticism — also enshrined in the mixture of alexandrines and octosyllables — does not necessarily imply disharmony.

Indeed, a unisonous cry emerges from the room (albeit not from the aforementioned objects themselves): '"Tout est frais dès qu'on veut comprendre la Nature"' (*OC*, I, 565). Rather than a Romantic appeal for harmony with nature as such, this is a denunciation of Classical aesthetics, which promote the idealization of nature rather than the depiction of things as they really are: 'tous ces idéaux [...] posent d'abord que l'art est chargé de corriger la nature, comme s'il pouvait être d'autres lois d'harmonie que celles du tel quel de la vie' ('L'Art moderne ou Allemagne', *OC*, III, 349 n. 3). This 'tel quel de la vie' with its shifting polyphony — the disparate, even anarchic character of modern life — is precisely what is celebrated in 'Complainte des pubertés difficiles'. The de-hierarchized, dilettantish juxtaposition of objects in the room is metonymic of Laforgue's mature aesthetic, and of his rejection of Classical hierarchies of cultural and artistic value.[41] This eclecticism is, equally, a critique of Eurocentrism. In dismissing Taine's notion that there is an artistic hierarchy that reflects that of the natural world, Laforgue specifically invokes Eastern art: 'Eh bien non! que devient votre idéal devant les merveilles des arts chinois et japonais?' (*OC*, III, 358). For Laforgue, Taine's vision of the world is 'trop étroit', since 'Tout l'Orient est laissé de côté' (*OC*, III, 361).

The openness to other cultures that is promoted in these notes is dramatized by 'Complainte des pubertés difficiles'.

The celebration of cultural difference is accompanied by a critique of exoticism, which reifies an absolute distinction between self and other. This repudiation is expressed by the jade elephant:

> Un éléphant de Jade, œil mi-clos souriant,
> Méditait sous la riche éternelle pendule,
> Bon boudha d'exilé qui trouve ridicule
> Qu'on pleure vers les Nils des couchants d'Orient,
> Quand bave notre crépuscule. (*OC*, I, 564)

This ridiculing of exoticism is again a response to *Le Sanglot*, and specifically — perhaps — to the poem 'Soleil couchant (*Le soleil s'est couché...*)' which features a sunset 'Sur les rives du Nil' (*OC*, I, 237). The fact that it is a Far Eastern figure commenting on a depiction of the Near East constitutes a crucial part of the mockery, since the exotic yearning of *Le Sanglot* is essentially for an undifferentiated 'là-bas'.[42] Of course, it is ironic that the critique of exoticism is voiced by the jade elephant, a figure whose presence in a Parisian drawing room is the result of this same exoticism; but this is a deliberate irony on the part of the poet, and, moreover, one of which the elephant itself is perhaps wryly aware ('œil mi-clos souriant'). Furthermore, it is only thanks to the elephant's presence in Paris that it can draw the comparison between the artistic idealization of the exotic and the banal reality of France ('Quand bave notre crépuscule'). The (literal) domestication of otherness is thus both mocked by the poem and, paradoxically, essential to the critique of exoticism.

If the elephant calls into question the fetishization of otherness, it is also — as we have seen — implicated in the poet's challenge to coherent selfhood. It thus encapsulates the twofold significance of Buddhism to Laforgue's work: the Buddhist idea of no-self, as mediated through the work of Hartmann, is crucial to his conceptualization of identity, and by consequence to his mature aesthetic; and the very presence in his work of Buddhist ideas and references is emblematic of his principle of openness to other cultures, a principle that embraces diversity while rejecting exoticism. In this sense, Laforgue's vision of a non-unitary self is tied to his vision of cultural multiplicity.

★ ★ ★ ★ ★

If the use of Buddhism in Laforgue's poetry suggests a challenge to conventional notions of selfhood, his notes on Buddhism also call into question individuality, albeit in a different sense. In these notes, he refers to the Buddhist idea that individuality is a mere illusion, the idea that Hartmann himself foregrounds (as we have seen); for Laforgue, Buddhist doctrine consists in

> la méditation de l'universelle apparence, arriver à la science du Bouddha, se préparer au nirvâna, arriver à briser par la suppression, l'extirpation en soi de l'être, arriver au non-être du Brahman (force, vouloir universel), [...] dépouiller le phénomène du moi, l'individuel, rentrer dans l'Éternel, dans l'Être. (*OC*, III, 1131)

In other words, Buddhism (for Laforgue) involves dispelling the illusion of selfhood in favour of recognizing one's unity with the underlying force — here labelled Brahman, but called the Unconscious ('l'Un-Tout') by Hartmann. Hartmann's image of the self as a rainbow is premised on the idea that the Unconscious is like the sun: that is, each individual self is merely an ephemeral reflection of a more fundamental presence (*PI*, II, 214). Elsewhere, Laforgue expresses the same idea: 'Il n'y a qu'une Substance, tout le reste n'est que modalité pure, phénomène passager de la vie divine. [...] L'individu n'est qu'un mode, un moment fugitif de l'existence absolue, unique. La substance seule existe et subsiste' (*OC*, III, 1138). Laforgue's interpretation of Buddhism thus replicates Schopenhauer's error: Brahman is, in fact, a *Hindu* principle signifying the 'world-soul', the underlying metaphysical reality that each individual soul is part of; Buddhism specifically rejects this notion of an eternal absolute just as it denies the existence of an essential human self, instead arguing that the world is ultimately empty. Nirvana is prompted by the realization of this idea of no-self. The confusion in Laforgue's understanding — one that is derived from his philosophical sources — is evident in the formulation 'arriver au non-être du Brahman'. Nonetheless, this use of Buddhism again shows its importance in challenging the notion of the sovereign self.

But despite this challenge, Laforgue repeatedly insists on the unattainability of this Buddhistic 'non-être': 'Le nirvâna prêché par Bouddha n'est que le privilège d'initiés ascétiques' (*OC*, III, 1131). Another section of notes reiterates this point:

> Se délivrer de la soif de l'être... (Bouddhisme-) renoncer, se pénétrer de ce que tout est phénomène, apparence que l'être seul existe. Illusion, rien n'existe en dehors de Brahma, — le remède philosophique, le vrai celui de Bouddha, n'est le privilège que d'un petit nombre. (*OC*, III, 1133–34)

Laforgue may grasp intellectually the illusion of selfhood, but actually achieving self-dissolution is another matter. He suggests that it is only in death that such annihilation is possible:

> Toute existence individuelle est pure apparence, une ombre de personnalité qui s'évanouit à la mort pour rentrer au sein du tout, de l'unique rayon dans le foyer de l'Être, goutte d'eau dans l'océan universel. [...] [La mort] fait tomber cette illusion d'une personnalité misérable qui tenait l'âme séparée et comme exilée de son principe. (*OC*, III, 1138)

These ideas are given their most explicit poetic form in 'L'Oubli', from *Le Sanglot*: here the poet dismisses his surroundings as 'des formes d'un jour, éphémère Existence' before concluding that 'Tout n'est qu'illusion' (*OC*, I, 364). The only reality is that of the Unconscious, 'la Loi': 'Toi seul peut dire: Moi, | Être Unique, Éternel, immuable Substance' (*OC*, I, 364). The poet expresses a desire for absorption into this ultimate reality: 'je vais me fondre en un désir | D'anéantissement dans l'océan de l'Être' (*OC*, I, 364). But then he wakes from his reverie and dismisses this as an impossible aspiration:

> Bah! des phrases! des vers! des souvenirs de livre!...
> — Impassibles bouddhas, je vous admire fort,

> Mais je tiens à ma vie et j'ai peur de la mort,
> Mon pauvre cœur humain si haut ne peut vous suivre. (*OC*, I, 365)

In 'L'Oubli', and in *Le Sanglot* more generally, the poet cannot relinquish his attachment to his individual self, despite his desire for fusion with the underlying unity of the Unconscious.

But in *Les Complaintes* he finds a way out of this impasse. Rather than seeking the absorption of the self into the underlying unity, the poet performs his dispersal into the multiple forms of the phenomenal world. The collection is thus premised on the demise of the self as fixed, enduring essence ('En deuil d'un Moi-le-Magnifique'); as 'Complainte des Complaintes' has it, these poems are the 'Gerbes d'ailleurs d'un défunt Moi' (*OC*, I, 621), the image of the bundle recalling the 'ensemble de rapports' of Hartmann's theory of selfhood, and thereby suggesting that each poem might, perhaps, constitute a provisional self. Poetic schizogony — the emergence of a proliferation of selves — requires the death of the old, lyrical 'Moi'.

'Deeps in him'[43]

In one of the prose fragments collected under the title 'Ennuis non rimés', Laforgue imagines the miserable life of a military musician forced to 'souffler dans un trombone des danaïdes, au jardin public' (*OC*, III, 1061); he contrasts this with what he considers to be ideal states of being, for example that of 'un bluet bleu, sur une faïence de Delf[t] au dessus d'un empilement d'étoles, dans la fraîche et toujours obscure arrière-boutique d'un bric-à-brac sur les quais de la Séquane!' (*OC*, III, 1061). This reprise of the bibelotic point of view adopted in 'Complainte des pubertés difficiles' articulates the fantasy of a passive, quietistic existence, the relinquishment of the burdens of selfhood. In a similar vein, Laforgue also imagines being 'une éponge passive, un corail au fond de la mer, incrusté à la même place voir le défilé de la nature marine' (*OC*, III, 1061). Laforgue's vision of sub-aquatic existence or exploration is a common one in his *œuvre*: it connotes, variously, a retreat from the endless cycle of willing, the dissolution or dispersal of the self, and the contemplation of the hidden recesses of the mind. The underwater realm thus stands for the Unconscious both as underlying unity, and as a domain with the self. It is a realm that is intrinsically other (in its disruption of sensory and kinetic experience, its hostility to human life, and its otherworldly flora and fauna). But Laforgue also associates this realm with specifically *cultural* others, and most frequently with India. Indeed, he suggests that India — like Germany — offers privileged access to the Unconscious. This appears to recuperate the exoticism critiqued by 'Complainte des pubertés difficiles', and this section explores whether this apparent tension can be resolved. First, though, it examines the image of the underwater world and its importance for Laforgue's conception of selfhood.

Laforgue's interest in the underwater world seems to have been inspired by the Berlin aquarium, one of his favourite haunts in the city.[44] The aquarium's allure was partly due to its cloistered quality: 'c'est l'Aquarium où l'on assiste aux dessous les plus vierges, aux scènes d'intérieur les plus perdues des mondes en question' (*OC*,

II, 501). Like the bibelot-cluttered Parisian drawing room, the aquarium's tanks appealed because of the visual qualities of their contents, Laforgue revelling in the descriptive possibilities presented by this space: 'Des landes à dolmens incrustés de joailleries visqueuses', 'des cultures de truffes en velours orange', 'des aiguilles de mer s'en allant comme des rubans frivoles' (OC, II, 502). For Pierre Jourde, this represents a domestication of otherness (and again there is a parallel with the drawing room here, sub-aquatic life constituting a kind of submerged *bibeloterie*):

> Dans cet univers de l'*autre côté*, l'étrangeté se miniaturise, se réduit à des dimensions qui lui confèrent à la fois la valeur dégradée d'une ornementation [...] et permettent de l'intérioriser. L'Autre, perdant l'incertitude par où il se rattache à la profondeur, peut donc aller jusqu'à se muer en objet décoratif, et cette mutation ne va pas sans une mièvrerie vaguement ridicule.[45]

But while Jourde may be right that Laforgue's over-lavish description represents a 'mauvais goût décoratif',[46] the poet's interest in the aquarium (and in the drawing room) goes beyond a dilettantish aestheticism. He does not merely look at the aquarium's tanks, but imagines being inside them, expressing regret that he cannot be an underwater creature himself:

> vous êtes dans le sous-marin, et nous, nous desséchons de fringales supra-terrestres; voilà la différence que je voulais signaler. Et pourquoi les antennes de nos sens, nous, ne sont-elles pas bornées par le Silence et l'Opaque et l'Aveugle? [...] et que ne savons-nous aussi nous incruster dans notre petit coin pour y cuver l'ivre-mort de notre petit moi? — Voilà ce que j'avais à dire, en quittant *ce monde de satisfaits*. (OC, II, 502; author's emphasis)

In imagining the restricted sensory experience ('le Silence et l'Opaque et l'Aveugle') of these denizens of the deep, Laforgue in fact presents an experience that is the opposite of aestheticism: the visual onslaught of his descriptions, with their catalogue of bizarre colours, shapes and textures, is replaced by the image of an anaesthetized existence, an existence almost devoid of sensory stimulation. This is a retreat from suffering, from the affliction of consciousness — the 'Lèpre originelle' ('Complainte propitiatoire à l'Inconscient', OC, I, 550) — and the yearning for the metaphysical ('fringales supra-terrestres'). This vision is recapitulated in 'Salomé': 'O monde de satisfaits, vous êtes dans la béatitude aveugle et silencieuse' (OC, II, 439). But it is more than a mere longing for serenity: this is also 'l'ivre-mort de notre petit moi', the dissipation of the self.

This is, of course, reminiscent of the use of Buddhist ideas examined in the previous section, and in fact Laforgue explicitly links animal tranquillity to Buddhism in another fragment of notes inspired by the Berlin aquarium:

> À l'aquarium de Berlin — devant le regard atone, gavé, sage, bouddhique des crocodiles, des pythons (les ophites), etc. — comme je comprends ces vieilles races d'Orient qui avaient épuisé tous les sens, tous les tempéraments, toutes les métaphysiques — et qui finissaient par adorer, béatifier comme symbole du Nirvâna promis ces regards nuls dont on ne peut dire s'ils sont plus infinis qu'immuables —
> Mais l'idéal c'est ces éponges, ces astéries, ces plasmas dans le silence opaque et frais, tout au rêve, de l'eau. (OC, II, 606)

In suggesting that reptilian equanimity is trumped by the even greater quietude of sub-aquatic fauna, Laforgue hints at an endorsement of the evolutionary relationship between cultures theorized by Hartmann: the doctrines of Buddhism lead towards, but are ultimately superseded by the philosophy of the Unconscious. But in another sense, this is a highly idiosyncratic Laforguian version of Hartmann's philosophy. For Hartmann, both biological and philosophical development are characterized by a gradual increase in consciousness, a process that will culminate — he argues — in the enlightened state necessary to bring the universe to an end. But for Laforgue, this movement is reversed: rather than aspiring to an increase in consciousness, he dreams of descending the chain of being to adopt a more primitive state.

This may be a subversion of Hartmannian doctrine, but it draws on the philosopher's own work for its imagery. Hartmann makes reference to 'le monde éloigné de nous des animaux aquatiques inférieurs' (*PI*, II, 166) to illustrate the degrees of consciousness within the animal kingdom, with these primitive aquatic organisms placed at the bottom of the scale. Even infusoria (protozoa, unicellular algae, and other microorganisms) have some level of consciousness according to Hartmann, but the less complex the animal, the less it responds to external stimuli: 'Plus nous descendons l'échelle animale, plus les sensations intérieures, se rattachant à la digestion ou aux fonctions de reproduction, acquièrent d'importance en comparaison des sensations qui proviennent d'excitations extérieures' (*PI*, II, 115). For Laforgue, this idea of a near-solipsistic existence is enthralling: 'Vivre au plus bas degré de l'échelle animale –' (*OC*, III, 980), he writes in his notebooks of 1884–85. At times, he (half-jokingly) makes use of the same image when he refers in his correspondence to the boredom of his existence in Berlin: 'Moi, je m'ennuie horriblement; je vais descendre peu à peu à l'état végétatif du corail' (to Mültzer, 14 April 1882, *OC*, I, 769); 'J'entre dans une période d'apathie, c'est pourquoi je me suis payé un néologisme: je me "madréporise"' (to Théophile Ysaÿe, June 1885, *OC*, II, 766). But boredom itself is philosophical: for Schopenhauer, it is symptomatic of an absence of willing (even if it only represents a brief pause in the cycle of desire, and one that itself causes suffering). In his poetry, Laforgue's aspiration to this beatific state of will-less serenity is obvious, although he regretfully recognizes the impossibility of achieving such a state (just as he does in his writings on the Berlin aquarium): '"Si c'était à refaire, | Chers madrépores, comme on ficherait le camp | Chez vous!"' ('Gare au bord de la mer', *OC*, II, 195); 'Or, ne pouvant redevenir des madrépores, | O mes humains, consolons-nous les uns les autres' ('Complainte d'un certain Dimanche', *OC*, I, 562). Given the unfeasibility of assuming a coralline existence, mutual consolation (suggesting, perhaps, Schopenhauerian sympathy) is the only option. This is also a recognition of the impossibility of returning to the comfort of the womb: the etymology of 'madrépore' links it to motherhood;[47] similarly, Laforgue describes the underwater plants in the aquarium as 'une flore fœtale' ('L'Aquarium', *OC*, II, 502). This is something akin to Freud's concept of the 'oceanic feeling', an expression suggested to him by his friend and correspondent Romain Rolland, who described this mystical feeling as 'a sensation of "eternity", a feeling as of something limitless, unbounded';[48] for Freud, this is a relic of the breast-feeding infant's inability to distinguish between the ego and the external world.[49]

But acknowledging the unattainability of this ideal does not entail simply accepting a vision of solid, stable selfhood. In fact, the aquatic biosphere offers a model of selfhood that Laforgue accepts as a given (rather than merely aspiring to in fantasy) and that is crucial to his aesthetics. This vision is adumbrated in his description of the aquarium's residents in terms of a body unpieced into its constituent parts: 'd'éponges en débris de poumons' (*OC*, II, 501), 'de bouts de tripes égarés là', 'de moignons dont les antennes clignent au corail d'en face, de milles verrues sans but apparent' (*OC*, II, 502). This physical disassembling offers, perhaps, a crude analogue for the challenge to individual integrity that is signalled by coral: despite appearing to be a single organism, a coral is in fact a colony of individual polyps. For Laforgue, this is an intriguing and productive metaphor for selfhood:

> Oyez, au physique comme au moral,
> Ne suis qu'une colonie de cellules
> De raccroc; et ce sieur que j'intitule
> Moi, n'est, dit-on, qu'un polypier fatal!
> ('Ballade', *OC*, II, 198)

The *rejet* of 'Moi' affords it a defamiliarizing effect, isolating and emphasizing the word and thus forcing us to rethink the concept of the self. The elision of 'Je' from 'Ne suis' also focuses attention on the self as object ('Moi') by eliminating the self as subject. This is a self constituted by a random ('De raccroc') assemblage of cells, and yet one that is also somehow predestined ('fatal'), part of the grander scheme of the Unconscious.

The image of the polypary is again derived from Hartmann's work, and, as Hiddleston notes, the poem in fact adapts many elements from the chapter 'Le Concept de l'Individualité' (*PI*, II, 153–90) in *La Philosophie de l'Inconscient*.[50] Here Hartmann argues that it is erroneous to 'tracer des limites, séparer absolument l'individu de ce qui l'entoure' (*PI*, II, 157). He illustrates this point with the example of polyps, particularly those that exist in colonies, like corals; he describes this colony (or 'polypier') as a 'petite république' (*PI*, II, 165), and argues that it constitutes an individual in itself, just as much as each of its members: 'Sur un polypier, chaque animal est aussi évidemment un individu que le polypier lui-même en est un' (*PI*, II, 163). The corollary of this argument is that what we commonly think of as an individual is only arbitrarily designated thus: it is possible to think of each organ or even cell in the human body as an individual, since each manifests a certain degree of independence. (As Salomé asks (rhetorically), '*O sectaires de la conscience, pourquoi vous étiqueter individus, c'est-à-dire indivisibles?*' (*OC*, II, 444).) Indeed, it is even possible to think of atoms as individuals. This argument operates in both directions, in that stars and planets can also be considered individuals. Ultimately, then, individuality (as we normally define it) is illusory, since every apparent individual is merely part of a larger individual — except for the only *true* individual, the Unconscious.

In the nineteenth century, the metaphorical use of the polypary was often associated with a different kind of philosophical discussion, namely the place of the individual within models of national belonging.[51] The metaphor was, in fact, common from the late eighteenth century onwards. Most notably, Friedrich Schiller praises 'les États grecs, où, comme dans un organisme de l'espèce des polypes, chaque individu jouissait d'une vie indépendante mais était cependant capable, en cas de nécessité, de s'élever à l'Idée de la collectivité'.[52] In the early twentieth century, the narrator of *À la recherche du temps perdu* makes use of a similar metaphor in describing the confrontation of Germany and France in World War I: just as human bodies are made up of 'des assemblages de cellules', so 'il existe d'énormes entassements organisés d'individus qu'on appelle nations'; these nation-bodies ('le corps Allemagne et le corps France') should be seen 'à l'échelle où verraient le corps d'un homme de haute taille des infusoires dont il faudrait plus de dix mille pour remplir un cube d'un millimètre de côté.'[53] The individual is to the nation what the polyp is to the polypary, and for Proust's narrator, this national belonging necessarily implies patriotism: 'Or dans les nations, l'individu, s'il fait vraiment partie de la nation, n'est qu'une cellule de l'individu-nation.'[54] For Proust, then, being a member of a nation inevitably involves a certain effacement of individuality, as Pauline Moret-Jankus points out.[55]

Laforgue's use of the polypary metaphor to describe the 'société un peu bien mêlée' (*OC*, II, 198) within himself, rather than the collectivity of the nation, might hint at his questioning of paradigms of nationhood. Indeed, Hartmann specifically challenges nationalism in his chapter on the second stage of illusion, the chapter in which he also invokes Buddhism's challenge to individuality: 'les individus comme les nations ne sont que des rouages ou des ressorts dans le grand mécanisme de l'univers, et n'ont comme tels d'autre tâche, d'autre devoir que de travailler à l'évolution universelle, l'unique fin qu'il faille poursuivre' (*PI*, II, 451). Read through Hartmann, Laforgue's exposure of the illusion of human individuality is also, by implication, a questioning of other forms of supposed individuality (such as the nation). Indeed, his portrayal of the individual as non-unitary, as a motley assortment of cells, challenges the idea of the individual as the monadic component of the national entity, and thereby undermines the patriotic vision of a mighty national whole: for Proust, and others, the vitality of the nation-polypary relies on the solidity of each individual polyp. In this sense, Laforgue takes Bourget's argument about Decadent society a stage further: Bourget sees excessive individual autonomy as threatening societal cohesion; Laforgue extends this vision of disaggregation to the individual herself. (This splitting of the atomic individual is a procedure analogous to that effected by Laforgue's neologistic *mots-valises*, which rupture what is for Bourget the most basic element of literary style — words themselves.)

Superficially, it seems ironic that Laforgue's most explicit questioning of cohesive selfhood takes place in *Des Fleurs de bonne volonté*, given that this is the collection in which he abandons the use of personae in favour of a return to the self, as dramatized by the playfully autobiographical sketch of the opening poem:

> Mon père (un dur par timidité)
> Est mort avec un profil sévère;
> J'avais presque pas connu ma mère,

> Et donc vers vingt ans je suis resté.
> Alors, j'ai fait d'la littérature [...].
> ('Avertissement', OC, II, 147)

But these lines do not signal that Laforgue has rehabilitated some atavistic notion of stable selfhood in this collection, since he remains 'un pauvre, un pâle, un piètre individu | Qui ne croit en son Moi qu'à ses moments perdus...' ('Dimanches (*C'est l'automne...*)', OC, II, 207). Moreover, there is a logical process at work in the shift away from the use of personae: the multiplicity that was previously externalized is now seen within the self.

★ ★ ★ ★ ★

For Laforgue, as for Hartmann, the only *true* individual is the supranational Unconscious. But despite the overarching unity of the Unconscious, Laforgue conceives of certain cultures as providing privileged access to it, as we saw in Chapter 3 with the case of Germany. In 'Complainte du Sage de Paris', which acts as a kind of provisional aesthetic manifesto, it is India that is represented as the land of the Unconscious, reinforcing the notion of an affinity between Germany and India. The poem dismisses a rationalist basis to aesthetics ('Des casiers de bureau, le Beau, le Vrai, le Bien' (OC, I, 618))[56] in favour of an unconsciously-inspired process ('Rime et sois grand, la Loi reconnaîtra les siens' (OC, I, 618)). This embrace of irrationalism is associated both with the East, and with immersion in water: 'Ah! démaillotte-toi, mon enfant, de ces langes | D'Occident! va faire une pleine eau dans le Gange' (OC, I, 618). These 'langes | D'Occident' are, precisely, the aesthetic standards of 'le Beau, le Vrai, le Bien', referred to in the previous couplet. But these moralizing aesthetic strictures represent not only a shibboleth for Western thought in general; Laforgue is also rejecting the orthodoxy of his specific cultural moment.

The triad of 'Le Beau, le Bien, le Vrai' originated in the work of Plato, but was most closely associated with Cousin in the nineteenth century: his *Du vrai, du beau, et du bien* (first published in 1836 with a second edition in 1854) represented the most important exposition of his philosophy. Propounding a rationalist form of spiritualism, it posited that God was the source of the true, the beautiful and the good. Under the Second Empire, as Digeon notes, Cousinian spiritualism was dominant in academia as well as in wider society, forming 'le fond de la morale bourgeoise moyenne'.[57] Indeed, it was still dogma in the Third Republic, with Sully Prudhomme stating that 'l'essence du bien, du beau, du vrai' is 'Dieu même' in his 1876 poem 'Le Zénith'.[58] (During World War I, Jean Richepin specifically referred to (two of) these qualities to evoke 'the superiority of the luminous Mediterranean civilization to that of the half-savages of northern Europe'[59] in his 1919 poem 'Aux Latins': 'c'est à travers Rome, et venus de la Grèce, | Que nous avons l'amour, le culte et l'allégresse | De marcher vers le Bien à la clarté du Beau'.[60]) In repudiating 'le Beau, le Vrai, le Bien', Laforgue was thus denouncing not only Western rationalism in general, but also the aesthetic orthodoxy of early Third-Republic France, and in particular its theistic (and, perhaps, proto-nationalistic) underpinning.

Does the fact that this repudiation is related to a turn to the East, with India constituting an escape from the rule-governed existence of the West, imply a recuperation of the exoticist discourse that is mocked by 'Complainte des pubertés difficiles'? In his early work, Laforgue certainly fantasizes about exotic escape and adventure, and not just in relation to India:

> Non! Je veux être heureux! Je n'ai que cette vie!
> J'irai vivre, là-bas, seul, dans quelque forêt
> D'Afrique, brute épaisse, et la chair assouvie,
> J'oublierai le cerveau que les siècles m'ont fait.
> ('Étonnement', *OC*, I, 298)

The notion of exchanging Old-World cerebralism for exotic sensuality is echoed in a letter to Charles Henry of February or March 1882 (although this time without the racist overtones inherent in the image of the 'brute épaisse'): 'Si j'avais de l'argent et pas de famille, je planterais l'Europe là, pour m'en aller dans des pays fous et bariolés oublier mon cerveau' (*OC*, I, 757). Indeed, a later poem — 'Albums' from *Des Fleurs de bonne volonté* — appears to perpetuate this vision of a liberation from civilization's strictures, this time in relation to the Wild West:

> On m'a dit la vie au Far-West et les Prairies,
> Et mon sang a gémi: 'Que voilà ma patrie!...'
> Déclassé du vieux monde, être sans foi ni loi,
> *Desperado!* là-bas, je serai roi!...
> Oh! là-bas, m'y scalper de mon cerveau d'Europe!
> (*OC*, II, 186; author's emphasis)

But a full reading of 'Albums' — written some three years after the letter to Henry and more than five after 'Étonnement' — confirms his critique of exoticism. The poem's utopian vision of a more primitive, sensuous, authentic existence is undermined by the final couplet, which recognizes it to be chimerical: 'Oh! qu'ils sont beaux les feux de paille! qu'ils sont fous, | Les albums! et non incassables, mes joujoux!...' (*OC*, II, 187). The uncritically primitivist exoticism that is occasionally evident in *Le Sanglot* is, like many of the other derivative aspects of his early work, renounced in his mature *œuvre*, and this renunciation is dramatized by poems like 'Albums', which draws the reader into exotic fantasy before abruptly deflating it, thus extending the critique beyond the poet's own juvenilia to encompass exoticism in general. As Dorothy Figueira comments, exoticism is premised on the search for 'compensation in and through the exotic for experiences of alienation and emptiness that are perceived as a function of Western society and culture'; the view of the exotic that motivates this search is 'a fantasy, which is seldom if ever understood as such'.[61] But 'Albums' suggests just such a recognition of this phantasmic premise.[62]

'Albums' adopts a similar pattern to certain poems in *Les Complaintes* which set up exotic reveries before undermining them with a moment of bathos. Most notably, 'Complainte d'une Convalescence en mai' imagines travelling 'pendant un an ou deux à l'étranger' (*OC*, I, 616) before invoking 'les Indes du Rêve aux pacifiques Ganges'; but then, in the poem's final couplet, the poem returns to the banality of the convalescent's lamp-lit supper of hard-boiled egg, and the poet dismisses his fantasies using the same adjective ('fou') as in 'Albums' ('Convalescence bien folle, comme on peut voir' (*OC*, I, 616)). Of course, the phantasmic nature of this vision of India is already implicit in the formulation 'les Indes *du Rêve*'. But in 'Complainte du Sage de Paris', the next poem in the collection, there is no such critique, or even acknowledgement of the constructed nature of the reference to India. Rather, the poet's appeal to 'faire une pleine eau dans le Gange' is the prelude to a liberating journey into the Unconscious as sub-aquatic domain: this is a realm of 'gisements d'instincts, virtuels paradis' (*OC*, I, 619), a realm where libidinal energies are released, where 'La logique, la morale' are dismissed.

The description that follows is characterized by an increasingly surreal visuality:

> [...] Et les bas-fonds sous-marins,
> Infini sans foyer, forêt vierge à tous crins!
>
> Pour voir, jetez la sonde, ou plongez sous la cloche;
> Oh! les velléités, les anguilles sous roche,
>
> Les polypes sournois attendant l'hameçon,
> Les vœux sans état-civil, ni chair, ni poisson!
>
> Les guanos à Geysers, les astres en syncope,
> Et les métaux qui font loucher nos spectroscopes!
>
> Une capsule éclate, un monde de facteurs
> En prurit, s'éparpille assiéger les hauteurs;
>
> D'autres titubent sous les butins génitoires,
> Ou font un feu d'enfer dans leurs laboratoires! (*OC*, I, 619)

The paratactic sequence of nominal clauses undermines linear logic, enshrining the rejection of reason that the poet has previously preached; perplexingly composite images, such as 'pelouses des Défaillances' and 'un monde de facteurs | En prurit', underline this irrationalist principle. The denunciation of rationality is presented explicitly through the image of 'les métaux qui font loucher nos spectroscopes!', which suggests that human control through science is undone in this domain. Social rules are also irrelevant, the image of 'Les vœux sans état-civil' pointing to a non-marital erotic relationship. This recalls the couple who 'gesticulent hors la loi' in the forest of 'Solo de lune', and the forest is, indeed, directly invoked here ('forêt vierge à tous crins'). The use of the adjective 'vierge' is ironic, with the sexual aspect of the 'gisements d'instincts' that reign over this world shown by the ejaculatory images of 'Les guanos à Geysers' and 'Une capsule éclate', and, more directly, in the line 'D'autres titubent sous les butins génitoires'. Here, the wealth of sexual possibilities is underlined phonetically by the chiastically patterned alliteration in [t] and [b] of 'titubent'/ 'butins'. This alliteration also highlights the presence in both words of 'but' and thereby underscores the Hartmannian principle at work here (since for Hartmann — as for Schopenhauer — sex is the ultimate goal of all human activity).[63]

The underwater domain in 'Complainte du Sage de Paris' thus represents an alternative reality, a world freed from the strictures of rational thought and sexual restraint. It is linked to the forest in the Laforguian imaginary, as the use of the image of the 'forêt vierge' makes clear: both are spaces of otherness, defined by their revolt against the logic of civilized society. The 'forêt vierge' image also connects this passage to Laforgue's note on the Unconscious in 'L'Art moderne en Allemagne',[64] and the poem itself specifically invokes the Unconscious as a watery realm: 'L'Inconscient, c'est l'Éden-Levant que tout saigne; | Si la Terre ne veut sécher, qu'elle s'y baigne!' (*OC*, I, 619). Although the imagery here is Christian ('l'Éden-Levant'), the rejection of Occidental rationalism remains intact: 'l'Éden' suggests a state that is far removed from analytical thought, while 'Levant' again suggests the East. But if the impetus for the poem's exploration of the depths was the reference to the Ganges, does this imply that India — like the underwater realm — is seen as a domain of otherness? If so, how can this be reconciled with the critiques of exoticism's illusory nature that are voiced by poems like 'Complainte des pubertés difficiles', 'Complainte d'une Convalescence en mai' and 'Albums'?

There is, undoubtedly, a tension between these positions. But in Laforgue's thinking there was perhaps a distinction between, on the one hand, picturesque exoticism and fantasies of travel and, on the other, the idea of India as the catalyst for self-exploration and a vision of an alternative reality. Of course, this use of India is still appropriative, its culture reduced to an exotic prop for omphaloscopy. For Laforgue, the journey inward is often connected to cultural otherness: the 'pleine eau dans le Gange' preached by the poet is, after all, a dive into the self. Rather than advocating the exploration of foreign territories, the poet is calling for us to survey the uncharted lands within. But in doing so, he draws on contemporary Orientalist discourse about India as a land of spirituality and mysticism. Moreover, in a passage from his philosophical notes (dated around 1884–85) that is reminiscent of 'Complainte du Sage de Paris' in its appeal to return to 'les grandes eaux de l'Inconscient', Laforgue suggests that his vision of the Ganges is connected to nineteenth-century ideas about India as the origin of European language and culture: here it is labeled the 'Gange des ancêtres' (*OC*, III, 1159). In Laforgue's thinking, then, this is not merely an exploration of the self, but a return to the source of civilization. Similarly, in his article on Bourget, he refers to the 'cuisante et douce réinfiltration du Vieux Bouddhisme' (*OC*, III, 127). This notion of return is a key feature of Orientalism: 'One always *returned* to the Orient', comments Said, quoting Goethe's statement that 'There in purity and righteousness will I go back to the profound origins of the human race'.[65]

Goethe's reference to 'purity' suggests a view of the Orient as the source of renewal, and this was again a recurring feature of the Orientalist imaginary: 'Certain Westerners believe that the West is in a state of decline, spiritually spent, and that the East possesses some spiritual or aesthetic *élan vital*, of which they hope to partake.'[66] Such a belief is evident in the passage where Laforgue refers to the 'Gange des ancêtres': his notion of a return to the source (of self and of culture) is fused with an optimistic vision of a possible future society based on liberation from Western rationalism:

> Aujourd'hui tout préconise et tout se précipite à la culture exclusive de la Raison, de la logique, de la conscience —

> La culture bénie de l'avenir est la déculture, la mise en jachère.
> Nous allons à la dessication [sic]: squelettes de cuir, à lunettes, rationalistes, anatomiques.
> Retournons mes frères vers les grandes eaux de l'Inconscient, et mêlons ce Jourdain dont le baptême à notre front ne serait pas effacé par 'tous les parfums d'Arabie', mêlons notre Jourdain au Gange des ancêtres. (*OC*, III, 1159)

This passage indicates that it is the present state of Western culture that Laforgue rejects; but he does not hold that we can effacer our cultural heritage entirely. This heritage may not be celebrated: the quotation from *Macbeth* suggests that it marks us like the smell of blood on Lady Macbeth's hand. Rather, he aspires to a synthesis of this heritage with that of the East, a confluence that is to take place within 'les grandes eaux de l'Inconscient'. In this sense, Laforgue's vision conforms to that of Hartmann, who holds that all philosophies — both Eastern and Western — feed into his own philosophy of the Unconscious.

This passage is echoed in Salomé's *vocéro* ('*Et vous, fatals Jourdains, Ganges baptismaux, courants sidéraux, cosmogonies de Maman! lavez-nous, à l'entrée, de la tache plus ou moins originelle du Systématique*' (*OC*, II, 444)), and Walzer, citing R. Schaffner, notes that the rejection of systematism is also part of Hartmannian doctrine: 'Quand l'homme perd la possibilité de percevoir les inspirations de l'Inconscient, il perd du même coup la source de la vie, sans laquelle il serait condamné à traîner une existence uniforme dans un schématisme desséchant' (*PI*, I, 358; quoted in *OC*, II, 586 n. 5). The term 'desséchant' corresponds to 'dessication [sic]' in the passage of notes quoted above. But there is also a crucial disparity with Hartmann's thought in this passage: while Hartmann's theory of evolution towards cosmic annihilation relies on an increase in human consciousness, Laforgue envisages a future progression towards *un*consciousness: 'S'il est possible d'atténuer la conscience dans le présent, on peut l'annihiler dans l'avenir: *prévision*, *attente*, par le culte devenu habituel de la Fatalité (voir les orientaux)' (*OC*, III, 1159; author's emphasis).

In general, though, Laforgue is not concerned primarily with grandiose visions of cultural renewal. For him, ideas of cultural otherness function first and foremost as proxies for 'the other within', and this is confirmed by another fragment from his 1884–85 notes. Here, he refers to Jean-Paul Richter's idea of 'l'Afrique intérieure', which is quoted in Hartmann (*PI*, I, 29), and he links this to both the forest and undersea domains; the passage makes clear that these are all metaphors for self-exploration:

> La rage de vouloir se connaître — de plonger sous sa culture consciente vers 'l'Afrique intérieure' de notre Inconscient domaine.
> Et c'étaient des épiements pas à pas, en écartant les branches, les broussailles de taillis, sans bruit pour ne pas effaroucher ces lapins qui jouent au clair de lune, se croyant seuls.
> Je me sens si pauvre si connu tel que je me connais moi, Laforgue en relation avec le monde extérieur — Et j'ai des mines riches, des gisements, des mondes sous-marins qui fermentent inconnus — Ah! c'est là que je voudrais vivre, c'est là que je voudrais mourir. Des fleurs étranges qui tournent comme des têtes de cire de coiffeurs lentement sur leur tige, des pierreries féériques comme celles où dort Galatée de Moreau surveillée par Polyphème, des coraux heureux sans

rêves, des lianes de rubis, des floraisons subtiles où l'œil de la conscience n'a pas porté la hache et le feu –. (*OC*, III, 1158)

Laforgue accepts that the state of permanent immersion enjoyed by a sponge or starfish is unattainable (in life, at least): the 'Ah!' of 'Ah! c'est là que je voudrais vivre' signals regret for an impossible ideal.[67] But he delights in the idea of exploring the underwater other-world of his own psyche like a diver: 'Il avait enregistré quelques menues fleur[s], rapporté, plongeur, quelques menus échantillons secs' (*OC*, III, 1158). This 'descente en Moi' ('Ballade', *OC*, II, 198) may necessarily imply a return to the surface world of everyday life, with all of its suffering, but it does at least suggest that there is a realm of wonders always available as a source of inspiration.

Conclusion

There are significant tensions in the ways that Laforgue conceives of the relationship between Eastern and Western cultures. Early syncretism gives way to eclecticism, a de-hierarchized model of cultural relations; the desire for cultural fusion is replaced by a playful randomness. Laforgue espouses openness to all cultural influences, but Buddhism holds a privileged place in his thinking. Its presence in his work — both his poetry and notes — bears the traces of Schopenhauer and Hartmann, both of whom draw on Buddhist ideas to support their own doctrines. For Hartmann in particular, Buddhism is important because of its challenge to the notion of stable, persistent selfhood, and it is in this sense that Buddhist ideas are crucial to Laforgue's thought. He makes use of Buddhist references in his various challenges to traditional models of the self: through the idea of multiple selves or avatars, as encapsulated by 'Complainte des pubertés difficiles'; through the erasure of self-consciousness in the underwater world; through multiplicity *within* the self. Buddhism's importance is thus twofold: it is influential in its questioning of selfhood, and it is emblematic of openness to non-European thought. The challenge to unitary selfhood *within* Buddhist thought also implies a challenge to unitary culture through the *use* of Buddhism.

But while such a challenge undermines the idea of otherness (in two senses), and while Laforgue's work offers a number of critiques of exoticism, there are moments when he recuperates the logic of Orientalism. Most notably, his references to India (in both 'Complainte du Sage de Paris' and in his notes) suggest an exoticizing view of it as the source of self-renewal and liberation from rule-governed existence. Although there is some logical consistency here — he critiques exoticism for its 'othering' of the East, instead seeing the East as the source of the self — this is nonetheless undeniably appropriative. His fascination for the mystical and sensual potentialities offered by India is simply a revalorization of the essentialist vision that is inherent to Orientalism.

Despite this exoticizing view, Laforgue's references to the East are characterized by a refusal to indulge the picturesque elements of exoticism — except where he is openly mocking such tendencies, such as in 'Salomé'. Instead he is concerned with the spiritual elements of the East; ultimately his interest lies not in exotic adventure, which he recognizes as fantasy, but in the other within. Moreover, he conceives of the East not as the source of a restored plenitude, of a return to a lost fullness of self, but as a way of *destabilizing* the self — as a strange, troubling world. In general, nineteenth-century exoticism is 'an evasive operation', argues Chris Bongie: 'In seeking out a realm of experience beyond the confines of a modernity that denies him the possibility of self-realisation, the "exotic subject" averts his gaze from the essential hollowness of his own phantasmic subjectivity.'[68] But for Laforgue, the exotic does not provide an escape from this emptiness; rather, it allows him to accept it.

Notes to Chapter 4

1. Foucher de Careil, p. 307.
2. Staël, II, 120.
3. Ibid., II, 152.
4. Ibid., II, 152.
5. Jules Michelet, *Introduction à l'histoire universelle* (1831); quoted in Carré, p. 56.
6. Jean Raynaud, *Revue Encyclopédique* (1832), vol. 53, pp. 16–17; quoted in Carré, p. 50.
7. Foucher de Careil, p. 306.
8. Victor Hugo, *L'Année terrible* (1872); quoted in Carré, p. 60.
9. Caro, p. 25.
10. Ibid., p. 26.
11. Ibid., p. 287.
12. Said, p. 99.
13. Max Müller, *Comparative mythology: an essay* (London: Routledge, [1856]).
14. See John Henry Barrows' inaugural speech (1893): 'The solemn charge which the Parliament preaches to all true believers is a return to the primitive unity of the world.' <http://parliamentofreligions.org/parliament/chicago-1893> [accessed 27 September 2016].
15. Founded in 1875, the Theosophical Society's French members included Édouard Schuré (who published *Les Grands Initiés* in 1889) and Camille Flammarion.
16. Droit, pp. 30–31.
17. Frank E. Reynolds and Charles Hallisey, 'Buddhism: An Overview', in *The Encyclopedia of Religion*, ed. by Lindsay Jones et al, 2nd edn, 15 vols (Detroit: Macmillan Reference USA, 2005), II, 1087–1101 (p. 1089).
18. Donald S. Lopez, *Buddhism: An Introduction and Guide* (London: Penguin, 2001), p. 12.
19. Ibid., p. 13.
20. Richard King, *Orientalism and Religion: Postcolonial Theory, India and 'the mystic East'* (London: Routledge, 1999), p. 69.
21. See, in particular, Edwin Arnold, *The Light of Asia* (London: Trübner, 1879).
22. Philip C. Almond, *The British Discovery of Buddhism* (Cambridge University Press, 1988), p. 55.
23. Jules Barthélemy-Saint-Hilaire, *Le Bouddha et sa religion* (Paris: Didier, 1860), p. 78.
24. Barthélemy-Saint-Hilaire, p. 89.
25. Ibid., p. v.
26. See p. 58.
27. Bourget, p. 36; see Hibbitt, p. 87.
28. Hibbitt, p. 89.
29. Jean-Pierre Bertrand, 'Petite mythologie portative', *Vortex*, 2 (2000) <http://www.orsini.net/laforgue/vortex2/bertrand2.htm> [accessed 30 April 2011] (para. 18 of 20). Laforgue himself describes *Les Complaintes* as a whole as an 'affaire de curiosité, de chinoiserie littéraire même' (*OC*, III, 153) in his pseudonymously written review of the collection.
30. Janell Watson, *Literature and Material Culture from Balzac to Proust: The Collection and Consumption of Curiosities* (Cambridge: Cambridge University Press, 1999), p. 2.

31. Bourget, p. 318.
32. Nordau, p. 10.
33. Ibid., p. 27. As Guy Ducrey points out, ancient earthenware statuettes were discovered in Tanagra, Greece, from the 1870s, although mass-produced fakes began to emerge not long afterwards. They became staples of literary descriptions of eclectic interiors. (Guy Ducrey, 'Tanagra ou les anamorphoses d'une figurine béotienne à la fin du XIXe siècle', in *Anamorphoses décadentes: l'art de la défiguration 1880–1914; études offertes à Jean de Palacio*, ed. by Isabelle Krzywkowski and Sylvie Thorel-Cailleteau (Paris: Presses de l'Université de Paris-Sorbonne, 2002), pp. 207–24 (p. 208).)
34. Theodor W. Adorno, 'On Lyric Poetry and Society', in *Notes to Literature*, ed. by Rolf Tiedemann, trans. by Shierry Weber Nicholsen, 2 vols (New York: Columbia University Press, 1991), I, 37–54 (p. 40).
35. Ibid., p. 44.
36. Jacques Rancière, 'The Politics of Literature', *SubStance*, 103, 33.1 (2004), 10–24 (p. 19).
37. Ibid., p. 23.
38. Stéphane Mallarmé, 'Ses purs ongles très haut...', *Poésies* (Paris: Gallimard, 1992), p. 59.
39. Bertrand (2000), (para. 16 of 20).
40. Rancière, p. 19.
41. See p. 68.
42. See, for example, 'Étonnement' (*OC*, I, 298).
43. Ezra Pound, *The Cantos*, 4th edn (London: Faber and Faber, 1987), 'CXVI', p. 810.
44. See Lefrère, p. 228.
45. Pierre Jourde, *L'Alcool du silence. Sur la décadence* (Paris: Champion, 1994), p. 164; author's emphasis.
46. Ibid., p. 164.
47. Pierre Loubier, *Jules Laforgue: l'Orgue juvénile* (Paris: Éditions Seli Arslan, 2000), p. 126.
48. Sigmund Freud, *Civilisation and its discontents*, trans. by Joan Riviere, 2nd edn, rev. by James Strachey (London: The Hogarth Press and the Institute of Psychoanalysis, 1963), p. 1.
49. Ibid., pp. 3–4.
50. J. A. Hiddleston, 'Dans l'intertexte laforguien: Hartmann et quelques autres', *Romantisme*, 19, no. 64 (1989), 47–52 (p. 49).
51. Judith Schlanger, *Les métaphores de l'organisme* (Paris: Vrin, 1971), pp. 71–77.
52. Friedrich Schiller, *Lettres sur l'éducation esthétique de l'homme (Briefe über die ästhetische Erziehung des Menschen)*, trans. by Robert Leroux (Paris: Aubier, 1943 [1794]), p. 107; quoted in Schlanger, p. 73.
53. Marcel Proust, *À la recherche du temps perdu*, 4 vols (Paris: Gallimard, 1987–89), IV, 350; quoted in Pauline Moret-Jankus, *Race et imaginaire biologique chez Proust* (Paris: Classiques Garnier, 2016), p. 144.
54. Proust, IV, 352; quoted in Moret-Jankus, p. 144.
55. Moret-Jankus, pp. 144–48.
56. See also 'Nobles et touchantes divagations sous la Lune': 'Trinité de Molochs, le Vrai, le Beau, le Bien' (*OC*, II, 108).
57. Digeon, p. 35.
58. Sully Prudhomme, 'Le Zénith', *Poésies de Sully Prudhomme* (Paris: Lemerre, [1879]), p. 260.
59. Howard Sutton, *The Life and Work of Jean Richepin* (Geneva: Droz, 1961), p. 140.
60. Jean Richepin, 'Aux Latins', *Poèmes durant la guerre (1914–1918)* (Paris: Flammarion, 1919), pp. 38–39; quoted in Sutton, p. 140.
61. Dorothy M. Figueira, *The Exotic: A Decadent Quest* (Albany: State University of New York Press, 1994), p. 12.
62. His critique of exoticism is reinforced by 'Salomé', which offers an example of how 'exotic writing often tends towards its own subversion in a *parody of exotic cliché*' (Jennifer Yee, *Exotic Subversions in Nineteenth-Century French Fiction* (Leeds: Legenda, 2008), p. 12; author's emphasis).
63. See Pan's punning on 'but' in 'Pan et la syrinx' (*OC*, II, 453).

64. See p. 84.
65. Said, p. 167; author's emphasis.
66. Figueira, p. 14.
67. Scott (1986), pp. 167–68.
68. Chris Bongie, *Exotic Memories: Literature, Colonialism, and the Fin de siècle* (Stanford: Stanford University Press, 1991), p. 10.

CHAPTER 5

The Eastern Other (2): Nothingness

In 'Climat, faune et flore de la Lune', one of the longest pieces from Laforgue's second published collection *L'Imitation de Notre-Dame la Lune*, the poet imagines a phantasmagorical lunar biosphere, presenting a litany of otherworldly landscapes and lifeforms that includes 'Étangs aveugles, lacs ophtalmiques, fontaines | De Léthé, cendres d'air, déserts de porcelaine' (*OC*, II, 78), 'paons blancs cabrés en aurores de prismes', and 'gélatines d'hippopotames en pâles | Flottaisons de troupeaux éclaireurs d'encéphales' (*OC*, II, 79). This logopoeic revel is reminiscent of Laforgue's descriptions of the underwater realm, which exude a similar delight in lexical play. Indeed, the moon's flora is directly compared to sub-aquatic organisms: 'Forêts de cierges massifs, parcs de polypiers, | Palmiers de corail blanc aux résines d'acier!' (*OC*, II, 79). The similarities go further: the lunar and undersea domains are both oneiric and timeless, representing an escape not just from the everyday world but also from the self. If there is a paradox implicit in Laforgue's account of underwater experience — this is a domain teeming with life, and yet it entails a kind of death of self — then the equivalent paradox is made explicit in 'Climat, faune et flore de la Lune': while this is an exuberantly vital world, it is also 'un miroir mort', a 'Radeau du Nihil' where 'Tout a l'air émané d'un même acte de foi | Au Néant Quotidien sans comment ni pourquoi!' (*OC*, II, 79). The concluding couplet of the poem, which states that 'c'est là qu'on en revient encore | Et toujours, quand on a compris le Madrépore' (*OC*, II, 79), reinforces the parallel between the two domains. It also suggests the same constitutive absence at the heart of profusion that is evident in the aquarium and the bourgeois drawing room:[1] once you have understood the fragmented nature of selfhood, the poem implies, you must recognize that the self (as fixed, enduring entity) is void.

Laforgue's writings, both published and private, return again and again to the idea of nothingness. This idea is consistently associated with Buddhism, and most often with the concept of nirvana. Again Laforgue's interpretations draw on his philosophical reading: in Schopenhauer and Hartmann's engagement with Buddhist thought, the idea of nirvana plays an important role, and its importance was heightened by the contemporary reception of the two philosophers in France, which placed considerable emphasis on their references to nirvana. In this sense, the French critics drew on the controversy surrounding Buddhism in the late nineteenth century, when the prevailing view cast the religion as fundamentally alien to the European mind because of its supposed worship of the void. In the European imaginary, Buddhism became 'un culte du néant', in the words of Cousin.[2] This 'néant' was understood variously as psychological, ethical, or ontological, but whatever the interpretation, it was deemed to be a profound threat to Western identity. For Laforgue, on the other hand, the idea of an escape from suffering through nirvana was intriguing, even if his attitude towards this possibility was subject to considerable ambivalence.

'La délivrance par l'anéantissement'[3]

The uncertainty surrounding the meaning of 'nirvana' for European critics was understandable. Despite being central to Buddhist doctrine, 'nirvana' — commonly understood as 'enlightenment' — has always been subject to contestation between the different Buddhist traditions:

> Some would claim that enlightenment requires the accumulation of merit over many lifetimes. Others would claim that enlightenment is possible in this very lifetime. Some would claim that enlightenment is a gradual process of purifying the mind of defilements. Others would claim that we are already enlightened, and simply need to recognize it.[4]

The difficulty of defining nirvana is compounded by the fact that those who claim to have experienced it 'stress its "otherness", placing it beyond all limited concepts and ordinary categories of thought':[5] it cannot be expressed in words. However, one thing that most, if not all, definitions of nirvana have in common is the idea of a release from desire. A frequently cited explanation of nirvana states, for example, that it is 'the complete cessation of craving (thirst), letting it go, renouncing it, being free from it, detachment from it'.[6] This description is essentially negative: it does not say what nirvana *is*, but what it brings to an end. Indeed, this negativity is implicit in the etymology of the term 'nirvana' itself, since it literally means 'blowing out', as of a flame. But as Moira Nicholls points out in a paraphrase of W. Sri Rahula,

> the use of such negative terms has given rise to the flawed idea that Nirvana itself is negative, expressing self-annihilation. He stresses that Nirvana is definitely no annihilation of self because there is no self to annihilate. Rather, if anything is annihilated, it is the illusion that such a self exists.[7]

In one interpretation of nirvana, then, enlightenment involves a psychological process: a profound change in attitude, a recognition of the non-substantiality of the self (the idea of 'no-self'). What is blown out, in this sense, is both craving and the ignorance that fuels this craving, and which in turn produces suffering. But this world of suffering is also characterized by the cycle of rebirth, and nirvana can equally be understood as the 'extinction [...] of what can be reborn, that is, as the dissolution of any continuing personal identity after death'.[8] There is thus a profound ambiguity in interpretations of nirvana: while it might be constituted by a *psychological* shift, it might also involve accession to a different *ontological* state, to 'a permanent state of bliss beyond the world of birth, death and rebirth'.[9] Some definitions of nirvana embrace this ambiguity by adopting a distinction between 'nirvana with remainder', an enlightenment that is attainable during a person's lifetime, and 'nirvana without remainder', which can only be achieved upon death.

Such complexities were elided by much of the nineteenth-century European scholarship on Buddhism. There was, however, some awareness of the different possible levels on which the extinction enacted by nirvana might operate, even if these levels were often conflated within the vague notion of 'anéantissement'. Nirvana was taken to be equivalent to a psychological, ethical, or ontological void:[10] an absence of hope or willpower, leading to a refusal of life itself; an absence of determined values or meanings; an absence of being, with the phenomena of superficial experience concealing an underlying emptiness. God and the soul were thus also absent. At worst, then, Buddhism was a kind of death cult; at best, it was a religion that promoted apathy. What united these different interpretations was the idea of Buddhism as 'un culte du néant';[11] almost all European scholars of Buddhism 'ont en commun d'avoir, plus ou moins, rapproché *nirvâna* et anéantissement, d'avoir considéré le bouddhisme comme un nihilisme, dont il fallait avoir peur ou d'autant plus attirant qu'il faisait peur'.[12] This irrevocable association between Buddhism and nothingness in the European imaginary owed much to the work of the leading European scholar of Buddhism, Eugène Burnouf. As 'Europe's acknowledged master of Sanskrit and Pali',[13] Burnouf spent much of his life translating and analysing the Buddhist texts that had been acquired by British civil servants under the Raj. His general introduction to Buddhism, *Introduction à l'histoire du buddhisme indien* (1844),[14] was the first major work on Buddhism in Europe and the benchmark for Buddhist studies throughout the nineteenth century. Until Burnouf, 'on en restait aux conjectures et déductions'.[15] In keeping with this scholarly rigour, he is cautious about defining nirvana, acknowledging that it is 'le terme qui revient le plus souvent dans les textes, le terme le plus important de tous' and that it is therefore 'celui que nous devons avoir le plus de peine à expliquer'.[16] Nonetheless, he consistently renders it as 'l'anéantissement complet',[17] signifying the annihilation of the self. Despite his circumspection, then, Burnouf was seen by most subsequent scholars as giving an erudite stamp of approval to the view of Buddhism as the religion of the void.[18]

In the 1850s, Catholic thinkers such as Antoine-Frédéric Ozanam lambasted the supposed nihilism of Buddhism, portraying it as barbarous and diabolical. Cousin was also horrified by 'cette déplorable idée de l'anéantissement qui fait le fond du bouddhisme',[19] and his condemnation influenced that of his close friend Saint-Hilaire, who portrays Buddhism as a nihilistic and hence monstrous religion in his 1860 work *Le Bouddha et sa religion*. Buddhism is particularly abhorrent, argues Barthélemy-Saint-Hilaire, because it lacks the concept of God, a concept it was thought possible to find 'jusque dans la grossièreté brutale des peuplades les plus sauvages.'[20] Such atheism can perhaps be explained by a fundamental difference in human nature:

> on peut demander si l'intelligence de ces peuples est faite comme la nôtre; et si dans ces climats où la vie est en horreur et où l'on adore le néant à la place de Dieu, la nature humaine est bien encore celle que nous sentons en nous.[21]

This ultra-Orientalist conclusion is at the heart of Barthélemy-Saint-Hilaire's interpretation of Buddhism. But while he establishes a clear demarcation between East and West at the most fundamental level, Barthélemy-Saint-Hilaire also laments the breaching of this boundary: 'Le malheur des temps veut que parmi nous les doctrines qui sont le fond du Bouddhisme retrouvent une faveur singulière, dont cependant elles sont si peu dignes.'[22] For Nordau, writing later in the century, the phenomenon of Western Buddhism was attributable to mental degeneracy:

> The degenerate who shuns action, and is without will-power, has no suspicion that his incapacity for action is a consequence of his inherited deficiency of brain [...]. In order to justify himself in his own eyes, he constructs a philosophy of renunciation and of contempt for the world and men, asserts that he has convinced himself of the excellence of Quietism, calls himself with consummate self-consciousness a Buddhist, and praises Nirvana in poetically eloquent phrases as the highest and worthiest ideal of the human mind. The degenerate and insane are the predestined disciples of Schopenhauer and Hartmann, and need only to acquire a knowledge of Buddhism to become converts to it.[23]

While for Barthélemy-Saint-Hilaire, Buddhism is an external other, threatening Europe from without, for Nordau it is relegated to the realm of the insane, an other within the bounds of Western culture. Despite the attempts of some European scholars to draw comparisons between Christianity and Buddhism (see Chapter 4), certain aspects of Buddhist thought proved resistant to assimilation. In particular, the European interpretation of nirvana as equivalent to self-annihilation engendered a discourse of ineradicable otherness.

★ ★ ★ ★ ★

Nordau was right to associate Schopenhauer and Hartmann with Buddhism, even if he draws the link through a specious diagnosis of mental illness: as we saw in Chapter 4, both philosophers draw on Buddhist thought to support their own ideas. As well as using Buddhism to bolster their monist metaphysics and pessimistic worldviews,[24] Schopenhauer and Hartmann both refer to the idea of nirvana when they theorize the end of the world. In his eschatology, which envisions the complete annihilation of the universe, Hartmann states that according to 'la doctrine bouddhique du Nirwana [sic]' there will be no state of benediction after the end of the world but simply 'le néant' (*PI*, II, 449). Bourdeau quotes a similar statement by Schopenhauer:

> Dans le bouddhisme, le monde naît par suite d'un trouble inexplicable, se produisant après un long repos dans cette clarté du ciel, dans cette béatitude sereine, appelée *Nirvana* qui sera reconquise par la pénitence.[25]

In fact, this is a mis-reading of nirvana, even within the spectrum of possible interpretations: Buddhist thought does not, in general, concern itself with eschatology, and on the rare occasions when it does, the idea of nirvana is not involved. Schopenhauer's above-quoted statement differs, in fact, from his interpretation of nirvana in *The World as Will and Representation*, where he refers to it as the extinction of the self (*WWR*, II, 508) and escape from the cycle of rebirth (*WWR*, I, 356). (Of course, Laforgue would not have been aware of these references, since he was not able to read *The World as Will and Representation*.) Schopenhauer's vision (as quoted by Bourdeau) also differs from Hartmann's, in that he asserts that nirvana will be achieved 'par la pénitence'. As we saw in Chapter 2, there is a crucial disparity between the two philosophers' ethical teachings, Schopenhauer advocating asceticism and Hartmann the acceptance of the life-process, and hence procreation. Schopenhauer's argument for the renunciation of bodily satisfaction draws on both Hinduism and Buddhism (*WWR*, I, 383 and 387) (although elsewhere he distinguishes between Hinduism, which preaches a 'strict and excessive asceticism', and Buddhism, which merely advocates 'celibacy, voluntary poverty, humility' and so on (*WWR*, II, 607)[26]. But Hartmann rejects the idea of self-denial ('le salut futur du monde ne s'obtiendra point par le renoncement, mais par le dévouement à la vie' (*PI*, II, 452)) and criticizes Schopenhauer for having adopted 'l'ascétisme suranné du bouddhisme' (*PI*, II, 453).

It is perhaps for this reason that French critics tend to insist on Schopenhauer's affinities with Buddhism much more strongly than they do for Hartmann. They even label Schopenhauer a Buddhist: he is 'Un Bouddhiste contemporain en Allemagne',[27] 'un bouddhiste égaré en Occident',[28] and an 'interprète exact de la pensée de Çakya-Mouni'.[29] By contrast, Hartmann's Indian sympathies are rarely foregrounded. Many of Schopenhauer's critics associate his principle of asceticism with Buddhism,[30] and this association no doubt served to intensify the controversy of this principle. Some extrapolate from the above-quoted statement from Bourdeau's collection, reinforcing the (spurious) link between nirvana and celibacy ('la pénitence'). Ribot refers to St. Augustine's statement that 'le mariage supprimé, la Cité de Dieu sera plus tôt remplie' before connecting this to Schopenhauer's supposedly Buddhistic promotion of chastity: 'Cette Cité de Dieu est ce que Schopenhauer appelle, faute d'un terme plus convenable, le nirvâna.'[31] Janet, likewise, links the Schopenhauerian idea of saving the world through sexual abstinence (an idea foregrounded by Challemel-Lacour) to the concept of nirvana: 'Voilà le célèbre *nirvana* dont on a tant parlé, et que Schopenhauer a emprunté au bouddhisme: il consiste en définitive dans la suppression du mariage.'[32] In broad terms, then, Buddhism's threatening 'otherness' was deployed to reinforce the perception that Schopenhauerian thought was a contaminating force within France because it undermined the institution of marriage, and hence national regeneration through demographic growth.[33]

If such associations suggest in oblique fashion the threat posed by Schopenhauerian thought, other critics make the danger of his Buddhistic philosophy more explicit. For Ribot, Schopenhauer's pessimism, if taken at face value, 'aurait le danger d'introduire chez nous le nirvâna bouddhiste, l'ataraxie complète de l'Orient';[34] that is, nirvana (interpreted psychologically as a state of tranquillity or *ataraxia*) would lead, he implies, to the complete relinquishment of willing, to apathy, and thus to the undermining of progress. Caro, too, warns against the threat posed by nirvana: 'Le nirvana ne lâche pas sa proie,' he states.[35] He also echoes the notion of an ontological divide between East and West that is hinted at by Ribot's use of the phrase 'chez nous', referring to the possibility that 'l'humanité civilisée s'abandonne à la mortelle séduction de ces conseillers du désespoir et du néant'.[36] Even if he seeks to minimize this possibility, the reference to 'l'humanité civilisée' reiterates Orientalist ideas of a fundamental, irrevocable binary between Western civilization and Eastern barbarism. For Foucher de Careil, it is Schopenhauer's elision of this boundary that is most troubling. He dismisses the philosopher's assimilation of Christianity's 'culte de la douleur'[37] to 'le nirvana indien':[38] Christian resignation, based on faith, hope and charity, has nothing to do with 'la torpeur du fakir ou l'engourdissement du Nirvana'.[39] Going beyond this psychological interpretation of nirvana, Foucher de Careil states that it is 'une extinction graduée, une cessation mystique ou savante de notre individualité, de nos facultés, de notre être enfin'[40] — that is, a threat to our very being. In short, Buddhistic quietism represents 'un véritable choléra de l'âme'.[41]

As we saw in Chapter 1, the metaphor of cholera is highly significant. O'Connor points out that victims of cholera 'absolutely disintegrated, their bodies dissolving so thoroughly into dead matter that their corpses bore little resemblance to the people that had once animated them';[42] Foucher de Careil implicitly compares this bodily obliteration to nirvana's supposed annihilation of the soul. But cholera also 'framed a horror story of *national* annihilation' (my emphasis), exposing 'the sheer fragility of white, Western identity'[43] and providing 'a figure for the threatening fluidity of cultural and bodily boundaries in an imperialist world economy':[44] for Foucher de Careil, Schopenhauer's insistence on this fluidity, on the interconnectedness of Eastern and Western ideas, is just as threatening as the ideas themselves. This is reiterated by his indignant statement that Schopenhauer only turns to European ideas 'pour aller chercher dans des hérésies décriées je ne sais quel souffle de mort venu de l'Orient bouddhiste',[45] the metaphor of the 'souffle de mort' recapitulating the miasmatic imagery examined in Chapter 1. Caro, too, makes use of imagery of disease in his description of how the idea of nirvana has been disseminated in Asia: 'cette folie métaphysique, cette ivresse de la mort, cette poursuite passionnée du non-être' has been spread amongst Eastern peoples 'par une sorte de contagion irrésistible'.[46] But he also uses the metaphor of intoxication when he remarks how strange it is that millions of Asians 'boivent à longs traits l'opium de ces fatales doctrines qui énervent et endorment la volonté'.[47] Just as cholera was believed to have originated in Asia, so opium too was primarily associated with the East in the nineteenth century (despite having been used medicinally in Europe for many centuries);[48] moreover, like cholera, opium was perceived as a threat to the nation itself:

> opiates were poisonous to the body not only of he who indulged in them but of the entire nation, whose very existence, in France, was understood to depend on the civic engagement of loyal republican citizens — a devotion that was seen as incompatible with opiate use.[49]

Indeed, opium also matched cholera's undermining of racial identity: it was seen to have 'Orientalizing' effects both mentally (leading to the supposedly Oriental qualities of placidity and indolence) and physically (with some commentators suggesting that opium use led to the user's facial features becoming more 'Eastern').[50] Buddhist ideas — and particularly the idea of nirvana — were thus seen to have contaminating effects on European bodies and minds, like cholera and opium; and this contamination was not merely a temporary infection or intoxication, but one that could fundamentally alter personal and ethnic identity, and thus the integrity of the nation itself.

Buddhism was, then, portrayed as radically other, as a threatening, contaminating force; and by associating it with Schopenhauer, critics sought to reinforce the perceived danger of his philosophy. For Laforgue, however, Buddhist ideas were fascinating, offering a possible way out of suffering. He interprets the concept of nirvana in various ways, reflecting his philosophical reading: as a state of tranquillity; as the erasure of the self; as the void at the end of the world, which will be brought about by sexual abstinence. But the allure of self-annihilation (whether that means simply the eradication of thought, or of the self altogether) is tempered by the knowledge that it may not be possible, or even beneficial.

'Vie ou Néant! choisir.'

In Laforgue's notes, there is a consistent association between nirvana and nothingness. In a fragment from his early (1881–82) notes, he describes 'Le Nirwana [sic]' as 'ni rien, ni absence de rien, le pur rien, rien' (*OC*, III, 1134), a definition that — as Hannoosh notes (*OC*, III, 1334 n. 3) — is derived from the work of Caro.[51] For Caro, nirvana is essentially a psychological void, but Laforgue also associates nirvana with asceticism, following his reading of Schopenhauer's other critics. As we saw in Chapter 2, Laforgue is fascinated by the possibility of self-denial, and the idea continues to emerge even after he has renounced the practice; in a crucial passage of his later notes, though, he seems to reject 'le néant' in favour of 'la vie' (signifying the life process and hence procreation). However, vacillation between these two poles persists: the dilemma is not resolved quite so emphatically as it may first appear.

Laforgue's association of Buddhism with ascetic practices is evident in his furious critique of Schopenhauer's (alleged) hypocrisy, where he argues that the philosopher '[n'a] rien du Bouddha sublime de la grande mansuétude, de l'ascétisme' (*OC*, III, 1137). Moreover, like some of Schopenhauer's French critics, he suggests that there is a link between nirvana and asceticism: 'Le nirvâna prêché par Bouddha n'est que le privilège d'initiés ascétiques' (*OC*, III, 1131). In establishing the link, he thus also acknowledges the difficulty of achieving the Buddhist solution to human suffering. He even suggests that Buddhist quietism — another form of the relinquishment of willing — is impossible in the West: 'l'indifférence suprême à tout [...] n'est possible malheureusement que dans le climat énervant de l'Inde' (*OC*, III, 1134). While there is an affinity here with Barthélemy-Saint-Hilaire's reference to 'ces climats où la vie est en horreur et où l'on adore le néant à la place de Dieu', for Laforgue there is a sense of regret at the unattainability of Buddhist devotion, in contrast to Barthélemy-Saint-Hilaire's sense of revulsion. Nonetheless, Laforgue suggests a view of Buddhism as 'other', despite his positive valorization of it.

Laforgue may view Buddhist asceticism as unattainable, but the interrelated ideas of nirvana (as nothingness) and asceticism remain important to his work as philosophical if not practical possibilities. In a crucial fragment of his notes, thought to have been written in 1884–85, he presents a dichotomy that is of central importance to his thinking, both ethically and aesthetically; this is a dichotomy between the Buddhistic renunciation advocated by Schopenhauer and the acceptance of the world process (and hence sexuality) advocated by Hartmann:

> En fait de religion, de vie organisée, systématique, il n'y a de choix qu'entre deux — ou bien vous voulez le néant, le repos — ou la vie. Le Repos — ou la bataille, aveugle substratum du Progrès indéfini sans but ni sanction, par la vertu de la Sélection naturelle. Si votre religion est le néant, la voie est toute tracée, — nirvanâ [sic] — opium de la marmotte — suicide — Platon Karataïeff —
> Si votre religion veut la vie — elle doit avant tout prendre son centre, sa clef, sa lumière dans ce qui est l'essence de la vie, de sa continuation — etc: l'amour des sexes.
> Or l'amour est chose inconsciente, universellement imprévue et inenregistrable en tragique, seconde-vue etc. Donc laissez le faire, laissez le passer — l'Amour Inconscient souffle où il veut 'Aimez et laissez faire le reste'. (OC, III, 1165)

While neither Schopenhauer nor Hartmann is mentioned by name, the choice between the Buddhist 'néant' of 'nirvanâ [sic]' on the one hand and 'la vie'/ 'l'amour des sexes' on the other reflects the ethical dichotomy between the two philosophers. The 'néant' option is implicitly associated with asceticism through its opposition to 'la vie' as sexual love; it is also associated with quietism ('le repos'). Its foreignness is suggested not only by the reference to nirvana, but also by the mentions of opium (which again implies a state of quietistic withdrawal) and Platon Karataev, a character from *War and Peace*.[52] The fragment seems to confirm the rejection of nirvana (and, by implication, 'l'ascétisme suranné du bouddhisme'). But it also implies that several years after the first mentions of Buddhism in his notes, he still considered Buddhist ideas worthy of serious philosophical consideration; indeed the idea of nirvana as 'le néant' — variously understood — continues to occupy a crucial role in his aesthetics.

Moreover, the apparent endorsement of Hartmannian ethics in this fragment must be nuanced, since Laforgue does not dogmatically accept the philosopher's call to embrace the life process (as we saw in Chapter 2).[53] Rather, he envisages a utopian condition in which sex is purely for pleasure, and is not restricted by the normative framework of marriage and reproductive teleology (with its concomitant taint of nationalism). Indeed, the provisional aesthetic manifesto of 'Complainte du Sage de Paris' suggests that liberated sexuality is a potential source of poetic creation. The poem endorses the idea of love inspired by the Unconscious that is propounded in the 'vie/néant' passage: 'Donc laissez le faire, laissez le passer — l'Amour Inconscient souffle où il veut "Aimez et laissez faire le reste"' (OC, III, 1165). 'Complainte du Sage de Paris' echoes this statement, firstly through an epigraph (later removed by Laforgue) that uses the same quotation from St. Augustine as above: 'Aimez, et laissez faire le reste' (OC, I, 620). In fact, the first part of the above statement is also repeated in the poem: 'Allez! laissez passer, laissez faire; l'Amour |

Reconnaîtra les siens [...]' (*OC*, I, 619). Within the poem itself these lines are linked to the notion that poetry is directed by the Unconscious, 'la Loi': 'Rime et sois grand, la Loi reconnaîtra les siens' (*OC*, I, 618). The poem thus suggests that there is some connection between sexual love and the writing of poetry, both of which are inspired by the Unconscious.

Indeed, the opening of the poem implies that it is *through* the sexual instinct that the Unconscious inspires creative expression.[54] The first line — 'Aimer, uniquement, ces jupes éphémères?' — seems to dismiss love, 'jupes' functioning metonymically. But while the transitory nature of his relationships with women precludes emotional attachment, sex is a different matter: 'leurs jardins d'un jour' — a euphemism for female genitalia — allow the poet to experience 'Les trucs Inconscients' by way of 'les rites réciproques' (the variant 'rites sexciproques' (*OC*, I, 620) making (too?) clear the implication here). That is, the experience of sex offers an insight into the ruse played by the Unconscious. While the poem also considers the possibility of sampling the Unconscious 'en pontifiant, avec toute ta foi | D'Exécuteur d'hautes-œuvres de la Loi', the turgid verbosity of this proposition renders it deliberately unappealing. It is, rather, 'en vivisectant ces claviers anonymes' — vivisection implying sexual penetration[55] — that the poet will experience the Unconscious. He associates sexual desire with the appetite for food: 'Déguster [...] | Les trucs Inconscients dans leur œuf, à la coque'; this association is reprised in a stanza where sexuality is also linked to creativity:

> Mais quoi, leurs yeux sont tout! et puis la nappe est mise,
> Et l'Orgue juvénile à l'aveugle improvise. (*OC*, I, 618)

Desire ('leurs yeux sont tout!') leads to the sexual encounter, 'la nappe' suggesting a bedsheet as well as a tablecloth;[56] indeed, it also figures the blank page on which poetry is written. The connection to creative expression is made clear by the following line, 'l'Orgue juvénile à l'aveugle improvise', the reference to improvisation implying a meta-poetic statement. This implication is reinforced by the phonetic echo of 'Jules Laforgue' in 'l'Orgue juvénile': the poet is (subtly) inscribing his aesthetic credo.[57]

The poem thus suggests that sexual desire is the driving force of the poet's work. This is, again, a subversion of Hartmannian aesthetics: while sex is the foremost manifestation of the Unconscious, and while the Unconscious is also the source of artistic inspiration, it is Laforgue who combines these arguments. It is also, as we have seen, a subversion of Hartmann's ethics, which call for the acceptance of sexuality not for its own sake (for pleasure) but solely for the purposes of procreation. This idea is alluded to in the poem in references that suggest the rejection of marriage ('sans noce', 'les vœux sans état-civil'); for Hartmann, casual, extra-marital sex is a betrayal of our instincts, and thus of the life process itself:

> la vie commune des époux dans le mariage est [...] chez l'homme une institution de l'instinct et non de la réflexion. [...] La résolution de ne cultiver que des amours passagères en dehors du mariage doit être regardée comme contraire à l'instinct, et comme un calcul de l'égoïsme. (*PI*, I, 248)

Laforgue's refusal of this aspect of Hartmann's philosophy is made clear in a passage from his notes which is linked to 'Complainte du Sage de Paris' through its use of the same expression, 'déguster... dans l'œuf, à la coque':

> Elle est belle en soi! je vais m'y ruer!
> Elle est le prototype de mon rêve! De celui qui naîtra de nous! Mais il restera tantale virtuel dans les Limbes des latences — il ne naîtra pas! et je détournerai dans mon impiété au-dessus des dieux et de l'univers pour mon spleen insatiable de ses fins divines cette fleur en trésor au calice merveilleusement aménagé. Tout pour moi.
> J'y dégusterai les plans de la nature dans l'œuf, et à la coque. Jusqu'à épuisement. Puis l'œuvre consommé j'irai me promener sur les boulevards les pouces aux entournures de mon gilet! (OC, III, 386)

Drawing on Schopenhauer's idea[58] that sexual attraction to a particular person is a manifestation of the will of the child who would be born from that union ('celui qui naîtra de nous'), the poet suggests he will subvert this process ('il ne naîtra pas'). He recognizes that this approach represents, in Hartmann's words, 'un calcul de l'égoïsme' — 'je détournerai dans mon impiété [...] de ses fins divines cette fleur en trésor au calice merveilleusement aménagé. Tout pour moi' — but is unapologetic. The link between this passage and 'Complainte du Sage de Paris' reinforces the idea that Laforgue conceives of his poetry as inspired by a liberated, uninstrumentalized sexual energy. In the context of the passage that dichotomizes 'la vie' and 'le néant', the poem suggests that creativity belongs firmly on the side of 'la vie'.

But 'Complainte du Sage de Paris' is by no means a definitive aesthetic manifesto. Moreover, there are significant tensions in Laforgue's attitude towards sex throughout his *œuvre*, it being characterized by both celebration and disapprobation, acceptance and doubt, joy and suffering. As such, the possibility of a release from the torments of sexuality through the denial of desire remains enticing: the choice between 'vie' and 'néant' is never definitively resolved. This choice is framed explicitly in another of *Les Complaintes*, 'Complainte des Voix sous le Figuier boudhique', a poem that was for Laforgue 'la plus importante (significative) en un sens du volume' (letter to Léon Vanier, 2 March 1885, OC, II, 740). Here, as in the passage examined above, Buddhism is presented as ethically opposite to the acceptance of sexuality. Firstly, 'Les Communiantes', having expressed the stirrings of sexual desire in comically euphemistic terms, appeal for the Buddha ('Çakya') to quell their concupiscence:

> Des ramiers
> Familiers
> Sous nos jupes palpitent!
> Doux Çakya, venez vite
> Les faire prisonniers! (OC, I, 554)

Similarly, the poem ends with a stanza (uttered by 'Le Figuier' itself) in which Buddhism is presented as an escape from the helter-skelter of sexual desire:

> Pauvres fous, vraiment pauvres fous!
> Puis, quand on a fait la crapule,
> On revient geindre au crépuscule,

> Roulant son front dans les genoux
> Des Saintes boudhiques Nounous. (*OC*, I, 554)

This opposition between sex and Buddhism is related to the dichotomy presented by 'Les Jeunes Gens' in the poem:

> — Vie ou Néant! choisir. Ah! quelle discipline! (*OC*, I, 554)

In the context of the passage of notes that presents the same dichotomy, it is clear that the opposition between sexuality ('l'amour des sexes') and Buddhism ('nirvanâ [sic]') maps onto the 'Vie ou Néant' choice. While the choice seems to be resolved (in favour of 'la vie') in these notes, 'Complainte des Voix sous le Figuier boudhique' suggests that there is no easy response to the dilemma. In fact, throughout Laforgue's work, he is torn between these two positions: 'vie' and 'néant', sex and self-denial, companionship and solitude.

The importance of this choice is reinforced by a consideration of the poem's intertext: it parodies 'Adieux' by Sully-Prudhomme,[59] a poem in which the bind of marriage is presented as inescapable. In this poem, 'Les Jeunes Gens' lament that their female childhood friends are all being married off, but ultimately tell them to go ahead and 'Mariez-vous', since 'on vous promet des hommes | D'un prospère foyer protecteurs économes'; 'Les Jeunes Filles', meanwhile, instruct their male friends to become good potential husbands:

> Luttez pour devenir plus tôt
> Des fiancés comme on les aime
> Et des hommes comme il en faut.[60]

Laforgue's parody presents an alternative to this vision of foreclosed gender roles and the inevitable normalization of sexuality within marriage: sexual desire can, perhaps, be cheated through Buddhistic renunciation.

But the poem also raises the possibility of circumventing this dilemma altogether. Having lamented the choice they are forced to make ('quelle discipline!'), 'Les Jeunes Gens' ask — rhetorically — whether there is not 'un Éden entre ces deux usines' (*OC*, I, 554). It is significant, moreover, that the 'vie/néant' fragment itself begins with a qualification that might open up the possibility of refusing the dichotomy altogether: '*En fait de religion, de vie organisée, systématique*, il n'y a de choix qu'entre deux' (my emphasis). Outside of the strictures of religion and other such systematizations, other options may be possible. Perhaps, in the context of 'Adieux', this 'Éden' is the innocent male-female friendship enjoyed by 'Les Jeunes Gens' and 'Les Jeunes Filles' before they reached 'l'heure fatale'[61] of marriageable age; this pre-sexual state accords, of course, with the Biblical Eden. But elsewhere 'Éden' can indicate a sexual paradise (see 'Complainte du pauvre Chevalier-Errant', *OC*, I, 576). What Laforgue seems to aspire to is a kind of *entre-deux*, a love that is both sexual and companionable:

> L'âme et la chair, la chair et l'âme,
> C'est l'esprit *édénique* et fier
> D'être un peu l'Homme avec la Femme.
> ('Dimanches (*Bref, j'allais me donner...*)', *OC*, II, 307; my emphasis)

This aspiration is related to a section of notes for his projected 'Nouvelles' which also deal with the question of sexuality; here, however, it is expressed through a reconfiguration of the 'vie/néant' dilemma. Rather than sex in the name of procreation, Laforgue dreams of a sexual mode based on an empathetic relation:

> Pendant la communion, nous n'aurons qu'une idée — non l'exaltation et la création de l'être idéal, mais l'infini de la compassion pour la créature éphémère et la misère de l'Histoire [...]. (OC, III, 926)

The reference to 'infini' here subverts Hartmann's chapter on love, which states that the race is 'l'infini' to the individual's 'fini'; Laforgue reimagines this 'infini' as existing in the relation between two individuals, rather than in the greater evolutionary purpose served by those individuals. Alongside this idea, Laforgue envisages a kind of faith: not in the endless cycle of reproduction ('l'affirmation de la vie indéfiniment renouvelée'), but in pure sensuality for its own sake, a faith that demands 'qu'il faut ramper, ramper au bras de l'autre vers le néant des voluptueuses stérilités immuables' (OC, III, 926). Again, this draws on Hartmann, who writes that the sexual urge is motivated in part by 'le désir d'anéantir [l]es limites de l'individualité, qui séparent les amants, pour se perdre, et disparaître avec toute sa personnalité au sein de l'être qui lui est plus cher que son être propre' (PI, I, 259). But true union, argues Hartmann, is only achieved in 'l'acte de la génération' (PI, I, 259). For Laforgue, by contrast, this 'néant' is attained in a pleasurable, non-generative sexual union. Laforgue thus reimagines the 'vie ou néant' dilemma as a choice between sexual reproduction, on the one hand, and unproductive but spiritually and sensually fulfilling sex on the other.

The idea of 'le néant des voluptueuses stérilités immuables' might, perhaps, be echoed in Salomé's hymn to the Unconscious, which begins by praising *'le Néant'* (OC, II, 443), before making the following appeal: *'broutez-moi, au jour le jour, de saisons en saisons, ces Deltas sans sphinx, dont les angles égalent quand même deux droits'* (OC, II, 444). As Philippe Bonnefis notes, 'Delta' was a common euphemism for the female pudenda in Greek eroticism;[62] the reference to geometry, meanwhile, is taken from Hartmann, who uses it as an example of *a priori* categories ('la somme des angles est égale à deux droits' (PI, I, 365).[63] Bonnefis thereby concludes that Salomé's appeal should be read as expounding the 'Fatalité de l'amour et du commerce entre les sexes'.[64] But the verb 'brouter', which signifies cunnilingus in modern slang,[65] might indicate that Salomé is preaching a subverted version of Hartmannian principles: not procreation, but pleasure. The notion of mutually fulfilling sexual pleasure might also be reflected in Salomé's praise of *'Amour'*, where she states that *'les choses sont les choses'* — the reality of sex must be accepted — but that *'il serait vrai de se faire des concessions mutuelles sur le terrain des cinq sens actuels, au nom de l'Inconscient!'* (OC, II, 443). Elsewhere in the *Moralités légendaires*, however, Andromède yearns for some 'sixième sens inconnu' in response to the dragon's 'petit poème sacré' (OC, II, 474), which celebrates the joys of our existing five senses (OC, II, 475); Hamlet, too, longs for something more: 'J'ai cinq sens qui me rattachent à la vie; mais, ce sixième sens, ce sens de l'Infini!' (OC, II, 386). But might this beyond, this 'infini', be attainable *through* the senses, and more specifically through sexual union? The reference to 'l'infini de la compassion' during sex in the above-quoted notes for the 'Nouvelles' certainly suggests that it might. Likewise, in 'Dimanches (*C'est l'automne...*)' (*Derniers vers*), which extols the 'merveille' (*OC*, II, 310) of sexual love,[66] the poet declares that 'Il ne s'agit pas de conquêtes, avec moi, | Mais d'au-delà!' (*OC*, II, 311).

The idea that sexuality is neither purely material nor purely spiritual is prominent in the 'Nouvelles' notes: sex is 'au fond le suprême éréthisme ni matériel, ni animique, mais unique'. This is a fragile vision, however. Ultimately we are caged in our bodies, unable to possess each other 'par les lèvres, par les yeux, par le cœur, par le cerveau, par là ce serait la possession en soi' (*OC*, III, 926). (In this sense, Laforgue adopts the point of view of 'Elle' in 'Complainte des formalités nuptiales', in which 'Lui' appeals — in pompously circumlocutory terms — for sexual congress ('Dis, veux-tu te vêtir de mon Être éperdu?' (*OC*, I, 577)), while 'Elle' argues for the sufficiency of the spiritual possession he has already effected ('ne m'as-tu pas | Prise toute déjà? par tes yeux, sans combats!' (*OC*, I, 578)).) Instead, sexual intercourse takes place through the genitals 'parce que par là seulement il y a semence, procréation, par là on nous vole'; we are paid in pleasure, but the profit is reaped by the species: 'la nature est le capitaliste, nous les salariés'. It is reproduction that forestalls the possibility of realizing a sexual paradise: 'C'est cette fatalité de la procréation qui gâte tout.' Laforgue can, nonetheless, continue to dream of a utopian realm where sex is without reproductive consequence: 'Oh, le pays des femmes aimant sans but et des fruits sans pépins' (*OC*, III, 926).

This idyll is somewhat reminiscent of the Edenic valley evoked in 'Complainte des Nostalgies préhistoriques', where the poet imagines sex with 'Une enfant bestiale et brûlée | Qui suce [...] | De juteux abricots'; as in the above vision, their sexual congress will be 'sans but': for pleasure alone, not bound to Hartmannian teleology. If this poem is overtly exoticist in temporal terms, it also hints at a vision of sensual fulfilment in tropical lands that belongs to the mainstream of geographical exoticism. Moreover, as we saw in Chapter 4, 'Complainte du Sage de Paris' establishes an association between sexual liberation and the East through its reference to 'une pleine eau dans le Gange'. The 'vie/néant' dichotomy cannot, then, be mapped onto a simple opposition between West and East, between Occidental progress and vigour and Oriental quietism and apathy. In fact, the East is associated with both sexual fulfilment and self-denial in Laforgue's work. Both of these possibilities represent alternatives to the hegemonic notion of sex within marriage for reproduction: while they may be associated with cultural others, what Laforgue is ultimately concerned with is not the otherness of exotic fantasy but a truly different way of approaching sexuality.

'[E]ntre lune et terre'

The provisionality of the aesthetic manifesto presented by 'Complainte du Sage de Paris' is confirmed by the poet's subsequent collection, *L'Imitation de Notre-Dame la Lune*: here, the poet draws inspiration not from 'la vie' but from 'le néant'. (As Laforgue wrote to his sister in May 1883, 'la destinée d'un artiste est de s'enthousiasmer et se dégoûter d'idéaux successifs' (*OC*, I, 822).) It is the eponymous moon, the dominant image of *L'Imitation*, that is primarily associated with 'le néant', representing, according to Marc Eigeldinger, 'escape into nirvana, aspiration to death in nothingness'.[67] In fact, references to Buddhism are entirely absent from the collection. But given the association that Laforgue consistently draws between nothingness and nirvana in his notes, the moon certainly belongs to the same side of the dichotomy as Buddhism. The moon, like the forest and the undersea realm, is inherently 'other' in its inaccessibility and its hostility to life, but Laforgue aspires to experience its otherness, just as he does for these other domains. This represents another manifestation of his desire to escape from the dominant contemporary discourse of pro-natalism: the moon is, after all, a cosmic pariah that has been 'mise au ban du Progrès | Des populaces des Étoiles' ('Petits mystères', *OC*, II, 101), a sterile misfit that cannot be co-opted into the narrative of progress. Pierrot, the lunar celebrant who dominates the collection, seems to be an outcast in a similar sense; but ultimately, Pierrot — like Laforgue — resists simple categorization within the 'vie/néant' binary.

Compared to 'le Néant' in several poems,[68] in 'Litanies des derniers quartiers de la Lune' the moon becomes the 'Vortex-nombril | Du Tout-Nihil' (*OC*, II, 113). This is an antonymic variation on the expression 'Tout-Un', used by Laforgue to designate the Unconscious (and itself an inversion of Hartmann's 'Un-Tout'). It implies that the All-One of the Unconscious is ultimately destined to become the void, just as 'l'une' — the homophone of 'Lune' — can be metathesized as the 'nulle' of the 'Néant'.[69] If this wordplay suggests Hartmann's eschatological vision of total annihilation, there is also a specific link to one of Schopenhauer's interpretations of nirvana. As we have seen, Bourdeau's collection includes Schopenhauer's statement that nirvana is equivalent to the state of nothingness that pertained before the creation of the world, the state that will return if mankind adopts his ethical doctrine of chastity: 'cette béatitude sereine, appelée *Nirvana* qui sera reconquise par la pénitence'.[70] This vision of tranquil emptiness finds an analogue in Schopenhauer's expression of longing for the lifelessness of the moon:

> on accordera qu'il vaudrait beaucoup mieux que [le soleil] n'ait pas plus de pouvoir sur la terre pour faire surgir le phénomène de la vie qu'il n'en a dans la lune, et qu'il serait préférable que la surface de la terre comme celle de la lune se trouvât encore à l'état de cristal glacé.[71]

Just as Schopenhauer interprets nirvana as the state of calm that will be attained if humanity dies out, so he declares that the lifelessness of the moon is the ideal condition for the earth. The extinction of human life is to be achieved through celibacy: for Schopenhauer, both means (asceticism) and end (void) are thus associated with Buddhism.

In the late nineteenth century, the idea of the earth becoming as desolate as the moon was not merely nihilistic whimsy: as Jean Pierrot notes, the recent astronomical discovery of the life-span of planets and stars had provoked fear that the Earth itself might be in decline, in which case 'La Lune [...] pouvait symboliser ce cadavre d'astre que la Terre était vouée à devenir un jour plus ou moins lointain'.[72]

But Laforgue's portrayal of the moon reflects Schopenhauerian yearning rather than contemporary disquiet: 'Clair de Lune', for example, opens with a statement of regret at the moon's unattainability (expressed in a typically jocular Laforguian melange of popular and technical registers): 'Penser qu'on vivra jamais dans cet astre, | Parfois me flanque un coup dans l'épigastre' (*OC*, II, 77). This expression of regret is echoed by a review of *L'Imitation* co-written pseudonymously by Laforgue and Kahn, which states that 'On éprouve une déception de n'y pouvoir aller' (*OC*, III, 156) (a disappointment enhanced, perhaps, by the portrayal of lunar travel in recent works by Jules Verne (*De la Terre à la Lune* (1865) and *Autour de la Lune* (1870))). The same poem insists on the moon's barrenness, even using the same adjective as Schopenhauer in its description of the moon as a 'Crâne glacé' (*OC*, II, 77).

The desire to relinquish terrestrial existence is expressed through the character of Pierrot, who is first introduced in *Les Complaintes* through a subversion of the popular rhyme 'Au clair de la lune':

> Au clair de la lune,
> Mon ami Pierrot,
> Filons, en costume,
> Présider là-haut!
> Ma cervelle est morte,
> Que le Christ l'emporte!
> Béons à la Lune,
> La bouche en zéro.
> ('Complainte de Lord Pierrot', *OC*, I, 584)[73]

As well as mimicking the shape of the full moon, the zero of Pierrot's mouth also offers an analogue of its nullity. This in turn reflects the emptiness of Pierrot's speech, which exposes the vacuity of everyday communication by taking 'banal, stereotyped phrases' and '[emptying] them of any last shred of meaning they may have had when used in their normal context'.[74] Likewise, as Hiddleston indicates, the behaviour of Laforgue's Pierrot ('La désinvolture, le manque d'à-propos, les pirouettes absurdes et inattendues, les soubresauts insensés de la conscience') serves to create 'ce sentiment d'irréalité et de liberté dans un univers où tout — hommes et choses — tourne à vide selon la seule loi du hasard'.[75] The Pierrots, who 'demandent *Rien* avec âme' ('Pierrots (III)', *OC*, II, 84; author's emphasis), are thus the earthly representatives of the moon's nothingness, transforming its blankness into a nihilistic philosophical credo.

Indeed, Hiddleston also argues that Pierrot's outlook demonstrates a similarity to Buddhism, stating that he displays 'a Buddhist resignation and a kind of inner detachment'.[76] This attitude is encapsulated in 'Pierrots (V)':

> L'art de tout est l'*Ainsi soit-il*;
> [...] le beau rôle
> Est de vivre de but en blanc
> Et, dût-on se battre les flancs,
> De hausser à tout les épaules.
> (*OC*, II, 86; author's emphasis)

The ecclesiastical reference of the first line belies an ethics that is closer to contemporary views of Buddhism as quietistic, as advocating withdrawal from active engagement in the world into a tranquil state of contemplation — 'l'ataraxie complète de l'Orient'[77] as Ribot has it. The image of Pierrot as passive and long-suffering (the foil to the mischievous and romantically successful Harlequin) was, of course, well established in the late nineteenth century, and Jean de Palacio even suggests it was a key reason for his popularity in melancholically-inclined literature of the *fin de siècle*.[78] In Laforgue's version of the character, the combination of Pierrot's resignation and his nihilism suggests a certain echo of Buddhism — an echo that is, however, never made explicit.

Pierrot also toys with asceticism, another practice deemed to be Buddhist in the late nineteenth century (and more particularly, as we have seen, by Schopenhauer, Hartmann and Laforgue). Pierrot's aspiration to fleshly mortification is evident from his first appearance in Laforgue's poetry: in fact, in the third stanza of 'Complainte de Lord Pierrot', Pierrot invokes the Eastern figure of the fakir in his call 'Tournons d'abord sur nous-même [sic], comme un fakir!' (*OC*, I, 584). He also declares that he has 'le cœur chaste et vrai' (*OC*, I, 584). In 'Pierrots (II)', Pierrot's apparent celibacy is alluded to euphemistically but unambiguously:

> [...] ils n'ont personne
> Chez eux, qui les frictionne
> D'un conjugal onguent. (*OC*, II, 83)

'Pierrots (I)' also indicates that they also subscribe to a regime of fasting: 'Ils vont, se sustentant d'azur!' (*OC*, II, 82). However, this assertion is undermined with typically Laforguian bathos by the following lines, which explain that they are far from rigorous in their abstention:

> Et parfois aussi de légumes,
> De riz plus blanc que leur costume,
> De mandarines et d'œufs durs. (*OC*, II, 82)

The reference to hard-boiled eggs recalls Laforgue's own memories of his long days in the library when he played the role of 'petit Bouddha' (*OC*, I, 763), but Pierrot's diet is hardly that of the dedicated ascetic. Suggestions of celibacy are also undermined: the fifth stanza of 'Complainte de Lord Pierrot' promises orgasmic pleasure to his female interlocutor:

> En costume blanc, je ferai le cygne,
> Après nous le Déluge, ô ma Léda!
> Jusqu'à ce que tournent tes yeux vitreux,
> Que tu grelottes en rires affreux [...]. (*OC*, II, 584)

This may be fantasy, but Pierrot's lust is unquestionable. In 'Pierrots (II)' from *L'Imitation*, meanwhile, the Pierrots have sex ('font la bête') but are motivated less by lust than by a need for affection and, perhaps, (metonymic) relief from the burdens of intellect:

> [...] ils font la bête
> Afin d'avoir des seins,
> Pis-aller de coussins
> À leurs savantes têtes. (*OC*, II, 83)

They are thus not 'dupes | Ça et là, de la Jupe' (*OC*, II, 83) — a phrase that echoes Schopenhauer and Hartmann's view of lust as a trick played by the species — since they are in control of their desires.

While the Pierrots (the 'Blancs enfants de chœur de la Lune' ('Pierrots (V)', *OC*, II, 85)) may appear to be the emissaries of the moon as void, their sexual indulgence means that they are not unequivocally on the side of 'le néant' in the 'vie/néant' dichotomy. We might thus read Laforgue's assertion that they are 'entre lune et terre' (*OC*, III, 157) as an expression of their interstitiality, their refusal of both postulates in the dilemma. In fact, their anarchic shifting between self-abnegation and self-indulgence — see also the Pierrot of *Pierrot fumiste*, who refuses to consummate his marriage until after a divorce has been granted (*OC*, I, 512) — shows that they represent a void of meaning, an absence of fixed values, rather than the 'néant' of celibacy. This Schopenhauerian 'néant' is definitively rejected in 'Lohengrin, fils de Parsifal', Lohengrin constituting in some senses the inverse of Pierrot: Pierrot uses breasts as pillows after sex, while Lohengrin prefers an ersatz pillowy Elsa to the real thing (*OC*, II, 428); Pierrot fantazises about being the swan to his partner's Leda, while Lohengrin is transported away from the nuptial bedroom to 'les altitudes de la Métaphysique de l'Amour' *by* a swan (*OC*, II, 428–29). Lohengrin is both a follower of Schopenhauer, in that he is aware of 'the deception by which the rest of humanity is manipulated' and thus 'pledges himself to the most rigorous chastity',[79] and also 'a self-professed feminist whose main task is to lead future crusades for the liberation of women';[80] when he appeals to his father, no less, to conclude this emancipatory mission (as he flees to 'the land of meditative freedom'),[81] the parody of asceticism as a self-deceiving enterprise is complete.

In Laforgue's later work, then, it is indulgence in the pleasures of (non-procreative) fornication — not the mortification of the flesh — that offers the means to transgress normative sexual morality. Moreover, this liberated sexual desire constitutes a source of creative energy. While Lohengrin argues that art merely serves the Will, accusing women of 'making [artists] sweat out masterpieces that will ensnare future generations of men for future generations of women',[82] Laforgue is parodying rather than endorsing this pseudo-Schopenhauerian logic: for him, the erotic principle underlying creativity is disconnected from any notion of generativity.

★ ★ ★ ★ ★

As well as standing for an eschatological vision of annihilation, the ethical principle of asceticism, and a void of meaning, the idea of 'néant' in Laforgue's work also signals the death of self. But the *entre-deux* to which Laforgue aspires in his writings on sexual ethics is also relevant, albeit in a different sense, to his thinking on selfhood.

It is in the foundational 'Préludes autobiographiques' that the poet's ambivalence on the question of the self is expressed, and the idea of nirvana plays a crucial role here. The poet presents a dilemma between two ways of attaining the ideal, referred to as 'l'Éden des Élus' (but which is not the same as the sexual Eden he envisages):

> Dilemme à deux sentiers vers l'Éden des Élus:
> Me laisser éponger mon Moi par l'Absolu?
> Ou bien, élixirer l'Absolu en moi-même?
> C'est passé. J'aime tout, aimant mieux que Tout m'aime.
> Donc Je m'en vais flottant aux orgues sous-marins,
> Par les coraux, les œufs, les bras verts, les écrins,
> Dans la tourbillonnante éternelle agonie
> D'un Nirvâna des Danaïdes du génie! (OC, I, 548)

This choice between the dissolution of self in the Unconscious ('éponger mon Moi par l'Absolu') and the distillation of the Unconscious within the self ('élixirer l'Absolu en moi-même') seems to be resolved in favour of the former option, since the poet describes himself floating underwater ('Donc Je m'en vais flottant aux orgues sous-marins'). The capitalization of 'Je' echoes that of 'Moi' and suggests the absorption of self into the absolute. This is the unmaking of identity, a reverse baptism, as the subsequent reference to the 'Sainte Piscine' suggests. For Jean-Pierre Richard, it is an act of flight that is both described and performed:

> Le *Je*, donc, dit qu'il s'en va, et [...] du même coup d'écriture, il opère réellement ce départ, il se trouve effectivement en allé.[83]

The 'Je' that Laforgue dismisses is 'le principe régnant d'une conscience, d'une conscience de soi, maîtresse d'elle-même et de son monde'.[84] Also connected to this abandonment of sovereign selfhood is the reference to the 'orgues sous-marins', since, as Richard points out, this provides an intertextual link to Jules Verne's *Vingt mille lieues sous les mers* (1869–70), in which Captain Nemo plays the organ in his submarine: 'Nemo' — of course — means 'nobody' in Latin; he is 'celui qui s'anonymise [...] par la plongée océanique, l'enfoncée inconsciente, et le charme du texte'.[85] Moreover, there is also a pseudo-anagram of the poet's name in 'Donc *Je* m'en vais *fl*ottant aux *or*gues',[86] which again enacts the disaggregation of the self.

But the dispersal, disintegration or dissolution of the sovereign subject do not necessarily imply complete annihilation. Indeed, an examination of the source of these lines problematizes the idea of self-annihilation in a different sense. As Grojnowski has noted, they are based on a passage from Laforgue's philosophical notes:[87]

> La désagrégation, l'abandon, la dissolution, la dilution du moi dans l'absolu — ou *de l'absolu dans le moi!* — de la conscience dans l'inconscient, son principe[,] but de toute religion, de tout besoin religieux, de tout idéal.
> Annihilation de la conscience dans l'inconscient, sauf un soupçon de juste persistance, de quoi jouir de son annihilation — une agonie perpétuelle. — le nirvâna des Danaïdes. (OC, III, 1148; author's emphasis)

The dichotomy of 'la dilution du moi dans l'absolu — ou *de l'absolu dans le moi!*' is the source of the lines 'Me laisser éponger mon Moi par l'Absolu? | Ou bien, élixirer l'Absolu en moi-même?' in 'Préludes autobiographiques'. Meanwhile, 'une agonie perpétuelle. — le nirvâna des Danaïdes' is transfigured as 'la tourbillonnante éternelle agonie | D'un Nirvâna des Danaïdes du génie!'. It is clear that 'Nirvâna' is the equivalent of 'annihilation' (and, as we have seen, Laforgue's notes confirm that he subscribes to the nihilistic interpretation of nirvana). However, Laforgue does not aspire to the complete effacement of consciousness, but rather to a paradoxical state wherein a grain of consciousness remains to enjoy its own annihilation: 'sauf un soupçon de juste persistance, de quoi jouir de son annihilation' (*OC*, III, 1148).

This passage of notes, and indeed the section of 'Préludes autobiographiques' that we have examined, can be further elucidated by Hartmann's chapter on mysticism in *La Philosophie de l'Inconscient*, as Hannoosh notes (*OC*, III, 1151 n. 12). Here Hartmann discusses the state of 'absorption de l'individu dans l'absolu', the eradication of consciousness (apparently) attained by certain mystics, such as 'bouddhistes' and 'quiétistes':

> Les mystiques nous disent que, dans cet état d'absorption, l'homme ne sent plus son corps, ni rien d'extérieur; qu'il ne perçoit même plus ses propres sentiments. 'Penser seulement à son état d'absorption, c'est cesser d'être absorbé.' Mourir à l'égoïsme, annihiler complètement sa personnalité, et se perdre au sein de l'être divin, tel est le but que poursuivent expressément les mystiques. (*PI*, II, 403)

Hartmann is in fact critical of the attempts of mystics to achieve a state of unity with the absolute; such attempts are unnecessary, he argues, since this state of unity already exists:

> L'unité de l'absolu et de l'individu, dont l'individualité ou le moi nous est connu par la conscience, en d'autres termes l'unité de l'Inconscient et du conscient nous est donnée une fois pour toutes; elle est indivisible, indestructible, autrement que par la destruction de l'individu. Aussi toute tentative pour rendre cette union plus intime qu'elle n'est doit être considérée comme insensée et vaine. (*PI*, II, 402)

He goes on to describe the manner in which mystics have traditionally sought to attain such union:

> La voie que l'histoire nous montre avoir été presque toujours suivie pour cela n'est que l'annihilation de la conscience, ou l'effort pour absorber l'individu dans l'absolu. Il y a là évidemment une grosse illusion: le but une fois atteint, et la conscience détruite, l'individu ne peut encore subsister. Le moi veut à la fois s'anéantir et persister pour jouir de son anéantissement. (*PI*, II, 402)

This is the source of Laforgue's notion of 'Annihilation de la conscience dans l'inconscient, sauf un soupçon de juste persistance, de quoi jouir de son annihilation'. For Hartmann it is 'une grosse illusion', but for Laforgue it describes the state of betweenness required for creative expression: the loss of self, witnessed by the self.

This is also a kind of torment, albeit one that is perhaps necessary for creativity. Suffering is inherent to the image of the Danaids,[88] and this is reinforced by the poet's description of their 'tourbillonnante éternelle agonie'; the idea that this is 'un nirvâna des Danaïdes *du génie*' (my emphasis) suggests that suffering is somehow essential to the creative faculty. Elsewhere it is the persistence of selfhood in itself that is associated with danaidean agony: '[...] j'ulule en détresse, | Devant ce Moi, tonneau d'Ixion des Danaïdes' ('Dimanches (*Je m'ennuie...*)', *OC*, II, 184), with the poet's own first name echoed, in stuttering form, in 'j'ulule'. The enduring existence of the self — painful as it is — may be needed to write. What Laforgue imagines in 'Préludes autobiographiques', then, is a state of paradox that enfolds both the liberation from self and its continuing presence, both joyous release and inescapable suffering.

Conclusion

For Barthélemy-Saint-Hilaire, the desire for self-annihilation that is central to Buddhism implies a fundamental schism in humankind, an irredeemable and essential otherness. While Laforgue is far from endorsing such essentialism, he also hints at the idea of Buddhist otherness through his assertion that Buddhism's 'remède philosophique' is unattainable for Westerners. But there is a tension between this notion that nirvana might in some way be alien to the European mind — a notion that is prevalent in the work of Schopenhauer's French critics — and a persistent concern with the dissolution of the self in his poetry. Laforgue does not aspire to self-annihilation unambiguously; but he does take seriously the Buddhist idea of nirvana (at least, as it was contemporarily understood in France) as a philosophical possibility.

Of course, it is only by examining Laforgue's notes that we can ascertain the depth and persistence of his engagement with Buddhism. The use of Buddhist and Hindu terms in his poetry seems, at first glance, to be typical of 'the virtual epidemic of Orientalia affecting every major poet, essayist, and philosopher'[89] of the nineteenth century. Indeed, Laforgue himself seems to bolster this point of view in a letter to Henry explaining his emendations to the latter's review of *Les Complaintes*: Laforgue states that he has added some quotations, the first of which is 'O Robe de Maïa' from 'Préludes autobiographiques', 'comme tenue boudhiste [sic] et curiosité de façon de dire' (OC, II, 778). But if this might suggest that Laforgue's engagement with Buddhism is merely a kind of *travestissement oriental*, his notes show that he did much more than try on Buddhist terminology because of its curiosity value. While Laforgue, like any other writer on the East in the era of colonialism, cannot 'unilaterally be detached from the general imperial context',[90] his interest in Buddhism goes deeper than the facile, picturesque exoticism of many of his contemporaries, showing a concern not merely with the unfamiliar contours of Buddhist lexis, but also with the profoundly different doctrines of Buddhist thought.

The heteroglossic elements of Laforgue's work do not, in fact, constitute the most important aspect of his engagement with Buddhism (despite Bakhtin's reference to Laforgue as one of the rare counter-examples to poetry's monoglossic character[91]). Laforgue engages with Buddhism *philosophically*, not merely on the level of language or imagery, even if his understanding of this philosophy — mediated as it is by Schopenhauer, Hartmann, and their critics — is partial and flawed. While initially framed using Buddhist terms ('nirvâna' etc), this engagement does not rely on these terms, as *L'Imitation* demonstrates: here, the use of Indian terms is rare, and there are no Buddhist ones whatsoever. But the persistent association between the moon and nothingness, which is in turn persistently associated with nirvana in Laforgue's notes, means that there are undoubtedly echoes of Buddhist thought in this collection. Laforgue himself reinforces the underlying principle at stake here in a passage of notes on Baudelaire. He praises Baudelaire for being 'chat, hindou, yankee, épiscopal alchimiste' (*OC*, III, 178), and for avoiding the kind of 'comparaison française, oratoire' (*OC*, III, 179) that Hugo or Gautier might have chosen in favour of jolting 'yankee' similes. He goes on to reiterate the idea of Baudelaire as 'Hindou — il l'a cette poésie plus que Leconte de Lisle avec toute son érudition et ses poèmes bourrés et aveuglants' (*OC*, III, 179). The phrase 'cette poésie' is unexplained; perhaps it signifies poetry that is concerned with exploring the depths of the self. In any case, what Laforgue suggests here is that it is possible to be a poetic 'Hindou' without writing poetry full of ostentatiously erudite Indian references, like Leconte de Lisle; that engagement with the ideas of Eastern philosophy goes beyond a desire to use them as poetic fodder.

Notes to Chapter 5

1. See Walter Benjamin, quoted by Pascal Durand: 'Nineteenth-century domestic interior. The space disguises itself — puts on, like an alluring creature, the costumes of moods. [...] In the end, things are merely mannequins, and even the great moments of world history are only costumes beneath which they exchange glances of complicity with nothingness, with the petty and the banal. Such nihilism is the innermost core of bourgeois coziness [...].' (Walter Benjamin, *The Arcades Project*, trans. by Howard Eiland and Kevin McLaughlin (Cambridge, MA: Harvard University Press, 1999), p. 216); quoted in Pascal Durand, 'Poésie et décor: l'intérieur, le trop, le rien. À propos de la "Complainte des puberités difficiles" ', in *Jules Laforgue: colloque de la Sorbonne: actes de la journée d'agrégation du 18 novembre 2000*, ed. by André Guyaux and Bertrand Marchal (Paris: Presses de l'Université de Paris-Sorbonne, 2000), pp. 143–58 (p. 149).)
2. Victor Cousin, *Histoire générale de la philosophie depuis les temps les plus anciens jusqu'au XIXe siècle*, 10th edn (Paris: Didier, 1873 [1863]), p. 94; quoted in Roger-Pol Droit, *Le Culte du néant: Les philosophes et le Bouddha* (Paris: Seuil, 1997), p. 131.
3. 'La vie était douleur, et il aboutissait à la morale des fakirs indiens, à la délivrance par l'anéantissement' (Zola, *La Joie de vivre*, XII, 71).
4. Lopez, p. 19.
5. Peter Harvey, *An Introduction to Buddhism: Teaching, History and Practices*, 10th edn (Cambridge: Cambridge University Press, 1998 [1990]), p. 62; see also Donald W. Mitchell, *Buddhism: Introducing the Buddhist Experience* (Oxford: Oxford University Press, 2002), p. 61.
6. *Samyutta-nikāya*, I, 136; quoted in Donald W. Mitchell, p. 60.
7. W. Sri Rahula, *What the Buddha Taught* (New York: Grove Weidenfeld, 1959), pp. 36–37; paraphrased in Moira Nicholls, 'The Influences of Eastern Thought on Schopenhauer's Doctrine of the Thing-in-Itself', in *The Cambridge Companion to Schopenhauer*, ed. by Christopher Janaway (Cambridge: Cambridge University Press, 1999), pp. 171–212.
8. Thomas P. Kasulis, 'Nirvāna', in *The Encyclopedia of Religion*, X, 6628–35 (p. 6628).
9. Ibid., p. 6629.
10. Droit, p. 39.
11. Ibid., p. 15.
12. Ibid., p. 16.
13. Guy Welbon, *The Buddhist nirvāna and its Western interpreters* (Chicago, IL: University of Chicago Press), p. 55.
14. Eugène Burnouf, *Introduction à l'histoire du buddhisme indien* (Paris: Maisonneuve, 1844).
15. Raymond Schwab, *La Renaissance orientale* (Paris: Payot, 1950), p. 121.
16. Burnouf, p. 17.
17. Ibid., p. 78, p. 83, p. 153 et al.
18. Philip Almond, writing about Great Britain, reinforces the idea that the nihilistic view of nirvana was widespread: 'The majority opinion throughout the nineteenth century was that Nirvana, essentially, entailed the annihilation of the previously suffering individual' (p. 102).

19. Jules Barthélemy-Saint-Hilaire, 'Rapport sur le tome I de l'*Introduction à l'histoire du buddhisme indien* par M. E. Burnouf. Suivi d'observations par M. Cousin' (Paris: Séances et Travaux de l'Académie des Sciences morales et politiques, 1847); quoted in Droit, p. 130.
20. Barthélemy-Saint-Hilaire, p. 165.
21. Ibid., p. 180.
22. Ibid., p. vi.
23. Nordau, pp. 20–21.
24. See p. 99.
25. Schopenhauer, trans. by Bourdeau, p. 42.
26. Schopenhauer is correct, broadly speaking, in establishing this distinction, since Buddhism does not preach extreme self-denial, but moderation.
27. Challemel-Lacour, p. 296.
28. Ribot, p. 5.
29. Caro, p. 220.
30. Challemel-Lacour, p. 327; Ribot, pp. 121–22; Caro, p. iii; Foucher de Careil, p. 271.
31. Ribot, p. 148.
32. Janet (June 1877), p. 623.
33. It is intriguing to note Andrew Counter's observation that in Zola's late, pro-natalist writings (the novels *Fécondité* and *Vérité*, and the article 'Dépopulation'), the author conflates his critique of certain non-procreative practices under terms suggesting negation: Santerre, the 'cynical heterosexual seducer' of *Fécondité* is labelled a seeker of 'l'anéantissement'; the literary figures reviled in 'Dépopulation' are 'les amoureux du néant'; Catholics in *Vérité* find only 'néant' in their religious devotions; Sérafine's hysterectomy reduces her to a 'néant de spectre' in *Fécondité* (Counter, p. 207).
34. Ribot, p. 174.
35. Caro, p. 229.
36. Ibid., p. iii.
37. Foucher de Careil, p. 299.
38. Ibid., p. 300.
39. Ibid., p. 355.
40. Ibid., p. 311.
41. Ibid., p. 300.
42. O'Connor, p. 11.
43. Ibid., p. 13.
44. Ibid., p. 10.
45. Foucher de Careil, p. 349.
46. Caro, p. 230.
47. Ibid., p. 26.
48. Harold Padwa, *Social Poison: The Culture and Politics of Opiate Control in Britain and France, 1821–1926* (Baltimore: The Johns Hopkins University Press, 2012), pp. 9–10.
49. Ibid., p. 7.
50. Ibid., p. 33.
51. See Caro: 'le vide de toute forme et de tout être, de tout concept: ni idées, ni absence d'idées. L'absence sentie d'idées serait encore une idée; ici plus rien, pas même le sentiment du rien, qui serait encore quelque chose: c'est l'absolu rien' (p. 229).
52. The reference to suicide problematizes the link to Schopenhauer to a certain extent, since the philosopher explicitly condemns suicide as ineffective in destroying the will; but despite this and other sporadic references, Laforgue never seriously considers suicide as a solution to suffering. (See, for example, the following passage from his early notes: 'les uns jouisseurs [...] auront recours au suicide matériel — les autres, sages, philosophes, artistes, curieux, vivront et arriveront au renoncement' (*OC*, III, 1129).)
53. Neither does he accept the philosopher's eschatology; such an acceptance would trouble the opposition established in this passage, since in Hartmann's vision the life process ultimately leads to the complete annihilation of the universe.

54. Bootle (2011), p. 172.
55. Hiddleston (1985), p. 69.
56. See 'Lohengrin, fils de Parsifal', where the couple's marriage is greeted by the chant '*la nappe est mise*' and '*Oh! La nappe | Des agapes!*' (*OC*, II, 422; author's emphasis).
57. Loubier, p. 25.
58. This idea is echoed by Hartmann (*PI*, I, 258).
59. Grojnowski (1988), p. 103.
60. Sully Prudhomme, *Poésies 1865–66: stances et poèmes* (Paris: Lemerre, [18??]), p. 76.
61. Ibid., p. 71.
62. Bonnefis (1988), p. 60.
63. Quoted in Bonnefis (1988), p. 61.
64. Bonnefis (1988), p. 61.
65. Guiraud, p. 194.
66. Sam Bootle, 'The Body Poetic: Laforgue's Translations of Whitman', *Dix-Neuf*, 20, no. 1 (2016), 25–44 (p. 31).
67. Marc Eigeldinger, *L'Évolution dynamique de l'image dans la poésie française du Romantisme à nos jours* (Neuchâtel: Seiler, 1943), p. 168.
68. See 'Au large' (*OC*, II, 76), 'Climat, faune et flore de la Lune' (*OC*, II, 79), 'Dialogue avant le lever de la Lune' (*OC*, II, 98), 'Nuitamment' (*OC*, II, 101) and 'Litanies des derniers quartiers de la Lune' (*OC*, II, 113).
69. Daniel Grojnowski, 'Poétique du Rien: L'Imitation de Notre-Dame la Lune', *Europe*, no. 673 (May 1985), 48–65 (p. 59); see also Lisa Block de Behar, *Jules Laforgue ou les métaphores du déplacement*, trans. by Albert Bensoussan (Paris: Harmattan, 2004), p. 151. Neither Grojnowski nor Block de Behar links this point to Hartmann's eschatology, however.
70. Schopenhauer, trans. by Bourdeau, p. 42.
71. Ibid., p. 40. Laforgue's poem 'Pataugement', from *Le Sanglot*, evokes a similar vision of the Earth 'Ne montrant tour à tour que steppes désolées, | Que vaste plaine blanche et qu'Océan polaire' (*OC*, I, 305).
72. Pierrot (1977), p. 63.
73. As Palacio comments, such transfigurations were common in the period (p. 29).
74. Elisabeth A. Howe, *Stages of Self: The Dramatic Monologues of Laforgue, Valéry and Mallarmé* (Athens: Ohio University Press, 1990), p. 79.
75. Hiddleston (1980), p. 83.
76. J. A. Hiddleston, 'Introduction', in Jules Laforgue, *Poems*, ed. by J. A. Hiddleston (Oxford: Blackwell, 1975), pp. 1–40 (p. 28).
77. Ribot, p. 174.
78. Palacio, p. 13.
79. Hannoosh, p. 131.
80. Ibid., p. 132.
81. Ibid., p. 132.
82. Ibid., p. 144; see *OC*, II, 426.
83. Jean-Pierre Richard, 'Donc je m'en vais', *Revue des Sciences humaines*, 178 (1980), 56–60 (p. 57); author's emphasis.
84. Ibid., p. 57.
85. Ibid., p. 59.
86. Ibid., p. 59; my emphasis.
87. Grojnowski, *Jules Laforgue, les voix de la Complainte*, p. 47.
88. See p. 61.
89. Said, p. 51.
90. Ibid., p. 334.
91. Mikhail Bakhtin, *Esthétique et théorie du roman*, trans. by Daria Olivier (Paris: Gallimard, 1978), p. 101.

CONCLUSION

Ideas of otherness are woven into Laforgue's reception of the philosophy of Schopenhauer and Hartmann in various ways. The pathologization of their philosophy as a plague sweeping across the border from Germany — an image that expresses the foreignness of their work in the most primal of terms — is redisposed by Laforgue, for whom the sickly body is a source of creative vitality. He also engages with the idealization of Germany inaugurated by Staël and perpetuated by the Wagnerian movement. This idealization is apparent above all in his article 'L'Art moderne en Allemagne', which casts Germany as the chosen land of the Unconscious. The wild German forest is contrasted to France's manicured gardens; in Laforgue's work more broadly, the forest image stands for the untamed realms of the human mind, for the domain where secret and, at times, disturbing fears and desires hold sway. The suffering and desiring body thus emerges as central to Laforgue's poetic project. In addition to its thematic importance, it also occupies a crucial role in his aesthetic principles. As he writes, programmatically, in one of his notebooks,

> faites de la vie, faites de tout, selon l'instinct qui a faim, soif, amoureux, las, froid, épileptique, tout, — et vous serez dans le vrai, dans la divine imperfection douloureuse mais touffue et incohérente de la créature éphémère. (OC, III, 380)

This liberation of bodily energies — both positive and negative — also has political importance, countering the dominant discourse that instrumentalized the body as the means to regenerate the French nation; in response to the nationalistic vision of a healthy, vigorous, generative physicality, Laforgue's poetry depicts our embodied condition as a discordant meld of pain and pleasure, suffering and joy. Moreover, he posits this condition as the very basis of artistic creation.

This principle is encapsulated by the final couplet of 'Préludes autobiographiques', in which the poet tells himself not to 'rester coi' but to let out 'un cri humain' (OC, I, 549). This responds to Hugo's 'Les Mages', a manifesto for Romantic lyricism, whose final stanza exhorts poets (addressed as 'prêtres' and 'génies') to 'Cherchez la note humaine'.[1] Laforgue replaces the musical 'note' with the visceral 'cri'. Salomé utters a similar cry — 'un cri enfin humain' (OC, II, 446) — although, ironically, this is only as she falls to her death. The cause of her demise is significant: having seemingly renounced her own aspirations to the status of lyrical poet (breaking her lyre over her knee at the end of her *vocéro*), she throws Iaokanann's decapitated head into the sea in an attempt to reanimate it so that it might sing like that of Orpheus — it lies 'sur un coussin, parmi les débris de la lyre d'ébène [...] comme jadis celle d'Orphée' (OC, II, 446) — and in the process overbalances and tumbles over the cliff. While she ends up dying in agony, 'le crâne défoncé' (*OC*, II, 446), the severed head of Iaokanann remains resolutely mum. The tale thus confirms the death of lyrical poetry, and suggests that any attempt to revive it is both futile and ridiculous.

Laforgue's work challenges not only the idea of the lyrical self, but also notions of stable selfhood in general. The human individual is merely a 'créature éphémère', as the above-quoted notes have it, rather than being grounded in any persistent essence or immortal soul. This ephemerality is underwritten by the Unconscious: each individual self is simply a provisional fragment of a larger whole. Throughout Laforgue's work, there exists the desire for complete absorption into this whole, for the relinquishment of selfhood and its concomitant sufferings; but alongside it, there is an acknowledgement (explicit or implicit) that such a state is not conducive to creativity, if it is even possible. The idea of the self as a solid, enduring entity may be illusory, but the idea of self-annihilation is equally chimerical. The vision of selfhood that emerges from Laforgue's work is, rather, one of a mutable and makeshift assemblage, an ever-changing multiplicity of constituent parts.

To a certain extent, this vision can be mapped onto his model of interculturality: his celebration of cultural difference, of eclecticism and a dehierarchized relationship between cultures, conforms to the same logic of multiplicity without defining order. While this model seems to undermine the notion of otherness altogether, as do his critiques of exoticism, there are also moments in Laforgue's *œuvre* when he seems to recuperate otherness, albeit in xenophile mode. Germany, in Laforgue's idealized image of it, provides a gateway to the Unconscious; the East, too, offers privileged access both to the Unconscious (as metaphysical principle) and to the individual unconscious. But this apparent tension can be at least partly resolved by the idea that the special status of such cultures is contingent rather than essential, since the Unconscious as All-One undermines all notions of otherness at the fundamental level, even if there are differences between cultures at the phenomenal level.

The supranational scope of the Unconscious is summarized by the epigram 'l'Inconscient souffle où il veut', a formulation that has a Biblical origin[2] but that also reappropriates the aeolian imagery used to demonise the influence of pessimism. This axiom features in both Laforgue's article on Impressionism and the passage of notes dichotomizing 'la vie' and 'le néant', and on both occasions it is accompanied by another pithy phrase: 'Laissez (le) faire, laissez (le) passer'. In 'L'Impressionnisme', he denounces the institutionalization of artistic activity, instead advocating 'le dilettantisme nihiliste, l'anarchie ouverte à toutes les influences, telle qu'elle règne parmi les artistes français en ce moment: "Laissez faire, laissez passer"' (*OC*, III, 334). He goes on to emphasize the overarching nature of the Unconscious: 'Au-dessus de l'humanité, la Loi suit son développement réflexe et l'Inconscient souffle où il veut' (*OC*, III, 334). Meanwhile, in the 'vie/néant' passage, the two expressions are even more closely connected: 'Donc laissez le faire, laissez le passer — l'Amour Inconscient souffle où il veut' (*OC*, III, 1165). As Mireille Dottin-Orsini notes, the former expression may have been inspired by the frequent use of a similar phrase, 'laissez dire, laissez faire', in articles of the late 1870s on Impressionist painters; this phrase may, in turn, have been derived from Manet's motto, 'faire vrai, laisser dire'.[3] But it is important to recall that the slogan 'Laissez faire, laissez passer' itself was coined in the seventeenth century as an appeal to finance minister Jean-Baptiste Colbert for the removal of governmental restrictions on trade, and was popularized in the eighteenth century by the Physiocrat Vincent de Gournay; Laforgue thus transposes this slogan for free trade from the discourse of economics to that of creativity, where it constitutes an appeal for openness to 'toutes les influences'. The repeated juxtaposition of the two phrases demonstrates that in Laforgue's aesthetics, such openness is a necessary corollary of unconscious inspiration.

The use of the phrase 'laissez faire, laissez passer' champions the principle of cultural diversity in aesthetics:[4] Laforgue's appeal for 'l'anarchie ouverte à toutes les influences' suggests, in itself, a global view of influence, and this is reinforced by his posthumously published article on the aesthetic theory of Taine, whose lectures Laforgue attended in 1880–81. This article, which also features the above-mentioned formulations ('L'Inconscient souffle où il veut et comme il veut, laissez le faire' (OC, III, 360)), offers a furious denunciation of Taine's Eurocentric neo-Classical aesthetics and an equally passionate appeal for aesthetic heterogeneity. In particular, Laforgue invokes Eastern art as a challenge to Taine's narrow idealism: firstly, Taine's notion that there is an artistic hierarchy reflecting that of the natural world provokes the retort 'Eh bien non! que devient votre idéal devant les merveilles des arts chinois et japonais?' (OC, III, 358); secondly, Taine's idea that the greatest art has 'un caractère bienfaisant' (OC, III, 359) is countered by the assertion that art is about being interesting, not moral, and that 'Une vieille civilisation décadente, l'humanité de Balzac, l'art japonais' are just as artistically interesting (if not more so) than 'une civilisation équilibrée' (OC, III, 359); finally, and more broadly, Laforgue argues that adherence to the Classical ideal takes no account of art's ceaseless innovation, an example of this being the paradigm shift effected by Manet's encounter with 'les albums japonais' (OC, III, 363). In summary, Laforgue argues that Taine's vision of the world is 'trop étroit' and that 'Tout l'Orient est laissé de côté' (OC, III, 361); moreover, Taine takes no account of the 'prodigieuses débauches de la *rêverie moderne*, élixir dernier de ce siècle épique' (OC, III, 361; author's emphasis). In Laforgue's notes for the article, a parallel is again drawn between the Eastern and the avant-garde, between 'l'Orient halluciné et anté-classique' and 'le monde halluciné des avancés' (OC, III, 370), the shared adjective suggesting that both worlds draw inspiration from the irrational depths of the unconscious. But while certain cultures (the East, Germany) are presented as having privileged access to this source of inspiration, ultimately the Unconscious as overarching metaphysical principle takes no account of national borders in its inspiratory action.

This vision is based, broadly speaking, on Hartmann's notion of the Unconscious as All-One; but once again Laforgue departs from the philosopher's doctrine in certain key respects. For Hartmann, the relationship between different cultures is defined by the principle of the survival of the fittest. He insists on the importance of 'la concurrence des races et des nations dans la lutte pour l'existence: les lois impitoyables de la nature y soumettent aussi bien les hommes que les animaux et les plantes'; nothing, therefore, can prevent 'la destruction des races d'hommes inférieures, qui ont végété jusqu'à nos jours, comme les représentants arriérés des forces primitives et dépassées par nous de la civilisation' (*PI*, II, 421–22). This disturbing suggestion that the demise of certain races is inevitable is followed by an even more shocking point: not only does Hartmann posit a Darwinian principle governing human culture, he also advocates active involvement in this process, effectively preaching genocide:

> Le vrai philanthrope, qui a une fois compris la loi du développement anthropologique, ne peut s'empêcher de souhaiter que l'on abrège les dernières convulsions de l'agonie d'un peuple; il n'hésite pas à y travailler lui-même. (*PI*, II, 422)

If there is any doubt as to the identity of these so-called inferior races, Hartmann makes it clear: these are 'des races incapables de soutenir la concurrence de la race blanche', and their 'suppression' will make the earth 'la possession exclusive des races actuellement les plus cultivées' (*PI*, II, 422). The Unconscious is utterly amoral in its pursuit of its ultimate goal:

> l'Inconscient n'est pas plus touché par les lamentations de plusieurs milliards d'êtres humains que par celles d'un nombre égal d'animaux: il lui suffit que ces plaintes sont nécessaires au progrès du monde et par suite à son but suprême. (*PI*, II, 423)

Laforgue's vision of open cultural exchange implicitly challenges the ruthless cruelty of Hartmann's doctrine, but in another fragment of notes he does concur with the underlying Darwinian logic: 'L'essence de la vie entre les individus est la concurrence vitale, se résumant dans la concurrence vitale entre les races pour le progrès, pour le bonheur' (*OC*, III, 1114). However, the inequality that this logic entails is not inevitable:

> Intervient une puissance suprême la fraternité, la Justice humaine sociale d'État corrigeant l'injustice nécessaire de la nature, pour le bonheur de chacun dans sa vie d'ici-bas, puisqu'il n'y en a pas une autre. (*OC*, III, 1114)[5]

Laforgue's response to Hartmann demonstrates his ethical commitment. It also shows the extent to which his reading of philosophy is defined by a critical approach. While the Unconscious (or, at least, Laforgue's idiosyncratic version of it) constitutes the ultimate aesthetic principle, implying liberation from both rational control and the restrictions of national culture, its power should not necessarily be accepted in every sphere of human existence.

* * * * *

Laforgue's appeal for a transnational aesthetics echoes his own migratory biography. His various displacements — from Uruguay to France at the age of 6, from Tarbes to Paris at the age of 16, from Paris to Germany at the age of 21 and back again at 26 — are referred to only occasionally and obliquely in his work, however. One such reference occurs in 'Préludes autobiographiques', where the poet describes himself as a 'Bon Breton né sous les Tropiques' (*OC*, I, 546). While this is factually inaccurate (as Lefrère points out, Montevideo is over a thousand kilometres south of the Tropic of Capricorn and Laforgue had no Breton ancestry),[6] it does hint at the ways in which Laforgue plays with the idea of foreign identity. What matters is not so much the veracity of Laforgue's Breton blood or tropical birth as the notion, conveyed in this formulation, that he is somehow out of place, that his point of origin cannot be fixed. Indeed, the possibility of reading this self-description as a mockery of earlier claims to outsider status (an interpretation supported by the fact that it appears at the head of a stanza parodying the grandiloquence of *Le Sanglot de la Terre*) itself points to the elusiveness of Laforguian identity: we cannot be sure if he is joking or being serious, just as we cannot be sure of where he really comes from.

There is a further level of significance to Laforgue's claim of Breton heritage. In the nineteenth century, as Heather Williams points out, Brittany was subject to a kind of internal exoticism, earlier discourses of Breton primitivism being perpetuated by Romantic conceptions of the region as wild, untamed and alluringly 'other', not least linguistically.[7] The association between Breton identity and what we might call 'outsider poetry' remained current in the late nineteenth century, as demonstrated by Verlaine's description of the Breton poet Tristan Corbière in *Les Poètes maudits*: 'Quel Breton bretonnant de la bonne manière!'[8] Indeed, Laforgue echoes this description and, moreover, connects it to his own work: in a letter to Léo Trézénik responding to accusations that his work was inspired by Corbière, he insists on his differences from the latter but goes on to suggest one point of affinity: 'si j'ai l'âme de Corbière un peu, c'est dans sa nuance bretonne' (*OC*, II, 786).[9] But this does not mean that we should recuperate his claim to Breton identity as genuine: rather, he asserts that his *poetry* has a 'Breton' quality, that it is in some sense 'other'.

In his early work, then, Laforgue aspires to the identity of outsider[10] just as he dreams of exotic adventure;[11] but his later work mocks these aspirations, instead enacting the idea of exploring otherness in and through language: 'L'ivresse du nomadisme sera [...] circonscrite et condensée sur la scène de l'écriture'.[12] For the early Laforgue, by contrast, language is felt to be limiting, with notes from 1880 registering his sense of being 'endolori par les luttes littéraires (lutte avec mes rêves dont je ne puis jouir et qu'il me faut matérialiser avec les vingt-cinq lettres de la langue humaine)' (*OC*, I, 655). If a sense of limitation also haunts Laforgue's later work, it is a limitation felt at the level of everyday life, not in the poetic world. In 'Complainte sur certains temps déplacés', for example, the sunset inspires exotic fantasies ('Ça vous fait le cœur tout nomade, | À cingler vers mille Lusiades!' (*OC*, I, 598)), but the poet is resigned to the restrictive banality of his existence:

> Je n'aurai jamais d'aventures;
> Qu'il est petit, dans la Nature,
> Le chemin d'fer Paris-Ceinture! (*OC*, I, 598)

The *rime redoublée* itself suggests repetition and constriction, encircling the tercet like the Paris-Ceinture loop line. But even outside of Paris there is no escape from the banality of human existence: 'Ah! que la Vie est quotidienne...' (*OC*, I, 586) declares 'Complainte sur certains ennuis', which is set in the aristocratic world that Laforgue experienced in Berlin. If the poet's yearning for exotic adventure does not entirely disappear in his mature work, it is most often ironized, and it sits alongside a desire to accept the facticity of the everyday:

> Oh! vivre uniment autochtones
> Sur cette terre (où nous cantonne
> Après tout notre être tel quel!)
> Et sans préférer, l'âme aigrie,
> Aux vers luisants de nos prairies
> Les lucioles des prés du ciel. (*OC*, II, 214)

But this 'tel quel' is not without its own wonders, underwritten as it is by the Unconscious.

Moreover, language itself provides a way to explore otherness in the here and now. The 'clownesque' manner of his mature *œuvre* suggests an irreverence for the conventions of French, and in a note written in late 1885 Laforgue openly expresses a desire to 'other' his national language:

> Écrire une prose très claire, très simple (mais en gardant toutes ses richesses) mais contournée non péniblement mais naïvement, du français d'africaine géniale, du français de Christ. Et y ajouter par des images hors de notre répertoire français, tout en restant directement humaines. Des images d'un Gaspard Hauser qui n'a pas fait ses classes mais a été au fond de la mort, a fait de la botanique naturelle, est familier avec les ciels et les astres, et les animaux, et les couleurs, et les rues, et les choses bonnes comme les gâteaux, le tabac, les baisers, l'amour. (*OC*, III, 1054)

What Laforgue aspires to, then, is a deterritorialization ('Être dans sa propre langue comme un *étranger*'),[13] a primitivistic re-working of the French language. This is reinforced by the reference to Gaspard Hauser, a supposedly feral child discovered in Germany in the early nineteenth century to whom Verlaine dedicated a poem in *Sagesse* (1880).[14] Indeed, Laforgue expresses his own sense of *dépaysement* in the German court through an identification with this outsider figure: 'je suis une série de bals, j'observe, tel un Gaspard Hauser' (*OC*, II, 821).

The lexical range of Laforgue's poetry and prose, which encompasses scientific, mythological, ecclesiastical, technical, Classical, medical, Buddhist and colloquial vocabulary, certainly fulfils his desire to incorporate 'des images hors de notre répertoire français'. Philosophical language itself constitutes a 'Parole venue d'ailleurs, et qui habite en étrangère le texte de Laforgue', as Bonnefis puts it.[15] Moreover, his use of French is unconventional in other ways, perhaps most notably in his creation of neologistic amalgamations such as 'Éternullité' ('Préludes autobiographiques', *OC*, I, 547) and 'sexciproques' ('Complainte à Notre-Dame des Soirs', *OC*, I, 551). He also ignores basic rules of French grammar, in particular the masculine plural form of the adjectival ending '-al' ('sentimentals' ('Complainte des Voix sous le Figuier boudhique', *OC*, I, 554), 'filials' ('Complainte d'un certain Dimanche', *OC*, I, 561), 'nuptials' ('Complainte sur certains temps déplacés', *OC*, I, 598)), as well as the contraction 'aux' ('à les seins dorloteurs' ('Complainte du fœtus de Poète', *OC*, I, 563), 'à lesquels' ('Les linges, le cygne', *OC*, II, 106)).. In addition, he constructs phrases with a word order far removed from standard French, perhaps most notably in the opening line of 'Complainte d'un autre Dimanche': 'C'était un très-au vent d'octobre paysage' (*OC*, I, 562). The line, which might almost be a *calque* from English syntax, certainly embodies Lord Pierrot's appeal to the Unconscious to 'Brouillez les cartes, les dictionnaires, les sexes' ('Complainte de Lord Pierrot', *OC*, I, 584).

Given these idiosyncrasies, it is no wonder that some of Laforgue's contemporaries opined that he wrote like a foreigner. Particularly vehement in his criticism was the poet and novelist Edmond Haraucourt, who wrote a letter to the journal *Lutèce* in response to the publication of 'Complainte propitiatoire à l'Inconscient' and 'Complainte-Placet de Faust fils' in March 1885:

> si ça continue, il suffira dans six ans: 1e de n'avoir rien à dire; 2e de le dire en mauvais vers et en vers faux; 3e d'écrire comme un Javanais: pour être un poète de génie. (*OC*, II, 746 n. 2)

Haraucourt's first point is reminiscent of Laforgue's notes on Baudelaire, written at around the same time, in which Laforgue lauds the absence of any conventional subject in the latter's work:

> faire des poésies détachées — courtes — *sans sujet appréciable* [...] mais vagues et sans raison comme un battement d'éventail, éphémères et équivoques comme un maquillage, qui font dire au bourgeois qui vient de lire 'Et après?' (*OC*, III, 172; author's emphasis)

While it is possible that this desire to *épater la bourgeoisie* was inspired in part by Haraucourt, Laforgue had in fact expressed a similar sentiment three years earlier; in a letter to Sabine Mültzer of 18 July 1882 he states that he aspires to write poetry about nothing:

> Moi je rêve de la poésie qui ne dise rien, mais soit de bouts de rêverie sans suite. Quand on veut dire, exposer, démontrer quelque chose, il y a la prose. (*OC*, I, 792)

Laforgue may thus have found perverse satisfaction in Haraucourt's first critique. However, in a letter to Kahn of 23 April 1885 responding to the criticism, he focuses not on this, but rather on the accusation of writing like a Javanese. Haraucourt — 'cet écervelé aux airs paternels' (*OC*, II, 755) — has, he states, inspired 'ce quatrain javanais':

> Les Haraucourt
> Sont moins rares
> Qu'un bon cigare
> Par le temps qui court. (*OC*, II, 755)

The simplicity of this piece of doggerel and the use of cliché in its final line seem designed to counter the charge of foreignness. Indeed, he is very evidently offended by a similar criticism from the editors of the *Revue illustrée*, to whom he had sent a novella (thought to be an early version of 'Les Deux Pigeons', a tale that was eventually excluded from *Moralités légendaires*): in a letter to Théophile Ysaÿe of April 1886, he writes:

> Il paraît que le comité bourgeois qu'on alimente dans les sous-sol[s] de chez Dumas a trouvé que j'écrivais 'comme quelqu'un qui serait étranger'! Allons, du moins la vieille gaîté française n'est pas morte. (*OC*, II, 845)

This is not to imply that Laforgue unironically claims the identity of 'honnête | poète | français' (*OC*, II, 822), the title he borrows from Pierrot (see 'Locutions des Pierrots (IX)', *OC*, II, 93) in signing off a letter to Kahn in March 1886. Rather, it bears witness to the distance that lies between the desire for subversion and the need for recognition. It is apt, in some sense, that in the years after his premature demise this recognition was to be found not in France, but abroad, in England, amongst the modernists Pound and Eliot.

Laforgue's resistance to being ascribed a foreign identity also shows the disparity between, on the one hand, celebrating the artist's capacity to accept 'toutes les influences' and to step beyond the bounds of his own national culture, and, on the other, the exclusionary logic used to 'other' undesirable elements (literary or otherwise) of society. After all, for Laforgue there *is* no otherness at the most fundamental level. His desire to elude binary thinking is often premised on an appeal to the Unconscious as monist metaphysical principle; but he is also fascinated by states of betweenness, such as that constituted by dreaming. In a section of his later notes, he returns to the 'vie/néant' dichotomy:

> Est-ce dormir? En ce cas, vive le Néant! Mais non! Est-ce alors vivre. Hélas non — vivre est souffrir par essence, en effet qu'on recense — mais le rêve, le sommeil, le demi sommeil qui rêve — ni vivre ni dormir. (*OC*, III, 1166)

This liminal, penumbral state permits a refusal of the choice between self-annihilation and suffering. For Laforgue, dream is, moreover, inextricably associated with writing. In December 1881, in a letter to Henry, he expresses his vision of 'une poésie qui serait de la psychologie dans une forme de rêve' (*OC*, I, 757); in May 1883, writing to his sister Marie, he reiterates this idea, stating that 'Une poésie ne doit pas être une description exacte (comme une page de roman), mais noyée de rêve' (*OC*, I, 821). Indeed, if in Laforgue's thinking each art-form is responsible for the refinement of its related sensory faculty — music improves the ear, visual art the eye and so on — and thus the evolution of humanity, then the task of writing is, Laforgue suggests, to develop the capacity to dream. This idea emerges in his notes on Taine, where he refers to Bourget's theory of artistic sensibilities:

> Selon la formule de Bourget chaque sensibilité extraordinaire a son mirage personnel de l'univers. Cela s'applique au philosophe (principe, essence, solution des choses), artiste optique (un certain sentiment et une certaine excitabilité devant la couleur et les formes des choses et des êtres), musicien (symphoniste ou mélodiste, etc.), poète (telle ou telle habitude de rêves). (*OC*, III, 361)

This 'habitude de rêves', this capacity to inhabit and explore the inner world of the soul, is what marks out the poet.

If this inner world is, in one sense, the most fundamental element of the self, its unfamiliarity, even strangeness, mean it is also an other within. Laforgue's interest in this world is central to his reception of philosophical ideas. But we might, perhaps, extend the idea of the poet's 'rêves' to his dreams of different social forms, especially in the realm of sexuality. Laforgue may be fascinated by the inner domain of the self, but this is certainly not to the exclusion of a concern for the outer world. Indeed, for Laforgue writing is a means to pass between inner and outer, just as it represents a way of breaching the boundaries between different cultures and different disciplines: between France and Germany, between West and East, between poetry and philosophy.

Notes to the Conclusion

1. Victor Hugo, *Les Contemplations* (Paris: Gallimard, 1973), p. 383.
2. The phrase is adapted from Jean 3:8: 'Le vent souffle où il veut' (the wind representing the Holy Spirit).
3. Mireille Dottin-Orsini, *OC*, III, 336.
4. Indeed, J. J. Clarke suggests that the phrase 'laissez-faire' was borrowed by de Gournay from fellow Physiocrat François Quesnay's writings on China, which discussed the term 'wu wei' and translated it as 'laissez-faire'; in this sense, the phrase embodies its own principle of transnational openness (J. J. Clarke, *Oriental Enlightenment: The Encounter Between Asian and Western Thought* (London: Routledge, 1997), p. 50).
5. On this point, I am indebted to Bertrand Marchal, who offered an illuminating analysis of Laforgue's response to Hartmann's doctrine in his paper 'Laforgue, Hartmann, l'Inconscient: quelques remarques' at the *journée d'études* of the Centre de Recherches sur les Poétiques du XIXème siècle entitled 'Les Philosophes de Jules Laforgue', held at the Université Sorbonne Nouvelle-Paris III on 31 May 2016. This paper was subsequently published as 'Laforgue et Hartmann, quelques remarques sur "les vers philo."' in *Revue d'histoire littéraire de la France*, 117, no. 2 (2017), 283-97, after the completion of this manuscript.
6. Lefrère, p. 19.
7. Heather Williams, 'Writing to Paris: Poets, Nobles and Savages in Nineteenth-Century Brittany', *French Studies*, 57, no. 4 (2003), 475–90.
8. Paul Verlaine, *Les Poètes maudits*, ed. by Michel Décaudin (Paris: SEDES, 1982), p. 22; quoted in Williams (2003), p. 487. See also des Esseintes' description of Corbière's poetry as 'à peine français' (Joris-Karl Huysmans, *À rebours* (Paris: Gallimard, 1977 [1884]), p. 316).
9. He also reinforces the idea of Brittany's otherness in his description of the region as 'le "Far-West" de la France' ('Notes d'un carnet de 1885', *OC*, III, 1013).
10. See, for example, the paratextual reference in the poem 'Mémento. Sonnet triste' from *Le Sanglot*, which is signed 'Jules Laforgue — Mouni' (*OC*, I, 419). A 'mouni' designates an ascetic sage, from the Hindu or Buddhist traditions.
11. See p. 116.
12. Loubier, p. 141.
13. Gilles Deleuze and Félix Guattari, *Kafka. Pour une littérature mineure* (Paris: Minuit, 1975), p. 48; authors' emphasis. For a more general Deleuzian reading of Laforgue, see Scott (2016).
14. Paul Verlaine, *Sagesse; Amour* (Paris: Rombaldi, 1937), pp. 101–02.
15. Bonnefis (1988), p. 62.

BIBLIOGRAPHY

ADORNO, THEODOR W., 'On Lyric Poetry and Society', in *Notes to Literature*, ed. by Rolf Tiedemann, trans. by Shierry Weber Nicholsen, 2 vols (New York, NY: Columbia University Press, 1991), I, 37–54
ALMOND, PHILIP C., *The British Discovery of Buddhism* (Cambridge University Press, 1988)
ANDERSON, BENEDICT, *Imagined Communities: Reflections on the Origin and Spread of Nationalism*, 2nd edn (London: Verso, 1991)
ARKELL, DAVID, *Looking for Laforgue: an informal biography* (Manchester: Carcanet, 1979)
ARNAUD, PIERRE, 'Dividing and uniting: sports societies and nationalism, 1870–1914', in *Nationhood and Nationalism in France from Boulangism to the Great War*, ed. by Robert Tombs (Oxford: Routledge, 1991, repr. 2006), pp. 182–94
ARNOLD, EDWIN, *The Light of Asia* (London: Trübner, 1879)
BAILLOT, ALEXANDRE, *Influence de la philosophie de Schopenhauer en France (1860–1900)* (Paris: J. Vrin, 1927)
BAJU, ANATOLE, *Le Décadent*, 1 (10 April 1886)
BAKHTIN, MIKHAIL, *Esthétique et théorie du roman*, trans. by Daria Olivier (Paris: Gallimard, 1978)
BALDWIN, PETER, *Contagion and the State in Europe, 1830–1930* (Cambridge: Cambridge University Press, 1999)
BALIBAR, ÉTIENNE, 'The Nation Form: History and Ideology', in Étienne Balibar and Immanuel Wallerstein, *Race, Nation, Class: Ambiguous Identities* (London: Verso, 1991), pp. 86–106
BANVILLE, THÉODORE DE, *Œuvres de Théodore de Banville; Les Cariatides; Roses de Noël* (Paris: Lemerre, 1889)
BARNES, DAVID S., *The Making of a Social Disease: Tuberculosis in Nineteenth-Century France* (Berkeley and Los Angeles, CA: University of California Press, 1995)
BARROWS, JOHN HENRY, 'Inaugural Speech' (1893) <http://parliamentofreligions.org/parliament/chicago-1893> [accessed 27 September 2016]
BARTHÉLEMY-SAINT-HILAIRE, JULES, *Le Bouddha et sa religion* (Paris: Didier, 1860)
BARTH, FREDRIK, 'Introduction', in *Ethnic Groups and Boundaries: The Social Organization of Culture Difference*, ed. by Fredrik Barth (Prospect Heights, IL: Waveland, 1998), pp. 9–38
BAUDELAIRE, CHARLES, *Œuvres complètes*, ed. by Marcel A. Ruff (Paris: Seuil, 1968)
BEAUVOIR, SIMONE DE, *Le deuxième sexe*, 2 vols (Paris: Flammarion, 1973)
BECKER, NICOLAS, 'Le Rhin allemand', trans. by Alfred de Musset, *Poésies complètes*, ed. by Maurice Allem (Paris: Gallimard, 1957)
BEM, JEANNE, *Le texte traversé: Corneille, Prévost, Marivaux, Musset, Dumas, Nerval, Baudelaire, Hugo, Flaubert, Verlaine, Laforgue, Proust, Giraudoux, Aragon, Giono* (Paris: Champion, 1991)
BÉNICHOU, PAUL, *Le sacre de l'écrivain, 1750–1830* (Paris: Gallimard, 1996)
BERNHEIMER, CHARLES, *Figures of Ill Repute: Representing Prostitution in Nineteenth-Century France* (Cambridge, MA; London: Harvard University Press, 1989)
BERTRAND, JEAN-PIERRE, *Les Complaintes de Jules Laforgue. Ironie et désenchantement* (Paris: Klincksieck, 1997)

———'Petite mythologie portative', *Vortex*, 2 (2000) <http://www.orsini.net/laforgue/vortex2/bertrand2.htm> [accessed 30 April 2011]
BERTRAND, JEAN-PIERRE, and HENRI SCEPI, ' "Le rêve d'une langue bornée, mais infinie": Laforgue poète langagier', in *La Littérature symboliste et la Langue. Actes du colloque organisé à Aoste les 8 et 9 mai 2009*, ed. by Olivier Bivort (Paris: Classiques Garnier, 2012), pp. 121–39
BILLIG, MICHAEL, 'Socio-psychological aspects of nationalism: imagining ingroups, others and the world of nations', in *Nationalism, Ethnicity and Cultural Identity in Europe*, ed. by Keebet von Benda-Beckmann and Maykel Verkuyten (Utrecht: European Research Centre on Migration and Ethnic Relations, 1995), pp. 89–105
BIVORT, OLIVIER, 'Obscurité de la langue, clarté de la poésie', in *La Littérature symboliste et la Langue. Actes du colloque organisé à Aoste les 8 et 9 mai 2009*, ed. by Olivier Bivort (Paris: Classiques Garnier, 2012), pp. 75–88
BLOCK DE BEHAR, LISA, *Jules Laforgue ou les métaphores du déplacement*, trans. by Albert Bensoussan (Paris: Harmattan, 2004)
BONGIE, CHRIS, *Exotic Memories: Literature, Colonialism, and the Fin de siècle* (Stanford, CA: Stanford University Press, 1991)
BONNEFIS, PHILIPPE, 'Entre Laforgue et Hartmann: le monologue de Salomé', *Lendemains*, 49 (1988), 57–69
———'Faire parler l'inconscient', *La Quinzaine Littéraire*, 488 (16–30 June 1987), 13–15
BOOTLE, SAM, 'The Body Poetic: Laforgue's Translations of Whitman', *Dix-Neuf*, 20, no. 1 (2016), 25–44
———'Jules Laforgue and the Illusion of Spontaneity', *Dix-Neuf*, 15, no. 2 (2011), 166–76
BOURDEAU, JEAN, 'Introduction', in Arthur Schopenhauer, *Pensées, maximes et fragments*, ed. and trans. by Jean Bourdeau (Paris: Germer-Baillière, 1880), pp. 1–26
BOURDELAIS, PATRICE and ANDRÉ DODIN, *Visages du choléra* ([Paris?]: Belin, 1987)
BOURGET, PAUL, *Essais de psychologie contemporaine* ([Paris]: Gallimard, 1993)
BOWIE, ANDREW, *Aesthetics from Kant to Nietzsche* (Manchester: Manchester University Press, 2003)
BRICHE, GÉRARD, 'Mal de Mère. Portrait de l'artiste en malade: Jules Laforgue', in *Littérature et Pathologie*, ed. by Max Milner (Paris: Presses universitaires de Vincennes, 1989), pp. 205–11
BURNOUF, EUGÈNE, *Introduction à l'histoire du buddhisme indien* (Paris: Maisonneuve, 1844)
BURROW, J. W., *The Crisis of Reason: European Thought, 1848–1914* (New Haven, CT: Yale University Press, 2000)
CANTACUZÈNE, J. A., *Le Monde comme volonté et comme représentation* (Leipzig: F. A. Brockhaus, 1886)
CARO, ELME-MARIE, *Le Pessimisme au XIXe siècle* (Paris: Hachette, 1878)
CARRÉ, JEAN-MARIE, *Les Écrivains français et le mirage allemand, 1800–1940* (Paris: Boivin, 1947)
CATY, MARGUERITE POULIN, 'Poétique du spleen dans l'œuvre de Jules Laforgue', *The French Review*, 65, no. 1 (1991), 55–63
CÉARD, HENRY, 'Clowns et philosophes', *Le Siècle*, 19 October 1888
CHALLEMEL-LACOUR, PAUL, 'Un Bouddhiste Contemporain en Allemagne', *Revue des deux Mondes*, 86 (March 1870), 296–332
CHAMBERS, ROSS, *Room for Maneuver: Reading (the) Oppositional (in) Narrative* (Chicago, IL: University of Chicago Press, 1991)
CHAMPOD, OLIVIER, '*Tessa*, ou comment brûler Schopenhauer', *Revue de littérature comparée*, 324 (2007), 427–38
CLARKE, J. J., *Oriental Enlightenment: The Encounter Between Asian and Western Thought* (London: Routledge, 1997)

COLIN, RENÉ-PIERRE, *Schopenhauer en France: un mythe naturaliste* (Lyon: Presses universitaires de Lyon, 1979)
COLLIE, MICHAEL, *Jules Laforgue* (London: The Athlone Press, 1977)
COLLIER, PETER, 'Poetry and Cliché: Laforgue's "L'Hiver qui vient"', in *Nineteenth-century French poetry: Introductions to close reading*, ed. by Christopher Prendergast (Cambridge: Cambridge University Press, 1990), pp. 199–224
CONSTABLE, LIZ, MATTHEW POTOLSKY and DENNIS DENISOFF, 'Introduction', in *Perennial Decay: On the Aesthetics and Politics of Decadence*, ed. by Liz Constable, Matthew Potolsky and Dennis Denisoff (Philadelphia: University of Pennsylvania Press, 1999)
CONVERSI, DANIELE, 'Reassessing current theories of nationalism: nationalism as boundary maintenance and creation', in *Nationalism: Critical Concepts in Political Science*, ed. by John Hutchinson and Anthony D. Smith (London: Routledge, 2000), pp. 420–33
COUNTER, ANDREW, 'Zola's fin-de-siècle reproductive politics', *French Studies*, 68, no. 2 (2014), 193–208
CUISINIER, JEANNE, *Jules Laforgue* (Paris: Albert Messein, 1925)
DALE, PETER, *Poems of Jules Laforgue* (London: Anvil Press Poetry, 2001)
DARNOI, DENNIS N. KENEDY, *The Unconscious and Eduard von Hartmann* (The Hague: Martinus Nijhoff, 1967)
DELANTY, GERARD, 'Nationalism and Cosmopolitanism: The Paradox of Modernity', in *The SAGE Handbook of Nations and Nationalism*, ed. by Gerard Delanty and Krishan Kumar (London: Sage, 2006), pp. 357–68
DELEUZE, GILLES, and FÉLIX GUATTARI, *Kafka. Pour une littérature mineure* (Paris: Minuit, 1975)
DIERX, LÉON, *Les Lèvres closes* (Paris: Lemerre, 1868)
DIGEON, CLAUDE, *La Crise allemande de la pensée française, 1870–1914* (Paris: Presses universitaires de France, 1959)
DROIT, ROGER-POL, *Le Culte du néant: Les philosophes et le Bouddha* (Paris: Seuil, 1997)
DUCREY, GUY, 'Tanagra ou les anamorphoses d'une figurine béotienne à la fin du XIXe siècle', in *Anamorphoses décadentes: l'art de la défiguration 1880–1914; études offertes à Jean de Palacio*, ed. by Isabelle Krzywkowski and Sylvie Thorel-Cailleteau (Paris: Presses de l'Université de Paris-Sorbonne, 2002), pp. 207–24
DUFOUR, MÉDÉRIC, *Étude sur l'esthétique de Jules Laforgue: une philosophie de l'impressionnisme* (Paris: Vanier, 1904)
DUJARDIN, ÉDOUARD, *Les Premiers Poètes du vers libre* (Paris: Mercure de France, 1922)
DUNSTAN MARTIN, GRAHAM, 'Introduction', in Jules Laforgue, *Selected Poems*, trans. by Graham Dunstan Martin (London: Penguin, 1998), pp. ix–xxxviii
DURAND, PASCAL, 'Poésie et décor: l'intérieur, le trop, le rien. À propos de la "Complainte des pubertés difficiles"', in *Jules Laforgue: colloque de la Sorbonne: actes de la journée d'agrégation du 18 novembre 2000*, ed. by André Guyaux and Bertrand Marchal (Paris: Presses de l'Université de Paris-Sorbonne, 2000), pp. 143–58
DURRY, MARIE-JEANNE, *Jules Laforgue* (Paris: Seghers, 1966)
EIGELDINGER, MARC, *L'Évolution dynamique de l'image dans la poésie française du Romantisme à nos jours* (Neuchâtel: Seiler, 1943)
ELIOT, T. S., *The Varieties of Metaphysical Poetry*, ed. by Ronald Schuhard (London: Faber and Faber, 1993)
ESPAGNE, MICHEL and MICHAËL WERNER, 'La construction d'une référence culturelle allemande en France: genèse et histoire (1750–1914)', *Annales*, 42 (1987), 969–92
FÉDI, LAURENT, 'Le clair-obscur: La philosophie française et l'inconscient', in *Un débat sur l'Inconscient avant Freud: la réception de Eduard von Hartmann chez les psychologues et philosophes français*, ed. by Serge Nicolas and Laurent Fédi (Paris: Harmattan, 2008)

FIGUEIRA, DOROTHY M., *The Exotic: A Decadent Quest* (Albany: State University of New York Press, 1994)
FLAUBERT, GUSTAVE, *Bouvard et Pécuchet: avec un choix des scénarios, du Sottisier, L'Album de la Marquise et Le Dictionnaire des idées reçues*, ed. by Claudine Gothot-Mersch ([Paris]: Gallimard, 1979 [1881])
——*Madame Bovary* (Paris: Nelson, 1950 [1856])
FOUCHER DE CAREIL, ALEXANDRE, *Hegel et Schopenhauer* (Paris: Hachette, 1862)
FREUD, SIGMUND, *Civilisation and its discontents*, trans. by Joan Riviere, 2nd edn, rev. by James Strachey (London: The Hogarth Press and the Institute of Psychoanalysis, 1963)
GARDNER, SEBASTIAN, 'Eduard von Hartmann's Philosophy of the Unconscious', in *Thinking the Unconscious: Nineteenth-Century German Thought*, ed. by Angus Nicholls and Martin Liebscher (Cambridge: Cambridge University Press, 2010), pp. 173–99
GAUNT, SIMON, 'The Chanson de Roland and the Invention of France', in *Rethinking Heritage: Cultures and Politics in Europe*, ed. by Robert Shannan Peckham (London: Tauris, 2003), pp. 90–101
GAUTIER, THÉOPHILE, *Spirite* (Paris: Nizet, 1970 [1886])
GIRARDET, RAOUL, *Le nationalisme français, 1871–1914* (Paris: Armand Colin, 1966)
GOBINEAU, ARTHUR DE, *Ce qui est arrivé à la France en 1870* (Paris: Klincksieck, 1970 [1870])
GROJNOWSKI, DANIEL, *Jules Laforgue et 'l'Originalité'* (Boudry-Neuchâtel: La Baconnière, 1988)
——*Jules Laforgue, les voix de la Complainte* (La Rochelle: Rumeur des Âges, 2000)
——'Poétique du Rien: L'Imitation de Notre-Dame la Lune', *Europe*, no. 673 (May 1985), 48–65
——'La première des "Complaintes"', in *Jules Laforgue: colloque de la Sorbonne: actes de la journée d'agrégation du 18 novembre 2000*, ed. by André Guyaux and Bertrand Marchal (Paris: Presses de l'Université de Paris-Sorbonne, 2000), pp. 43–54
GUIRAUD, PIERRE, *Dictionnaire historique, stylistique, rhétorique, étymologique, de la littérature érotique* (Paris: Payot, 1978)
GUY, MADELEINE, 'De la réécriture musicale dans *Moralités légendaires*', *Dix-Neuf*, 20, no. 1 (2016), 66–80
——'Jules Laforgue, Hartmann and Schopenhauer: From Influence to Rewriting', in *Questions of Influence in Modern French Literature*, ed. by Thomas Baldwin, James Fowler and Ana de Medeiros (Basingstoke; New York, NY: Palgrave Macmillan, 2013), pp. 58–70
Le Hanneton, July 1867
HANNOOSH, MICHÈLE, *Parody and Decadence: Laforgue's 'Moralités légendaires'* (Columbus: Ohio State University Press, 1989)
HARRISON, ROBERT POGUE, *Forests: The Shadow of Civilisation* (Chicago, IL: University of Chicago Press, 1992)
HARROW, SUSAN, *Zola, The Body Modern: Pressures and Prospects of Representation* (London: Legenda, 2010)
HARTMAN, ELWOOD, *French Literary Wagnerism* (New York; London: Garland, 1988)
HARTMANN, EDUARD VON, *La Philosophie de l'Inconscient*, 2 vols, trans. by D. Nolen (Paris: Germer Baillière, 1877)
——*Philosophy of the Unconscious: speculative results according to the inductive method of physical science*, trans. by William Chatterton Coupland, 2nd edn (London: Kegan Paul, 1931)
HARVEY, PETER, *An Introduction to Buddhism: Teaching, History and Practices*, 10th edn (Cambridge: Cambridge University Press, 1998 [1990])
HENRY, ANNE, 'Actualité d'un vieux prophète', in *Schopenhauer et la création littéraire en Europe*, ed. by Anne Henry (Paris: Méridiens Klincksieck, 1989), pp. 11–14

—— 'L'Expansion du schopenhauérisme', in *Schopenhauer et la création littéraire en Europe*, ed. by Anne Henry (Paris: Méridiens Klincksieck, 1989), pp. 15–19
—— 'La Réception française de Schopenhauer', in *Schopenhauer et la création littéraire en Europe*, ed. by Anne Henry (Paris: Méridiens Klincksieck, 1989), pp. 32–26
HIBBITT, RICHARD, *Dilettantism and its Values: From Weimar Classicism to the fin de siècle* (London: Legenda, 2006)
HIDDLESTON, J. A., 'Dans l'intertexte laforguien: Hartmann et quelques autres', *Romantisme*, 19, no. 64 (1989), 47–52
—— *Essai sur Laforgue et les 'Derniers vers': suivi de, Laforgue et Baudelaire* (Lexington, KY: French Forum, 1980)
—— 'Introduction', in Jules Laforgue, *Poems*, ed. by J. A. Hiddleston (Oxford: Blackwell, 1975), pp. 1–40
—— 'Laforgue and Hartmann', in *Proceedings of the Xth Congress of the International Comparative Literature Association, 1982*, ed. by Anna Balakian (New York, 1985), pp. 66–72
HOBSBAWM, ERIC J., *Nations and Nationalism since 1780: Programme, Myth, Reality* (Cambridge: Cambridge University Press, 1990)
HOFFMEISTER, GERHART, 'De l'Allemagne', in *The Literary Encyclopedia* (1 November 2005). <http://www.litencyc.com/php/sworks.php?rec=true&UID=5708> [accessed 24 February 2014]
HOGAN, W. F., 'Syllabus of Errors', in *New Catholic Encyclopedia*, 15 vols (New York, NY: McGraw-Hill, 1967), XIII, 854–56
HOLMES, ANNE, '"De nouveaux rythmes": The Free Verse of Laforgue's "Solo de Lune"', *French Studies*, 62, no. 2 (2008), 162–72
—— *Jules Laforgue and Poetic Innovation* (Oxford: Clarendon Press, 1993)
HOWE, ELISABETH A., *Stages of Self: The Dramatic Monologues of Laforgue, Valéry and Mallarmé* (Athens: Ohio University Press, 1990)
HUGO, VICTOR, preface to *Les Burgraves*, in *Théâtre complet*, 2 vols, ed. by J.-J. Thierry and Josette Mélèze (Paris: Gallimard, 1963–64)
—— *Les Contemplations* (Paris: Gallimard, 1973)
HUTCHEON, LINDA, *A Theory of Parody: The Teachings of Twentieth-Century Art Forms* (New York: Methuen, 2000)
HUYSMANS, JORIS-KARL, *À rebours* (Paris: Gallimard, 1977 [1884])
ISRAEL, JONATHAN, *Radical Enlightenment: Philosophy and the Making of Modernity 1650–1750* (Oxford: Oxford University Press, 2001)
JANAWAY, CHRISTOPHER, *Schopenhauer* (Oxford: Oxford University Press, 1994)
JANET, PAUL, 'La Métaphysique en Europe depuis Hegel. II. Un philosophe misanthrope', *Revue des deux Mondes*, 21 (May 1877), 269–87
—— 'La Métaphysique en Europe depuis Hegel. III. La Philosophie de la Volonté et la Philosophie de l'Inconscient', *Revue des deux Mondes*, 21 (June 1877), 614–35
JANKÉLÉVITCH, VLADIMIR, 'La Décadence', in *Revue de Métaphysique et de Morale*, 55, no. 4 (October-December 1950) (Paris: Presses universitaires de France), 337–69
JOURDE, PIERRE, *L'Alcool du silence. Sur la décadence* (Paris: Champion, 1994)
KAHN, GUSTAVE, *Symbolistes et décadents* (Paris: L'Édition de Paris, 1902; repr. Geneva: Slatkine Reprints, 1977)
KASULIS, THOMAS P., 'Nirvāna', in *The Encyclopedia of Religion*, ed. by Lindsay Jones et al, 2nd edn, 15 vols (Detroit: Macmillan Reference USA, 2005), X, 6628–35
KING, RICHARD, *Orientalism and Religion: Postcolonial Theory, India and 'the mystic East'* (London: Routledge, 1999)
LAFORGUE, JULES, *Œuvres complètes*, ed. by Jean-Louis Debauve et al, 3 vols (Lausanne: L'Âge d'Homme, 1986–2000)
LAMARTINE, ALPHONSE DE, *Œuvres poétiques complètes*, ed. by Marius-François Guyard (Paris: Gallimard, 1963)

La Rochefoucauld, François de, *Réflexions ou sentences et maximes morales*, ed. by Dominique Secretan (Geneva: Droz, 1967 [1665])
Leclerc, Yvan, '"X en soi": Laforgue et l'identité', *Romantisme*, 19, no. 64 (1989), 29–38
Leclercq, Armelle, 'Jules Laforgue à la lisière des langages: Fonctions subversives du jeu intertextuel', in *(Ab)Normalities*, ed. by Catherine Dousteyssier-Khoze and Paul Scott, (Durham: Durham Modern Languages Series, 2001), pp. 139–50
Lefebvre, Jean-Pierre, 'L'introduction de la philosophie allemande en France au XIX siècle. La question des traductions', in *Transferts: les Relations interculturelles dans l'espace franco-allemand (XVIIIe et XIXe siècle)*, ed. by Michel Espagne and Michaël Werner (Paris: Éditions Recherche sur les civilisations, 1988), pp. 465–76
Lefrère, Jean-Jacques, *Jules Laforgue* ([Paris]: Fayard, 2005)
Lopez, Donald S., *Buddhism: An Introduction and Guide* (London: Penguin, 2001)
Loubier, Pierre, *Jules Laforgue: l'Orgue juvénile* (Paris: Éditions Seli Arslan, 2000)
Magee, Bryan, *The Philosophy of Schopenhauer* (Oxford: Oxford University Press, 1997)
Mallarmé, Stéphane, *Poésies* (Paris: Gallimard, 1992)
Marcowitz, Reiner, 'Attraction and Repulsion: Franco-German Relations in the "Long Nineteenth Century"', in *A History of Franco-German Relations in Europe: From 'Hereditary Enemies' to Partners*, ed. by Carine Germond and Henning Türk (New York: Palgrave Macmillan, 2008), pp. 13–26
Marmier, Xavier, *Poésies d'un voyageur* (Paris: F. Locquin, 1844)
Martin, Emily, 'Toward an Anthropology of Immunology: The Body as Nation State', *Medical Anthropology Quarterly*, New Series, 4, No. 4 (December 1990), 410–26
Mauclair, Camille, *Jules Laforgue, Essai* (Paris: Mercure de France, 1896)
Maupassant, Guy de, 'Auprès d'un mort', in *Contes et nouvelles*, 2 vols, ed. by Louis Forestier (Paris: Gallimard, 1974)
McGuinness, Patrick, 'Introduction', in *Symbolism, Decadence and the Fin de Siècle: French and European Perspectives*, ed. by Patrick McGuinness (Exeter: University of Exeter Press, 2000), pp. 1–15 and 281–84
Michelet, Jules, *La France devant l'Europe*, 2nd edn (Florence; Lyon: Successeurs Le Monnier, 1871)
Mitchell, Allan, *A Stranger in Paris: Germany's Role in Republican France, 1870–1940* (New York: Berghahn, 2006)
Mitchell, Donald W., *Buddhism: Introducing the Buddhist Experience* (Oxford: Oxford University Press, 2002)
Morel, Bénédict, *Traité des dégénérescences physiques, intellectuelles et morales de l'espèce humaine et des causes qui produisent ces variétés maladives* (Paris: Baillière, 1857)
Moret-Jankus, Pauline, *Race et imaginaire biologique chez Proust* (Paris: Classiques Garnier, 2016)
Morgan, Edwin, 'Notes on the Metaphysics of Jules Laforgue', *Poetry*, 69, no. 5 (February 1947), 266–72
Müller, Max, *Comparative mythology: an essay* (London: Routledge, [1856]).
Nicholls, Moira, 'The Influences of Eastern Thought on Schopenhauer's Doctrine of the Thing-in-Itself', in *The Cambridge Companion to Schopenhauer*, ed. by Christopher Janaway (Cambridge: Cambridge University Press, 1999)
Nordau, Max, *Degeneration*, trans. by George L. Mosse (Lincoln; London: University of Nebraska Press, 1968 [1895])
Nye, Robert A., *Crime, Madness, and Politics in Modern France: The Medical Concept of National Decline* (Princeton, NJ: Princeton University Press, 1984)
O'Connor, Erin, *Raw Material: Producing Pathology in Victorian Culture* (Durham, NC; London: Duke University Press, 2000)
Ordinaire, Dionys, 'La Jeune Génération', *La Revue politique et littéraire. Revue des cours littéraires*, 9 (January-July 1885), 706–10

PADWA, HAROLD, *Social Poison: The Culture and Politics of Opiate Control in Britain and France, 1821–1926* (Baltimore, MD: The Johns Hopkins University Press, 2012)

PALACIO, JEAN DE, *La décadence: le mot et la chose* (Paris: Les Belles Lettres, 2011)

PEARSON, ROGER, 'The Voice of the Unconscious: Laforgue and the Poet as Lawgiver', *Dix-Neuf*, 20, no. 1 (2016), 125–44

PERRAULT, CHARLES, *Contes*, ed. by Marc Soriano (Paris: Flammarion, 1989)

PIA, PASCAL, 'Notes et variantes', in Jules Laforgue, *Les Complaintes: suivies des Premiers poèmes*, ed. by Pascal Pia (Paris: Gallimard, 1979), pp. 338–438

PIERROT, JEAN, *L'imaginaire décadent (1880–1900)* (Paris: Presses universitaires de France, 1977)

——'Laforgue, décadent?', in *Laforgue aujourd'hui*, ed. by J. A. Hiddleston ([Paris]: José Corti, 1988)

POTOLSKY, MATTHEW, *The Decadent Republic of Letters: Taste, Politics and Cosmopolitan Community from Baudelaire to Beardsley* (Philadelphia: University of Pennsylvania Press, 2013)

POUND, EZRA, *The Cantos*, 4th edn (London: Faber and Faber, 1987)

PRÉVOST-PARADOL, LUCIEN-ANATOLE, *La France nouvelle* (Paris: Lévy, 1868)

PRICE, ROGER, *A Social History of Nineteenth-Century France* (London: Hutchison, 1987)

PRUDHOMME, SULLY, *Poésies 1865–66: stances et poèmes* (Paris: Lemerre, [18??])

——*Poésies de Sully Prudhomme* (Paris: Lemerre, [1879])

RAMSEY, WARREN, 'Introduction', in *Jules Laforgue: Essays on a Poet's Life and Work*, ed. by Warren Ramsey (Carbondale: Southern Illinois University Press, 1969), pp. xii-xxx

RANCIÈRE, JACQUES, 'The Politics of Literature', *SubStance*, 103, 33.1 (2004), 10–24

RASMUSSEN, CLAIRE and MICHAEL BROWN, 'The Body Politic as Spatial Metaphor', in *Citizenship Studies*, 9, no. 5 (2005), 469–84

RAUDOT, CLAUDE MARIE, *De la Décadence de la France* (Paris: Amyot, 1850)

REBOUL, PIERRE, *Laforgue* (Paris: Hatier, 1960)

REYNAUD, LOUIS, *L'Influence allemande en France au XVIIIe et XIXe siècle* (Paris: Hachette, 1922)

REYNOLDS, FRANK E., and CHARLES HALLISEY, 'Buddhism: An Overview', in *The Encyclopedia of Religion*, ed. by Lindsay Jones et al, 2nd edn, 15 vols (Detroit: Macmillan Reference USA, 2005), II, 1087–1101

RIBOT, THÉODULE, *La Philosophie de Schopenhauer* (Paris: Germer Baillière, 1874)

RICHARD, JEAN-PIERRE, 'Donc je m'en vais', *Revue des Sciences humaines*, 178 (1980), 56–60

——'Le Sang de la complainte', *Poétique*, 37 (February 1979), 487–95

RIVAROL, ANTOINE DE, *De l'universalité de la langue française* (Paris: Obsidiane, 1991 [1784])

ROWE, PAUL, *A Mirror on the Rhine? The Nouvelle revue germanique, 1829–1837* (Oxford; Bern: Peter Lang, 2000)

RUCHON, FRANÇOIS, *Jules Laforgue: sa vie — son œuvre* (Geneva: Éditions Albert Ciana, 1924)

SAID, EDWARD W., *Orientalism: Western Conceptions of the Orient* (London: Routledge and Kegan Paul, 1978; repr. London: Penguin, 2003)

SAKARI, ELLEN, *Prophète et Pierrot: thèmes et attitudes ironiques dans l'œuvre de Jules Laforgue* (Jyväskylä: University of Jyväskylä, 1974)

SCEPI, HENRI, 'La Complainte de tous les excès (de l'hypertrophie au fatras)', in *Jules Laforgue: colloque de la Sorbonne: actes de la journée d'agrégation du 18 novembre 2000*, ed. by André Guyaux and Bertrand Marchal (Paris: Presses de l'Université de Paris-Sorbonne, 2000), pp. 27–42

——*Poétique de Jules Laforgue* (Paris: Presses universitaires de France, 2000)

SCHLANGER, JUDITH, *Les Métaphores de l'organisme* (Paris: Vrin, 1971)

SCHOPENHAUER, ARTHUR, *Pensées, maximes et fragments*, ed. and trans. by Jean Bourdeau (Paris: Germer-Baillière, 1880)

—— *The World as Will and Representation*, trans. by E. F. J. Payne, 2 vols (New York: Dover Publications, 1966)
SCHWAB, RAYMOND, *La Renaissance orientale* (Paris: Payot, 1950)
SCOTT, CLIVE, *A Question of Syllables: Essays in Nineteenth-Century French Verse* (Cambridge: Cambridge University Press, 1986)
—— 'The Stuttering Poet: A Deleuzian Reading of a Laforguian Poetics', *Dix-Neuf*, 20, no. 1 (2016), pp. 9–24
SMITH, DOUGLAS, *Transvaluations: Nietzsche in France, 1872–1972* (Oxford: Clarendon Press, 1996)
SMITH-ROSENBERG, CARROLL, *Disorderly Conduct: Visions of Gender in Victorian America* (Oxford: Oxford University Press, 1985)
SONTAG, SUSAN, *Illness as Metaphor* (New York, NY: Farrar, Strauss and Giroux, 1978; repr. New York, NY: Doubleday, 1990)
SPACKMAN, BARBARA, *Decadent Genealogies: The Rhetoric of Sickness from Baudelaire to D'Annunzio* (Ithaca, NY; London: Cornell University Press, 1989)
STAËL, GERMAINE DE, *De l'Allemagne*, 2 vols (Paris: Garnier-Flammarion, 1968)
STRAUSS, JONATHAN, *Subjects of Terror: Nerval, Hegel and the Modern Self* (Stanford, CA: Stanford University Press, 1999)
SUTTON, HOWARD, *The Life and Work of Jean Richepin* (Geneva: Droz, 1961)
SWART, KOENRAAD W., *The Sense of Decadence in Nineteenth-Century France* (The Hague: Martinus Nijhoff, 1964)
SYMONS, ARTHUR, *The Symbolist Movement in Literature* (New York, NY: Dutton, 1919)
TAITHE, BERTRAND, *Defeated Flesh: Welfare, Warfare and the Making of Modern France* (Manchester: Manchester University Press, 1999)
TERDIMAN, RICHARD, *Discourse/ Counter-Discourse: the theory and practice of symbolic resistance in nineteenth-century France* (Ithaca, NY: Cornell University Press, 1985)
THOMPSON, HANNAH, 'A Battle in the Feminine? The Gendered Body and the Franco-Prussian War', in *Visions/ Revisions: Essays on Nineteenth-Century French Culture*, ed. by Nigel Harkness et al (New York, NY; Oxford: Peter Lang, 2004), pp. 157–73
VAN TIEGHEM, PHILIPPE, *Les Influences étrangères sur la littérature française (1550–1880)* (Paris: Presses universitaires de France, 1961)
VARIGNY, CHARLES DE, 'L'Amour, les Femmes et le Mariage d'après Schopenhauer', *La Revue Politique et Littéraire. Revue des cours littéraires*, 18 (January-July 1880), 702–10
VARLEY, KARINE, *Under the Shadow of Defeat: the War of 1870–1 in French Memory* (New York: Palgrave Macmillan, 2008)
VERLAINE, PAUL, *Sagesse; Amour* (Paris: Rombaldi, 1937)
VIAL, FERNAND, 'L'inconscient métaphysique et ses premières expressions littéraires en France: Jules Laforgue', in *Stil- und Formprobleme in der Literatur*, ed. by Paul Böckmann, (Heidelberg: Carl Winter, 1959), pp. 358–66
VIGNY, ALFRED DE, *Œuvres de A. de Vigny* (Bruxelles: Meline, Cans, 1837)
—— *Poèmes antiques et modernes* (Paris: Canel, 1826)
WAGNER, RICHARD, *Quatre poèmes d'opéras traduits en prose française, précédés d'une lettre sur la musique* (Paris: Librairie Nouvelle, 1861)
WATSON, JANELL, *Literature and Material Culture from Balzac to Proust: The Collection and Consumption of Curiosities* (Cambridge: Cambridge University Press, 1999)
WATSON, LAWRENCE, '"L'Hiver qui vient": Poème-Manifeste', in *Laforgue aujourd'hui*, ed. by J. A. Hiddleston ([Paris]: José Corti, 1988), pp. 135–53
—— *Jules Laforgue: Poet of His Age* (Mahwah, NJ: Office of Communication Services, Ramapo College of New Jersey, 1980)
WELBON, GUY, *The Buddhist nirvāna and its Western interpreters* (Chicago, IL: University of Chicago Press)

WHITE, CLAIRE, 'Laforgue, Beauvoir, and the Second Sex', *Dix-Neuf*, 20, no. 1 (2016), 110–24
—— *Work and Leisure in Late Nineteenth-Century French Literature and Visual Culture: Time, Politics and Class* (Basingstoke: Palgrave Macmillan, 2014)
WILLIAMS, HEATHER, *Mallarmé's Ideas in Language* (Oxford; New York: Peter Lang, 2004), pp. 37–38
—— 'Writing to Paris: Poets, Nobles and Savages in Nineteenth-Century Brittany', *French Studies*, 57, no. 4 (2003), 475–90
YEE, JENNIFER, *Exotic Subversions in Nineteenth-Century French Fiction* (Leeds: Legenda, 2008)
ZOLA, ÉMILE, *Œuvres complètes*, 21 vols, ed. by Henri Mitterand (Paris: Nouveau monde, 2002–2010)
—— *Le Roman expérimental* (Paris: Flammarion, 2006)

INDEX

Adorno, Theodor W. 105
Almond, Philip C. 101, 144 n. 18
Alsace-Lorraine 11, 37–38, 77
Amaury, Arnaud 56, 73 n. 13
Anderson, Benedict 11–12
Arkell, David 19 n. 13
Arnaud, Pierre 67
Arnold, Edwin, *The Light of Asia* 121 n. 21
asceticism 7–8, 9, 50, 53, 57–60, 130–31, 137, 139, 155 n. 10
atheism 2, 4, 5, 29, 51–52, 126

Baju, Anatole 40
Bakhtin, Mikhail 143
Balibar, Étienne 12
Balzac, Honoré de 149
    La Peau de chagrin 106
Banville, Théodore de 81
Barrows, John Henry 121 n. 14
Barth, Fredrik 12
Barthélemy-Saint-Hilaire, Jules 101–02, 126–27, 130, 143
Baudelaire, Charles 27, 44 n. 47, 68, 105–06, 144, 153
    'Richard Wagner et Tannhaüser à Paris' 27
Beauvoir, Simone de 20 n. 46
Becker, Nicolas 26
Bem, Jeanne 65
Benjamin, Walter 144 n. 1
Bernheimer, Charles 48 n. 159
Bertrand, Jean-Pierre 18 n. 1, 69, 105, 107
bibelot 102, 105, 106
Billig, Michael 12
Bismarck, Otto von 34, 80
Block de Behar, Lisa 146 n. 69
body politic 11, 13, 29, 35, 37–39, 41, 48 n. 161, 92, 114
Bonaparte, Napoléon 22, 23, 24, 25, 88
Bongie, Chris 121
Bonnefis, Philippe 18 n. 1, 19 n. 13, 135, 152
Boulanger, Georges Ernest 11
Bourdeau, Jean 28, 30, 31, 32, 33, 127, 128, 137
Bourget, Paul 5, 39, 58, 65, 67–68, 104, 105, 114, 118, 154
Bowie, Andrew 4
Brahmanism, *see* Hinduism
Bréal, Michel 41
Briche, Gérard 62, 68

Brown, Michael 48 n. 161
Buddha:
    comparison to Christ 101–02, 102–03
    life 101
Buddhism:
    German affinity with 97–98
    nirvana 125–26
    reception by Laforgue 15–16, 102–04, 106, 108–09, 111–12, 120, 124, 130–31, 133–34, 137, 138–39, 143
    reception by Schopenhauer and Hartmann 7, 15, 99–100, 104, 127–28
    reception in Europe 101, 124–25, 126–27, 128–30
Burnouf, Eugène 126

Caro, Émile 28, 30–31, 31, 33, 34, 36, 51, 53, 54, 55, 58, 73 n. 10 & 34, 74 n. 64, 76, 80, 98, 128–29, 129, 130, 145 n. 51
Carré, Jean-Marie 24, 25, 43 n. 22
Caty, Marguerite Poulin 63
Céard, Henry 32
Challemel-Lacour, Paul 5, 29–30, 32, 40, 52, 53, 57, 128
Chambers, Ross 13
Champod, Olivier 57
Champsaur, Félicien, *Lulu, pantomime clownesque* 32
Christianity:
    reception by Laforgue 5, 102, 103–04
    reception by Schopenhauer and Hartmann 7, 15, 99–100
la clarté française 21, 24, 32, 41, 72, 77
Clarke, J. J. 155 n. 4
Colbert, Jean-Baptiste 149
Colin, René-Pierre 33, 35, 46 n. 113, 59
Conversi, Daniele 12
Corbière, Tristan 151, 155 n. 8
Counter, Andrew 48 n. 174
Cousin, Victor 21, 25, 36, 115, 125, 126
cultural difference 15, 97, 107–08, 148–49

Darnoi, Dennis N. Kenedy 19 n. 14 & 20
Darwinism 8, 36, 56, 86, 87, 149–50
Daudet, Alphonse, 'La dernière classe' 77
decadence 36, 37, 39, 68, 81, 114
Decadent movement 13, 22, 23, 39–42, 51, 61–62, 63, 64, 67–68, 72
decline of France 13, 22, 28, 36–37, 41, 42, 61, 91–92

Deleuze, Gilles 35, 152
demographic problems 11, 13, 37, 39, 42, 92, 128
Diderot, Denis 32
Dierx, Léon 90, 91
Digeon, Claude 35, 37, 80, 115
dilettantism 17, 68, 104–05
disease 11, 13, 16, 29, 33–36, 38, 40–41, 50–51, 61–63, 67, 69, 72, 85, 89, 92, 147
    cholera 33, 34, 129–30
    tuberculosis 63, 67, 72, 89–90
Dottin-Orsini, Mireille 148–49
Ducrey, Guy 122 n. 33
Dujardin, Édouard 85
Dunstan Martin, Graham 19 n. 13

Eigeldinger, Marc 137
Eliot, T. S. 154
Ephrussi, Charles 62
Espagne, Michel 14
Eurocentrism 102, 107, 149
exoticism 14, 15, 16, 22, 83, 93, 108, 116, 118, 120–21, 122 n. 62, 136, 143

Fénelon, François 55
Fichte, Johann 25
Figueira, Dorothy 116
Flaubert, Gustave 48 n. 161
    Le Dictionnaire des idées reçues 26
    Madame Bovary 84
Foucher de Careil, Alexandre 33, 34, 36, 97, 98, 129
Foustel de Coulanges, Numa Denis 11
France, Anatole 40
Franco-Prussian War 11, 13, 21, 28, 35, 36–37, 38, 48 n. 159, 76, 78–79, 92
free verse 14, 72, 84, 85, 93
Freud, Sigmund 112

Gardner, Sebastian 5, 19 n. 14
Gautier, Théophile 26, 27, 144
Gide, André 27
Girardet, Raoul 77
Gobineau, Arthur de 38, 41, 95 n. 72
Goethe, Johann Wolfgang von 26, 118
Goncourt, Edmond de 62
Gournay, Vincent de 149, 155 n. 4
Groddeck, Georg 90
Grojnowski, Daniel 64, 65, 141
Guattari, Félix 152
Guy, Madeleine 18 n. 8, 45 n. 52

Hannoosh, Michèle 2, 53, 58, 73 nn. 7, 10 & 25, 74 n. 64, 130, 142
Haraucourt, Edmond 153
Harrison, Robert Pogue 81, 83, 84
Harrow, Susan 48 n. 158
Hartmann, Eduard von:
    aesthetics 10, 56, 60, 106–07, 132
    eschatology 5–6, 30–31, 53, 54–55, 93, 112, 119, 127
    ethics 6, 8–9, 42, 50, 54, 69–70, 85, 128
    life 31
    reception of Eastern thought 15, 99–100, 104, 127–28
    reception in France 22, 28
    theory of individuality 15, 100, 110, 113, 114
    Unconscious 2, 3–4, 4–5, 6, 8, 14, 15, 16, 52, 55–56, 67, 68, 69, 79, 81, 82, 86–87, 93, 103, 132, 137, 150
Hauser, Gaspard 152
health 51, 62, 69, 72, 84–85
Heine, Heinrich 24
Helmholtz, Hermann von 56
Henry, Anne 27
Henry, Charles 10, 69
Hibbitt, Richard 58, 104
Hiddleston, J. A. 1, 6, 87, 88, 89, 90, 113, 138
Hinduism 7, 99, 108–09, 128, 155 n. 10
Hobsbawm, Eric J. 44 n. 38, 77
Hoffmann, E. T. A. 26
Holmes, Anne 10, 45 n. 52
Hugo, Victor 26, 54, 98, 144, 147
    L'Année terrible 98
    Odes 54
Huysmans, Joris-Karl, *À rebours* 27, 155 n. 8

illness, *see* disease
India 15, 16, 80–81, 97–100, 110, 115, 116–17, 118, 120

Janaway, Christopher 19 n. 14
Janet, Paul 31, 32, 33, 73 n. 25, 128
Jankélévitch, Vladimir 41
Jourde, Pierre 111

Kahn, Gustave 2, 138
Kant, Immanuel 4, 12, 25, 68, 80, 99

Laforgue, Jules:
    life:
        death 63
        family 114
        heritage 151
        life in Germany 16, 75–76, 76–77, 78–79, 93, 112
        life in Paris 1, 58
        marriage 79
        migrations 150
    works:
        'L'Aquarium' 110–11, 112
        'L'Art moderne en Allemagne' 55–56, 75, 79–83, 93, 98, 118, 147
        Berlin, la cour et la ville 75, 77–79, 80, 82, 93, 94 n. 12
        Les Brins d'Herbe:
            'O Étoile de France'/ 'O Star of France' 92

Les Complaintes 1, 10, 16, 17, 55, 59–60, 62, 64, 65, 66, 69, 102, 103, 104–05, 106, 110, 116, 121 n. 29, 143

'À Paul Bourget' 64, 104, 110; 'La chanson du petit hypertrophique' 64, 65; 'Complainte à Notre-Dame des Soirs' 9, 152; 'Complainte de l'Automne monotone' 91; 'Complainte de l'Orgue de Barbarie' 84, 89; 'Complainte de Lord Pierrot' 138, 139, 153; 'Complainte des Complaintes' 64, 110; 'Complainte des formalités nuptiales' 9, 63, 136; 'Complainte des grands Pins dans une villa abandonnée' 77; 'La Complainte des montres' 65; 'Complainte des Mounis du Mont-Martre' 65–66; 'Complainte des Nostalgies préhistoriques' 136; 'Complainte des pubertés difficiles' 105–08, 110, 116, 118, 120; 'Complainte des Voix sous le Figuier boudhique' 133–34, 152; 'Complainte d'un autre Dimanche' 153; 'Complainte d'un certain Dimanche' 112, 152; 'Complainte d'une Convalescence en mai' 55, 116–17, 118; 'Complainte du fœtus de Poète' 153; 'Complainte du pauvre Chevalier-Errant' 95 n. 65, 134; 'Complainte du pauvre corps humain' 62–63, 92; 'Complainte du roi de Thulé' 95 n. 65; 'Complainte du Sage de Paris' 18, 56, 95 n. 65, 95 n. 67, 115, 117–18, 120, 131, 133; 'Complainte du soir des Comices agricoles' 9, 90; 'Complainte-Litanies de mon Sacré-Cœur' 61, 66; 'Complainte-Placet de Faust fils' 153; 'Complainte propitiatoire à l'Inconscient' 5, 55, 103, 111, 153; 'Complainte sur certains ennuis' 152; 'Complainte sur certains temps déplacés' 105, 151, 152; 'Préludes autobiographiques' 17, 18, 54, 61, 64–65, 103, 107, 140–43, 152

Derniers vers 1, 60, 63, 81, 84–85

'Dimanches (*Bref, j'allais me donner...*)' 87, 134; 'Dimanches (*C'est l'automne...*)' 136; 'L'hiver qui vient' 18, 63, 84, 85, 88–93; 'Légende' 63; 'Le mystère des trois cors' 90, 92; *Noire bise, averse glapissante*' 63; 'Ô géraniums diaphanes' 85, 86; 'Pétition' 88; 'Simple agonie' 66; 'Solo de lune' 63, 71, 85, 87–88, 117

Des Fleurs de bonne volonté 114

'Albums' 116–17, 118; 'Arabesques de malheur' 71; 'Avertissement' 115; 'Ballade' 113, 120; 'Dimanches (*C'est l'automne...*)', 115; 'Esthétique (*Je fais la cour à ma Destinée*)' 1; 'Gare au bord de la mer' 112; 'Mettons le doigt sur la plaie' 70–71

L'Imitation de Notre-Dame la Lune 16, 62, 136–37, 138, 143

'Au large' 89, 146 n. 68; 'Clair de Lune' 138; 'Climat, faune et flore de la Lune' 124, 146 n. 68; 'Dialogue avant le lever de la Lune' 146 n. 68; 'Les linges, le cygne' 65, 153; 'Litanies des derniers quartiers de la Lune' 137, 146 n. 68; 'Locutions des Pierrots' 154; 'Un mot au Soleil pour commencer' 89; 'Nuitamment' 146 n. 68; 'Petits mystères' 137; 'Pierrots' 138, 139, 140

'L'Impressionnisme' 83

Moralités légendaires 1, 2, 135

'Hamlet ou les suites de la piété filiale' 2, 66, 135; 'Lohengrin, fils de Parsifal' 2, 27, 140, 146 n. 56; 'Le Miracle des roses' 63, 72; 'Pan et la syrinx' 85–88, 122 n. 63; 'Persée et Andromède ou le plus heureux des trois' 2, 135; 'Salomé' 2, 3, 66, 111, 113, 119, 120, 122 n. 62, 135, 147

Pierrot fumiste 140

Premiers Poèmes:

'Ce qu'aime le gros Fritz' 76; 'Soleil couchant (*Le soleil s'est couché...*)' 108

Un raté 54, 57

Le Sanglot de la Terre 1, 17, 50, 51–52, 53–54, 55, 57, 58, 65, 102–03, 104, 106, 107, 108, 110, 116, 151

'Berceuse' 58; 'Les Boulevards' 106; 'Cauchemar' 103; 'Éclair de gouffre' 106; 'Étonnement' 116, 122 n. 42; 'Fantaisie' 89; 'Fragments' 51, 58; 'Hypertrophie' 65; 'Justice' 51–52; 'Lassitude' 52; 'Marche funèbre pour la mort de la Terre' 94 n. 3, 102–03; 'L'Oubli' 53, 58, 109–10; 'Pâle soleil d'hiver' 91; 'Pataugement' 53, 60, 102, 146 n. 71; 'Suis-je?' 52; 'Trop tard' 57, 58

Stéphane Vassiliew 63

Tessa 50, 57, 59, 61, 72

Lamartine, Alphonse de 26
Laprade, Victor de 28
La Rochefoucauld, François de 33, 35, 46 n. 105
Laurent, Émile 40
Le Nôtre, André 82
Leconte de Lisle, Charles Marie René 144
Lefebvre, Jean-Pierre 25
Lefrère, Jean-Jacques 94 n. 11, 151
Lopez, Donald 101

Magee, Bryan 7, 19 n. 14, 28, 32
Malherbe, François de 81
Mallarmé, Stéphane 67, 106
Manet, Édouard 149
Marcowitz, Reiner 37
Marmier, Xavier 26, 44 n. 44

Mauclair, Camille 85
Maupassant, Guy de 27, 29, 31
McGuinness, Patrick 49 n. 191
Mérimée, Prosper 26
Michelet, Jules 38, 41, 98
misogyny 7, 9, 30, 31
Montaigne, Michel de 35
moon 124, 137–38, 143
Morel, Bénédict 47 n. 143
Moret-Jankus, Pauline 114
Morgan, Edwin 89
Müller, Max 101
Mültzer, Sabine 58
music 25–26, 82–83, 85
Musset, Alfred de 26
mysticism 80, 98, 100, 118, 142

Napoleonic Wars 35, 36
nationalism 11–12, 14, 15, 26, 51, 66–67, 72, 75, 77, 79, 94, 114, 147
   German 24, 79, 82
Nerval, Gérard de 26, 44 n. 37
Newton, Isaac 68
Nicholls, Moira 125
Nietzsche, Friedrich 27, 35
Nordau, Max 36, 40, 41, 105, 127
Nye, Robert 36, 42

obscurity 21, 24, 26, 27, 28, 32, 33, 41, 76
O'Connor, Erin 34, 129
opium 129–30, 131
Ordinaire, Dionys 33, 34
Orientalism 12–13, 100, 118, 120, 127, 129
otherness 3, 11, 12–13, 13–14, 21, 23, 33–34, 40–41, 75, 82, 83, 88, 97, 108, 117–18, 119, 128, 137, 141, 147, 148, 151, 152
Ozanam, Antoine-Frédéric 126

Palacio, Jean de 41, 139
pantheism 19 n. 20, 33, 36
Pascal, Blaise 35
Pearson, Roger 18 n. 8, 85, 87
Perrault, Charles 91
pessimism 2, 11, 28–29, 30, 36, 40, 51, 54, 59, 67, 72
   comparison to Buddhism 99, 128
   as disease 11, 22, 33–34, 41, 43, 46 n. 113, 61
Pia, Pascal 76
Pierrot 17, 42, 60, 66, 105, 137, 138–40, 153, 154
Pierrot, Jean 61, 137
Plato 99, 115
Pound, Ezra 154
Prévost-Paradol, Lucien-Anatole 47 n. 143
pro-natalism 14, 16, 137, 145 n. 33
Proust, Marcel 27, 114
Prudhomme, Sully 115, 134

Quinet, Edgar 24

Ramsey, Warren 18 n. 13, 56
Rancière, Jacques 106
Rasmussen, Claire 48 n. 161
Raudot, Claude Marie 37
Renan, Ernest 11
revanchisme 11, 34, 37, 67, 72, 76
Reynaud, Louis 24, 25
Rhine Crisis 11, 26
Ribot, Théodule 31, 32, 42, 89, 128–29, 139
Richard, Jean-Pierre 64, 65, 141
Richepin, Jean 115
Richter, Jean-Paul 119
Rimbaud, Arthur 10
Rivarol, Antoine de 24, 41
Rolland, Romain 112
Romanticism 26, 39, 54, 61, 67, 81–82, 83, 147
Rowe, Paul 44 n. 44
Ruchon, François 4

Said, Edward 12–13, 118
Sakari, Ellen 4
Scepi, Henri 69
Schelling, Friedrich 4, 19 n. 20, 25
Schiller, Friedrich 114
Schopenhauer, Arthur:
   aesthetics 9–10, 50, 60, 70, 71
   eschatology 5, 29–30, 53, 54, 93, 127
   ethics 6–8, 9, 29–30, 40, 42, 50, 54, 57–58, 62, 85, 128
   life 31
   as *moraliste* 32–33
   reception of Eastern thought 7, 15, 99–100, 127–28
   reception in France 22, 27–28
   rumoured licentiousness 29, 31–32, 59
   theory of tragedy 52–53
   Will 3–4, 52, 69, 71
Scott, Clive 61, 62, 155 n. 13
Shakespeare, William 102
   A Midsummer Night's Dream 83
   Macbeth 119
Smith, Douglas 35
Smith-Rosenberg, Carroll 48, n. 162
Sontag, Susan 34
Spackman, Barbara 40, 41
Staël, Germaine de 12, 14, 21, 22, 23–25, 26, 27, 43, 76, 80, 82, 93, 97, 98, 147
Strauss, Jonathan 44 n. 37
Swart, Koenraad 37
Symons, Arthur 43
syncretism 101, 102, 103, 107

Taine, Hippolyte 68, 69, 84, 107, 149, 154
Taithe, Bertrand 38
Terdiman, Richard 14
Thiers, Adolphe 26, 38
Thompson, Hannah 38
Tolstoy, Leo, *War and Peace* 131
translation 21, 25–26, 27, 28

transnationalism 12, 15, 21, 23, 26, 34, 150, 155 n. 4

unconscious (individual) 3, 6, 69, 84, 93, 148, 149
underwater world 110–12, 117–18, 119–20, 124, 141

Van Tieghem, Philippe 26
Varigny, Charles de 31, 33
Verlaine, Paul 49 n. 191, 67, 74 n. 58, 151, 152
Verne, Jules:
    De la Terre à la Lune 138
    Autour de la Lune 138
    Vingt mille lieues sous les mers 141
vers libre, *see* free verse
Vigny, Alfred de 48 n. 169, 92
Vincens, Charles 27
Voltaire, *Candide* 24

Wagner, Richard 26–27, 35, 45 n. 53, 76, 82–83
    'Lettre sur la musique' 27, 82
    Tannhaüser scandal 26–27

Wagnerian movement 22, 147
Walzer, Pierre-Olivier 4, 78, 79, 119
Watson, Janell 105
Watteau, Jean-Antoine 88–89
Werner, Michaël 14
Whitman, Walt 92
Williams, Heather 151
Willm, Jean 25–26

Yee, Jennifer 122 n. 62

Zola, Émile 38, 41
    Au Bonheur des Dames 46 n. 113
    La Débâcle 38
    'Dépopulation' 39–40, 42, 145 n. 33
    Fécondité 144 n. 3
    La Joie de vivre 30, 46 n. 113, 144 n. 3
    Nana 48 n. 159
    Le Roman expérimental 39
    Vérité 144 n. 3